Why Teach Philosophy in Schools?

Bloomsbury Philosophy of Education

Series Editor: Michael Hand

Bloomsbury Philosophy of Education is an international research series dedicated to the examination of conceptual and normative questions raised by the practice of education. There is a particular focus on philosophical dimensions of current policy debates, though work of a less applied nature will also have a place.

Editorial Board
Sigal Ben-Porath (University of Pennsylvania, USA)
Randall Curren (University of Rochester, USA)
Doret de Ruyter (Vrije Universiteit Amsterdam, the Netherlands)
Dianne Gereluk (University of Calgary, Canada)
Judith Suissa (UCL Institute of Education, UK)
Christopher Winch (King's College London, UK)

Also available in the series:
Wonder and Education, Anders Schinkel
Cherishing and the Good Life of Learning, Ruth Cigman
A Critique of Pure Teaching Methods and the Case of Synthetic Phonics, Andrew Davis
Philosophical Reflections on Neuroscience and Education, William H. Kitchen
Children, Religion and the Ethics of Influence, John Tillson

Why Teach Philosophy in Schools?

The Case for Philosophy on the Curriculum

Jane Gatley

BLOOMSBURY ACADEMIC
LONDON • NEW YORK • OXFORD • NEW DELHI • SYDNEY

BLOOMSBURY ACADEMIC
Bloomsbury Publishing Plc
50 Bedford Square, London, WC1B 3DP, UK
1385 Broadway, New York, NY 10018, USA
29 Earlsfort Terrace, Dublin 2, Ireland

BLOOMSBURY, BLOOMSBURY ACADEMIC and the Diana logo are trademarks of
Bloomsbury Publishing Plc

First published in Great Britain 2023
Paperback edition published 2024

Copyright © Jane Gatley, 2023

Jane Gatley has asserted her right under the Copyright, Designs and Patents Act, 1988, to be identified as Author of this work.

For legal purposes the Acknowledgements on p. viii constitute
an extension of this copyright page.

Series design by Clare Turner

All rights reserved. No part of this publication may be reproduced or transmitted in any form or by any means, electronic or mechanical, including photocopying, recording, or any information storage or retrieval system, without prior permission in writing from the publishers.

Bloomsbury Publishing Plc does not have any control over, or responsibility for, any third-party websites referred to or in this book. All internet addresses given in this book were correct at the time of going to press. The author and publisher regret any inconvenience caused if addresses have changed or sites have ceased to exist, but can accept no responsibility for any such changes.

A catalogue record for this book is available from the British Library.

A catalog record for this book is available from the Library of Congress.

ISBN: HB: 978-1-3502-6835-7
PB: 978-1-3502-6839-5
ePDF: 978-1-3502-6836-4
eBook: 978-1-3502-6837-1

Series: Bloomsbury Philosophy of Education

Typeset by Newgen KnowledgeWorks Pvt. Ltd., Chennai, India

To find out more about our authors and books visit www.bloomsbury.com
and sign up for our newsletters.

Contents

Series Editor's Foreword   vi
Acknowledgements   viii

Introduction   1

Part 1 Philosophy in Schools

1   A History of Philosophy in Schools   7
2   Existing Arguments for Teaching Philosophy in Schools   25

Part 2 The Aims of Education

3   The Aims of Education   55
4   A Utility Account of Education   91

Part 3 Two Arguments for Teaching Philosophy

5   Teaching Philosophy to Clarify Ordinary Concepts   127
6   Teaching Philosophy to Make Sense of the Curriculum   149

Conclusion   183

References   189
Index   199

Series Editor's Foreword

Bloomsbury Philosophy of Education is an international research series dedicated to the examination of conceptual and normative questions raised by the practice of education.

Philosophy of education is a branch of philosophy rooted in and attentive to the practical business of educating people. Those working in the field are often based in departments of education rather than departments of philosophy; many have experience of teaching in primary or secondary schools; and all seek to contribute in some way to the improvement of educational interactions, institutions or ideals. Like philosophers of other stripes, philosophers of education are prone to speculative flight, and the altitudes they reach are occasionally dizzying, but their inquiries begin and end on the ground of educational practice, with matters of immediate concern to teachers, parents, administrators and policymakers.

Two kinds of questions are central to the discipline. *Conceptual* questions have to do with the language we use to formulate educational aims and describe educational processes. At least some of the problems we encounter in our efforts to educate arise from conceptual confusion or corruption – from what Wittgenstein called 'the bewitchment of our intelligence by means of language'. Disciplined attention is needed to such specifically educational concepts as learning and teaching, schooling and socializing, training and indoctrinating, but also to the wider conceptual terrain in which educational discourse sits: what is it to be a person, or to have a mind, or to know or think or flourish, or to be rational, intelligent, autonomous or virtuous? *Normative* questions have to do with the justification of educational norms, aims and policies. What educators do is guided and constrained by principles, goals, imperatives and protocols that may or may not be ethically defensible or appropriate to the task in hand. Philosophers of education interrogate the normative infrastructure of educational practice, with a view to exposing its deficiencies and infirmities and drawing up blueprints for its repair or reconstruction. Frequently, of course, the two kinds of questions overlap: inappropriate aims sometimes rest on conceptual muddles, and our understanding of educational concepts is liable to distortion by ill-founded pedagogical norms.

In terms of scholarly output, philosophy of education is in rude health. The field supports half a dozen major international journals, numerous learned societies and a busy annual calendar of national and international conferences. At present, however, too little of this scholarly output finds a wider audience, and too few of the important ideas introduced in journal articles are expanded into fully developed theories. The aim of this book series is to identify the best new work in the field and encourage its authors to develop, defend and work out the implications of their ideas, in a way that is accessible to a broad readership.

It is hoped that volumes in the series will be of interest not only to scholars and students of philosophy of education and neighbouring branches of philosophy, but also to the wider community of educational researchers, practitioners and policymakers. All volumes are written for an international audience: while some authors begin with the way an educational problem has been framed in a particular national context, it is the problem itself, not the local framing of it, on which the ensuing arguments bear.

Michael Hand

Acknowledgements

This book is based on my PhD thesis, and would not have been written without the support of my supervisor, Michael Hand, and many others who have supported me in a variety of different ways since beginning my PhD. I would like to thank everyone who has taken an interest in my work and invited me into the academic community.

I also owe thanks to the Economic and Social Research Council for their generous financial support over the course of my PhD, and for providing further funding for a year-long postdoctoral fellowship to adapt my thesis into this book. I am very fortunate to have been able to devote myself fully to this project, and have enjoyed every moment of it.

Finally, I want to thank my friends and family for their support. In particular, my husband who made the process of writing this book a small part of a much wider adventure in life.

I would like to acknowledge the published work that this book draws upon. This has been reused according to the permissions granted by the original copyright agreements. The previously published papers present in this work are mentioned below:

Gatley, J. (2020a). 'The Educational Value of Analytic Philosophy', *Journal of the American Philosophical Association*, 7(1), pp. 59–77, doi: 10.1017/apa.2020.9.

Gatley, J. (2020b). 'Philosophy for Children and the Extrinsic Value of Philosophy', *Metaphilosophy*, 51(4), pp. 548–63, doi: 10.1111/meta.12445.

Gatley, J. (2020c). 'A Utility Account of Liberal Education', *Philosophy of Education*, 74(2), pp. 28–38, available at: https://www.philofed.org/copy-of-issue-2.

Gatley, J. (2021). 'Intrinsic Value and Educational Value', *Journal of Philosophy of Education*, 55 (4-5), pp. 675–87, doi: 10.1111/1467-9752.12555.

Introduction

This book makes the case for teaching philosophy in schools. In one sense, the task ought to be straightforward. Philosophy is an established discipline with a long and distinguished provenance. Other disciplines such as history, physics and literature appear to earn their place on the curriculum on these merits alone. However, unlike history, physics and literature, philosophy is not often a regular or protected part of school curricula around the world.

Another sense in which making the case for teaching philosophy in schools ought to be straightforward is that there is evidence that teaching philosophy in schools leads to a range of benefits. It is commonly held to contribute to students' critical thinking skills and social skills. It touches on important questions that students face about identity, morality and religion. Again, while other disciplines' positions on the curriculum are often justified by appeals to similar benefits, philosophy continues to be excluded from mainstream teaching in many countries.

This is not to say that philosophy has been unfairly maligned, or that it ought to be included on grounds of parity with other disciplines. The underlying issue is that the school curriculum is rarely a well-planned, logical or coherent affair. Disciplines are taught, or not taught according to chance factors such as historical happenstance, societal trends or the preferences of policymakers. While there is research into curriculum theory, in practice schools and policymakers often follow previous curricula and make piecemeal adjustments. It is not merely the case that philosophy has been left off an otherwise well-planned curriculum, the problem is that in many cases, the curriculum is not well-planned.

As such, an argument for teaching philosophy in schools is going to require a normative account of the curriculum; in other words, an account which makes claims about how the curriculum ought to look. This normative account of the curriculum is going to need to appeal to the aims of education. Any case for teaching philosophy in schools with thus rest on the aims of education, and a normative account of the curriculum.

School teachers experience first-hand the influences of political, economic and societal trends on the curriculum. During my time as a Religious Education teacher in English secondary schools between 2010 and 2017, external forces led to the steady loss of philosophy from Religious Education syllabi in schools. One of the motivations behind this book is to make a case for teaching philosophy in schools, which is resistant to these political, economic and societal curriculum influences. First, I set out why the existing reasons and arguments for teaching philosophy in schools do not add up to a failsafe case for teaching philosophy, and in response I present two arguments which, I believe, do.

The case presented here is limited to the claim that at some point during a person's education, they ought to be taught some philosophy. I do not argue that all education ought to be philosophical, whatever that might mean. Nor do I argue that philosophy ought to be present throughout someone's entire education. I limit my argument to the claim that schools should teach philosophy to their students at some point, likely when students are old enough to be able to engage with philosophical ideas relatively easily. I also limit my argument for teaching philosophy to the claim that philosophy should be taught to the extent that is needed to meet whichever aims of education it is well-suited to meet. I do not argue that philosophy should be taught in a comprehensive way or that all aspects of philosophy need to be covered.

The case that I present is motivated by two concerns about education and curricula. The first is that curricula take up children's time and liberty. As such, any proposed use of school time ought to be justified and should provide something valuable or some educational good. Whatever this is, it needs to be important enough to claim a space for itself on a curriculum which is necessarily limited in terms of the time and resources available. The second concern is that any educational activity which is under consideration for curriculum inclusion can only have a failsafe case for its inclusion if it is the best or only way of achieving the specified educational good. When it comes to making a case for teaching philosophy in schools, the case must meet two criteria: (1) that teaching philosophy provides some specifiable educational good and (2) that there is reason to hold that this specified good is only or best delivered by teaching philosophy.

After outlining the history and current state of philosophy in schools in Chapter 1, I outline why existing arguments for teaching philosophy in schools do not meet these two criteria. For example, a commonly held reason for teaching philosophy in schools is that it promotes students' academic and social skills. I argue that these reasons fail to show that teaching philosophy is the only or best way of bringing about improvements in students' academic and social skills. The common argument that teaching philosophy improves critical thinking abilities in students does not establish that other possible curriculum activities would not be able to achieve the same results. Similarly, claims that teaching philosophy can help students to communicate clearly or work well in groups do not amount to a failsafe argument for teaching philosophy in schools because other activities might be able to achieve the same results. A class discussion about a poem in an English lesson might have the same effect on social skills. Spending more curriculum time studying scientific methods might have the same effect on critical thinking skills.

I also discuss religious reasons for teaching philosophy in schools, disciplinary reasons, reasons relating to moral and political education, a collection of underdeveloped reasons pointing to a role for philosophy at the core of the curriculum, and the possibility of defining the nature of philosophy and arguing for its educational value on that basis. I conclude that the existing cases for teaching philosophy in schools do not specify educational goods that are clearly best met by teaching philosophy.

I then embark on a project to establish the aims of education with a view to be able to specify a set of valuable educational goods. This is important because it is only in relation to educational aims that claims about educational goods can be established. An educational good is something that has educational value, and in turn, educational value is determined by the aims of education. Later in the thesis, I will argue that there are two educational goods sitting at the heart of the aim of education identified that are best met by teaching philosophical content and skills.

Chapter 3 focuses on the educational practice of providing students with a broad array of theoretical content. By theoretical content, I mean information and ideas about the world. As a matter of fact, this is something that schools spend a lot of curriculum time doing. I discuss existing literature dealing with this phenomenon, mostly through the lens of liberal education. I examine the educational aims ascribed to a broad theoretical education and outline why none of the aims given provide a plausible and coherent account of why teaching a broad array of theoretical content is educationally valuable. Chapter 4 provides such an account by appealing to the utility of theoretical content. Here, I provide an original account of the value of theoretical content, which claims that a broad theoretical education is valuable insofar as it helps students to interact with the world by providing them with different ways of understanding it. I then argue that all students ought to be provided with at least some theoretical education, as being able to interact effectively with the world underlies a range of different aims of education, from promoting individual flourishing to contributing to social justice.

If effective interaction with the world is an aim of education, and a broad theoretical education helps people to interact effectively with the world by providing them with a plurality of effective ways of understanding it, then two arguments emerge for teaching philosophy in schools. The first is that students are faced with a range of questions based on ordinary concepts which they need help thinking clearly about and answering. Some aspects of philosophy, particularly analytic philosophy, are concerned with the systematic study of ordinary concepts. Based on this, I argue that students ought to be taught philosophical skills and content relating to ordinary concepts. The second argument is that a broad theoretical education involves studying content from different disciplines, and these disciplines employ different conceptual schemes. This means that students are required to make sense of different conceptual schemes over the course of their education. I argue that there are philosophical content and skills which are best placed to help students to make sense of the different conceptual schemes they encounter. Furthermore, I argue that a broad theoretical education might fail to help students to interact effectively with the world if students are not helped to make sense of this conceptual fragmentation.

I conclude that all students ought to be taught some broad, theoretical education to help them to interact effectively with the world. This broad theoretical education ought to include philosophical content, which helps them to address ordinary concept questions. Secondly, unless they are also taught how to make sense of the conceptual fragmentation of their broad theoretical education, it is less likely to help them to interact effectively with the world, and so loses its educational value. I argue that a course in philosophy is best placed to help students to make sense of a broad theoretical education. As such, all students ought to be taught some philosophical content and skills over the course of their education.

Part 1

Philosophy in Schools

1

A History of Philosophy in Schools

This chapter introduces the role that philosophy has previously played and currently plays in schools around the world. I briefly summarize the history of philosophy in schools to the present day. I then outline some of the main principles underlying the Philosophy for Children (P4C) method of teaching philosophy, which is commonly used in schools and has been widely written about. I go on to outline criticisms and challenges to teaching philosophy in schools, followed by a more in-depth case study based on philosophy teaching in the UK. Finally, I summarize existing reasons and arguments given for teaching philosophy in schools. These will be subjected to critical analysis in Chapter 2. This chapter provides the necessary background for more philosophical discussion later in the book.

UNESCO Reports and Philosophy in Schools

UNESCO has published a series of reports on the status of philosophy in schools between 1953 and the present day. These reports provide the most comprehensive account of the place of philosophy in schools over this time period. They are global in their reach, and do not narrowly focus on P4C as some other sources do, but cover all ways of teaching philosophy in schools that they encountered. The UNESCO reports incorporate survey data and commissioned reports from different countries. They reveal information about the presence, purpose and history of teaching philosophy across the world.

UNESCO has been a dedicated advocate of teaching philosophy: 'The very mission of UNESCO, dedicated to serving the intellectual and moral solidarity of humanity, is to embrace and promote knowledge as a whole. In an open, inclusive and pluralistic, knowledge-oriented society, philosophy has its rightful place. Its teaching alongside the other social and human sciences remains at the heart of our concerns' (UNESCO, 2007, p. ix). The following outline of reasons for introducing a world philosophy day reveals UNESCO's commitment to including philosophy in education:

1. *Recalling* the Universal Declaration of Human Rights, which stipulates in Article 26 that 'everyone has the right to education' (para. 1) and that 'education shall be directed to the full development of the human personality …. It shall promote understanding, tolerance and friendship among all nations, racial or religious groups … for the maintenance of peace' (para. 2),
2. *Recalling* also the Constitution of UNESCO, which declares that

    the States Parties to this Constitution, believing in full and equal opportunities for education for all, in the unrestricted pursuit of objective truth, and in the free exchange of ideas and knowledge, are agreed and determined to develop and to increase the means of communication between their peoples and to employ these means for the purposes of mutual understanding and a truer and more perfect knowledge of each other's lives,

3. *Mindful* of the eminent role played by philosophy in the development of humanity,
4. *Convinced* of its importance and concerned about the need to protect it from the dual threat represented by obscurantism and extremism,
5. *Recalling* the fundamental role of philosophy in the promotion of tolerance and peace,
6. *Underlining* UNESCO's aim of imbuing public opinion with moral and philosophical ideas that would strengthen respect for the human person, the love of peace, solidarity and the attachment to a cultural ideal,
7. *Recalling* UNESCO's aim of encouraging progress in philosophical studies, supporting the activities of associations, universities and all other institutions with a similar goal, and fostering international exchanges and publications in the field, in particular through the holding of Philosophy Day at UNESCO, which has been celebrated since 2002 at the Organization's Headquarters and in more than 70 Member States,
8. *Urges* Member States to:

    (a) pursue their efforts to promote philosophy within their countries. (UNESCO, 2005, p. 2)

Philosophy is present on secondary curricula across the world. However, whether it is compulsory, optional or only available to a few select students differs widely, as does the stability of philosophy as a school subject going into the future. I explore four key influences highlighted by UNESCO's reports regarding whether philosophy is taught in schools or not. These are the influences of Catholicism, the influence of the French education system, the Anglo-American philosophical tradition and the P4C movement. I will go through these in turn.

Catholicism and Philosophy in Schools

Historically, Catholic countries, like Italy, Spain, ex-Spanish colonies in Latin America, and African countries with large missionary influences have tended to emphasize the importance of philosophy in schools. A UNESCO report into teaching philosophy in Latin America and the Caribbean sums up this influence:

> The strong historical influence of the Catholic Church has long been in favour of philosophy. For the Church, which has always considered education as one of its principal attributes, philosophy constitutes, still today, the essential precondition of theological studies. The programme of Catholic secondary education thus traditionally grants a great place to philosophy. As for public education, it has remained attached to the humanities, classics, general knowledge, and there too philosophy finds its place quite naturally. (UNESCO, 2009, p. 26)

As a result, philosophy has traditionally been present on the school curriculum in a range of countries with Catholic connections.

The case of philosophy teaching in Cuba illustrates the influence of the Catholic Church. Philosophy was part of the school curriculum in pre-revolutionary Cuba due to the influence of the Catholic Church. As is the case in many countries, secondary education mirrored higher education. In higher education, 'philosophy was taught in the university from its foundation in 1728, in seminaries...and in monasteries... The philosophy taught was scholastic, of the Aristotelian – Thomist School, harmonizing with the requirements and aims of the Catholic Church' (Llera, 1953, p. 27). After 1900, with the independence of Cuba, philosophy was largely erased from higher education; however, in 1938 philosophy was introduced back into universities, and back onto the school curriculum as part of reforms to education. In secondary schools, 'the fifth-year programme on the arts side includes an introductory course in philosophy and logic' (p. 28). By 1995, possibly linked to Castro's secular regime, philosophy was no longer taught in Cuban schools (Droit, 1995, p. 181). Although there are many other factors at play, Cuba shares similarities with Latin American countries where Spanish colonization alongside the introduction of Catholicism created a link between education and philosophy, making philosophy a ready contender for inclusion on school curricula.

A similar example is that of the Democratic Republic of Congo, formerly Zaire. A report from 1980 about philosophy teaching in Zaire summarizes its history:

> During the colonial era, philosophy teaching was introduced by the missionaries when they set up the Roman Catholic seminaries (Grands Seminaires) to train young men for priesthood . . . the philosophy taught in the seminaries took its inspiration from Thomism . . . it was taken seriously, since the missionaries held the conviction that bad philosophy could but produce bad theology. (Elungu, 1980, p. 2)

From 1959, schools came under the influence of the Belgian education system, which itself was influenced by the French system. Combined, these influences meant that 'the syllabus provide[d] for thirty hours of philosophy teaching ... the three main subjects taught [were] logic, psychology and schools of philosophical thought, with the study of a few authors such as Plato, Descartes, Comte, Bergson and Mounier ... philosophy in secondary schools [was] generally taught by philosophy graduates or priests' (Elungu, 1980, p. 3).

The centrality of the Catholic Church in Latin America correlates with the fact that many countries teach philosophy in secondary schools. It is taught during secondary education in the following countries: Argentina, Brazil, Colombia, Chile, Ecuador, Haiti, Honduras, Mexico, Uruguay and Venezuela (UNESCO, 2009, p. 27). Recently, the place of philosophy on these curricula has become tenuous: 'In Peru, despite strong protests by teachers, the teaching of philosophy was withdrawn from the curriculum in 2002, criticised as being a Western mode of expression without any national roots. The partisans of sciences, from their perspective accused it of not distinguishing itself from literature' (p. 27). The Dominican Republic phased out philosophy teaching when it reduced the number of disciplines taught at secondary level because 'philosophy could be found in a transversal way in other disciplines such as history, literature or civic education' (p. 27). The same process took place in Mexico, where philosophical content was absorbed into civic courses, or ethics and values courses (p. 30). In Uruguay, philosophy teaching in secondary schools was challenged by 'the weight of market society's demands, the attempts to reduce the space of philosophy by reforms to the curriculum and the danger of the weakening of philosophy teaching in the classrooms' (p. 32).

The importance of philosophy in Catholic education accounts for the presence of philosophy on curricula in countries which have been historically influenced by Catholicism. However, as education becomes more secular in some of those countries, the position of philosophy loses its original justification and risks being lost from the curriculum.

The French *Baccalaureat*

In France, and countries influenced by or colonized by France, philosophy is taught as a core part of the final years of students' education. In 1953, Canguilhem commented that 'the *Baccalaureat*, or higher completion certificate, is awarded only at the conclusion of courses of study which have included in the final stages, a more or less extensive introduction to philosophy. A certain amount of philosophical training is thus required in France, of anyone following a career for which the *Baccalaureat* is necessary' (Canguilhem, 1953, p. 53). Canguilhem's report to UNESCO quotes responses to the survey citing the rationales at play when it comes to teaching philosophy in French secondary schools. These responses highlight the importance of students thinking for themselves, the importance of reflection in education and of pursuing self-knowledge. One response claims that 'the teaching of philosophy is the really distinctive feature of French secondary education. The teaching in our secondary schools is not encyclopaedic, with the emphasis on knowledge. It is, above all, a training which seeks to stir and exercise thought; knowledge itself is merely a stimulant and a subject for this exercise' (Monod in Canguilhem, 1953, p. 195, p. 55).

Philosophy remains at the heart of the French *Baccalaureat*, with students sitting a final exam in it regardless of their chosen *Baccalaureat* strand. The exam consists of two general philosophical questions, and a text for explication. In 2019, the literature strand of the *Baccalaureat* asked students: (1) Is it possible to escape time? (2) What is the point of explaining a work or art? and to (3) Explicate an extract from Hegel (Le Parisien, 2019). Pepin's study guide *Les Dix Philosophes Incontournables du Bac Philo* covers the following philosophers: Plato, Aristotle, Descartes, Spinoza, Kant, Hegel, Kierkegaard, Nietzsche, Freud and Sartre (2010). This gives some idea of the sort of course taught during the final two years of French schooling today.

The French *Baccalaureat* combined with the Catholic influence, may have influenced Italian and Spanish curricula, which also teach philosophy in schools.

Francophone countries in Africa often teach philosophy as a core element of secondary education. In 1984, Francophone countries teaching philosophy included Burundi, the Congo, Gabon, Guinea, Ivory Coast, Madagascar, Mali, Mauritania, Morocco, Senegal, Togo, Tunisia and Zaire (UNESCO, 1984). The influence of the French system is also visible in Quebec, where philosophy is taught at secondary level (UNESCO, 2011, p. 40). North African countries including Morocco, Algeria and Tunisia place much emphasis on philosophy, as might be expected of ex-French colonies. Egypt and Turkey have also taught philosophy as part of secondary education, following a French *Baccalaureat* model, possibly influenced by the proximity of French colonies in the region (UNESCO, 1953).

Where philosophy is taught in schools using the *Baccalaureat* model, the place of philosophy on the curriculum has been robust in the face of political, economic and societal pressures. For example, Morocco increased the amount of philosophy taught in secondary schools and responded to worries about the colonial nature of European philosophy by introducing Arabic philosophy (UNESCO, 1984, p. 196).

The Anglo-American Tradition

Philosophy is not a compulsory subject in schools in Anglophone countries. This is despite it being well-represented in British, American and Australasian universities. Traditionally, Anglophone countries in Africa, Asia, Australasia and the Americas have not taught philosophy in schools, although this is changing with the introduction of P4C programmes in schools in some of these countries.

The 1953 UNESCO survey illuminates one rationale behind the absence of philosophy in secondary schools in the UK. This early survey is interesting because it coincides with a peak in the analytic philosophy tradition in the UK. British responses to the survey highlight the idea that analytic philosophy is at odds with public philosophy and philosophy in schools. There is a strong kickback against the idea that philosophy has any instrumental value, rather it should only be pursued for its own sake. The analytic slant of Anglo-American philosophy is also flagged as inappropriate for fulfilling the sort of aims alluded to by UNESCO in their survey. These opening paragraphs of the British report to UNESCO demonstrate the tense attitude towards including philosophy on school curricula:

It was not a matter of surprise to the British consultants that one of the recipients of the questionnaire (Professor Emmet of Manchester) included in her reply the following statement:

'I ought to say, I think, that most of my colleagues felt rather indignant that an alleged fact-finding questionnaire should be framing questions in a way which suggested continually that philosophy ought to be ideologically directed. We cannot share this view, not because we disagree with the democratic ideology, but because this is to us a false view of the nature of philosophy.'

Professor Emmet certainly spoke for many others than herself in the United Kingdom when she wrote thus. It is not however an implication of her argument that philosophical work in Britain today is irrelevant to the confusions and questions of the market-place: merely that as philosophical work, its service to the everyday world must be indirect. We are admittedly, in Britain, living in a period when the dominant temper of academic philosophy is analytic and critical rather than speculative and constructive. (MacKinnon, 1953, p. 119)

MacKinnon continues that,

The impact of philosophy on the community at large must be largely indirect; the philosopher or philosophers cannot usurp the function of the priest or the preacher, the doctor or the psycho-analyst. He can neither give men a faith to live by; nor in the optimistic style of the thirties, believe that by the dissemination of textbooks of applied logic he can alter materially the springs of political or social decision. (MacKinnon, 1953, p. 120)

This means that

The teaching of philosophy is very uncommon in schools. Indeed, it is generally felt that except for a brief course of the most general kind, it is much better left to the more mature age at which a student proceeds to the university. (p. 123)

The British response demonstrates a principled objection to teaching philosophy in schools.

Philosophy has since been introduced as an A-level in the final years of secondary education in the UK. However, this course is optional and its uptake is small (NATRE, 2018). Similarly, philosophy is rarely an established part of secondary curricula in the United States. Later UNESCO reports claim that 'in African Francophone countries, teaching philosophy is obligatory and takes place during the last year of secondary school … [in] Anglophone countries, philosophy is not a required course' (UNESCO, 2009b, p. 22). This includes Australia and New Zealand, where philosophy is not part of the secondary curriculum (UNESCO, 1986). The influence of the Anglo-American analytic tradition and its aversion to philosophy in schools in the Anglophone world is such that UNESCO reports: 'One thing that stands out overall is the absence of philosophy as a mandatory subject in English-speaking countries. As one Malawian writer put it, "Malawi being an English-speaking country, philosophy is only taught here at university"' (UNESCO, 2007, p. 76).

It is worth noting that many countries fall outside of the themes discussed. For example, Finland is neither under the sole influence of the Anglo-American analytic tradition, nor is it a Catholic country or influenced by the French *Baccalaureat*. Here, philosophy has historically always played a role in some parts of the religious education provision. More recently, a philosophy and ethics course has been added for all students during their last two years of school.

Philosophy for Children (P4C)

P4C is a much discussed approach to teaching philosophy, which is taught in schools across the world. P4C originated in the late 1960s with Matthew Lipman's pioneering work, and P4C approaches have brought philosophy into both secondary and primary schools across the world. P4C stands in contrast to more traditional approaches to philosophy teaching. It comes with its own distinctive pedagogy based on the Community of Inquiry (CoI), which promotes a certain type of dialogue. P4C has an international presence and is an associated body of literature setting out its aims, methods and virtues.

In 2007, UNESCO recorded case studies of P4C teaching in primary schools from across the world. These include Germany, Austria, Belgium, Canada, Spain, France, Italy, Norway, Czech Republic, the UK, the United States, Argentina, Brazil, Chile, Colombia, Mexico, Peru, Uruguay, Venezuela, Japan and Malaysia. P4C is not part of any compulsory curriculum in these countries, but tends to be associated with grass-roots initiatives to bring P4C into schools. UNESCO reports that 'according to our research and the responses to the UNESCO questionnaire, virtually no P4C initiatives appear to have been instigated in schools in the region of Africa and the Arab states – or if they have, they have yet to be publicized via the Internet or in journal articles' (UNESCO, 2007, p. 42).

As of 2019 the International Council of Philosophical Inquiry with Children (ICPIC) lists sixty-three countries involved in P4C (ICPIC, 2019). The Society for the Advancement of Philosophical Enquiry and Reflection in Education (SAPERE), the largest P4C organization in the UK, has sixty registered trainers and train 5,500 teachers a year in the UK (SAPERE, 2008. Hand and Winstanley note that 'it is difficult to find reliable figures on just how many schools are currently offering P4C programmes to pupils', but cite an ICPIC estimate that 2,000 primary schools and 200 secondary schools offer P4C in the UK (Hand & Winstanley, 2008, p. xiii).

Although P4C is predominantly aimed at primary-aged students, P4C approaches have proved malleable and have been used in secondary schools and other community groups such as prisons and homeless shelters. P4C advocates also provide some of the most detailed discussions available of why philosophy ought to be incorporated into school curricula. Compared to the other influences on the presence of philosophy in schools, the influence exerted by the P4C movement is relatively new and promising in terms of its popularity and growth in recent years.

Challenges to Philosophy in Schools

Besides the influence of Catholicism, the French *Baccalaureat*, the Anglo-American tradition and P4C, various other local factors have influenced attitudes towards philosophy in schools. I will outline some of the difficulties faced by philosophy in schools in terms of: the tension between different philosophical traditions; the conflation of political ideology and philosophy; poorly thought out, or under-resourced teaching and global pressure to educate for technological advancement.

The Western origins of the model of philosophy that has been exported with colonial education systems creates tension where it meets other philosophical traditions. Where philosophy is taught in secondary schools, it tends to follow a European conception of philosophy. UNESCO asked survey participants to list ten philosophers who, in their opinion, were the most important to cover. These lists were largely identical, with slight differences between those in the Anglo-American tradition and those from the more continental French tradition (Droit, 1995, pp. 145–51). It is no surprise then, that philosophy has been accused of being imperialistic and at odds with a country's national identity. Hountondji points out that 'in this chronicle of works and discourse, the names which incontestably dominate – in the present state of our knowledge – are those of non-African authors. When the African pupil or student studies the history of philosophy under these conditions, does he not further alienate himself from his own culture? Likewise does not the teaching of philosophy become a teaching of dependence?' (Hountondji, 1984, p. 20). In India, the disparity between traditional philosophies and Western philosophy has caused difficulties relating to the content and nature of philosophy teaching: 'The conference recognised the urgent need for the reorganisation of courses in philosophy so as to correct the excessive emphasis laid on occidental systems and to accord an appropriate place to the study of oriental systems' (Nikam, 1953, p. 99).

Another complication for philosophy in schools is the tension between political ideologies, which are often labelled 'philosophies', and the sort of philosophy taught at universities and schools: 'The proclamation by the public authorities of doctrines of ideologies which, rightly or wrongly, are claimed as philosophies' are at odds with academic philosophical traditions (UNESCO, 1984, p. 14). In a report on the problems faced by philosophy teaching in Africa from 1980, UNESCO states as follows

> This gives rise to real or potential conflictual situations or, at the least, creates a malaise between professional philosophers, who see themselves as more qualified than non-specialists to deal with philosophical questions, and representatives of the public authorities, who are shocked by such pretensions and view them as a legacy of the liberal ideology dispensed by the Western universities where the majority of them studied or as a manifestation of elitism or corporatism. (UNESCO, 1980, p. 3)

A related issue is the use of philosophy departments to further state ideology. In 1986, a description of the largest university philosophy department in China showed that it emphasized political ideology over other aspects of the philosophical canon: 'There are 11 research offices in the Philosophy Institute, devoted to: dialectical materialism; historical materialism; dialectics of nature (philosophy of science); history of the philosophy of Marxism; philosophy of Mao Zedong's thought; history of Chinese philosophy; history of Western philosophy; logic; ethics; aesthetics and the editorial board of the Journal of Philosophical Research, which publishes professional journals in philosophy' (Fensi, 1986, p. 81). The relationship between philosophical thought and ideology makes philosophy courses natural grounds for peddling state-endorsed political and ideological agendas. A similar point might be made about recent changes in Spain where

> philosophy is traditionally taught in the last two years of secondary school (Bachillerato), in two courses: one is called Philosophical Concepts (Filosofía I) and the other The History of Philosophy (Filosofía II) … In 2006, the Organic Law of Education (Ley Orgánica de Educación, LOE) changed the title of Filosofía I to Philosophy and Citizenship, skewing it towards a course in civic education and severing its connections with the sister subject, History of Philosophy. (UNESCO, 2011, p. 42)

Using a philosophy course to teach citizenship illustrates the idea that philosophy courses are easily adapted to further political aims. Regardless of whether or not this is justifiable, it pushes other philosophical content off the curriculum.

Conversely, some countries have avoided teaching philosophy precisely because it raises questions about political and ideological neutrality. One of the problems identified in the 1980 report into philosophy in Africa is that 'in some countries there is a real mistrust of philosophy which is considered as utopian and subversive dreaming' (UNESCO, 1980, p. 3). In countries facing internal conflict, this might be perceived as a threat to peace. The report asks whether it is

> possible to conceive of a neutral, uncommitted philosophy, a philosophy akin to a "rigorous science" transcending political conflicts, a philosophy uninvolved in the class struggle, in the struggle between the people and its exploiters, between the subjected nations and the imperialist home countries and, perhaps it should be added, in the struggle between the State and the people, the machinery of repression and its victims within the same nation. (UNESCO, 1980, p. 4)

If this is not possible, then it seems that philosophy teaching in schools is going to conflict with some aim or another espoused by the state.

A further problem faced by philosophy teaching is that of non-ideal teaching conditions. One student, interviewed in Tunisia, described her situation: 'In class students try harder to receive than to participate because it is a heavy curriculum and there's not enough time. Students are only thinking about remembering what is being taught so that they can use it later. Given how little time there is, from the moment he or she enters the classroom the teacher tries to dictate the lesson to us and that's it' (UNESCO, 2009a, p. 30). Similarly, 'in a study of the Organization of Ibero-American States devoted to the curricula of philosophy at secondary level in 18 Latin American countries in 1992, it appeared that "where philosophy is still taught, the education process emphasizes the history of philosophy rather than philosophy itself. Too often, in fact, philosophy is taught in a pompous, even pedantic way, by summoning up the great names of the history of philosophy. This way of teaching tends to discourage students and to deaden their interest in the field"' (UNESCO, 2009, p. 31).

Philosophy is sometimes seen as at odds with certain aims of education. In particular, where countries place a strong emphasis on the role of education as a means of strengthening the economy and future prospects of the nation. For example, 'testimonials from South Africa report a growing disenchantment with regard to philosophy, which is often regarded as unable to contribute to the economic and scientific progress of their country' (UNESCO, 2007, p. 124). In these circumstances, philosophy appears a poor contender for curriculum space.

Philosophy in Schools in the UK

To place the global picture painted by the UNESCO surveys into context, the situation in the UK illustrates many of the factors discussed. Despite home-grown arguments to the effect that philosophy should not be taught to children, there are multiple instances where philosophy plays a role in schools.

Alongside Emmet's already mentioned scepticism about the value of philosophy in education, other British philosophers have expressed doubts about the role of philosophy in schools. Wilson considers the growing influence of P4C poorly thought through. He thinks that P4C is unclear about what philosophical thinking is, what it contributes to education and what it is that P4C advocates hope students will learn (Wilson, 1992, p. 17). White makes a similar point, suggesting that philosophy should only be taught in schools if it clearly meets an educational aim (White, 2005). Another line of thought which has been influential is Kitchener's scepticism about whether children are capable of doing philosophy. He argues that, although P4C might help children with their critical thinking skills, the evidence does not show that it helps them with abstract philosophical thought. He follows Piaget in suggesting that children under the age of ten may not be capable of properly engaging with abstract philosophy (Kitchener, 1990, p. 430). Nonetheless, philosophy still plays a role in various parts of school curricula in the UK.

P4C is widely practised at primary level, but is not part of any of the national curricula. It is usually introduced with the aim of bringing about improved social skills, or critical thinking abilities. There is some presence of P4C in secondary schools. For example, the organization *Thinking Space* received funding to take philosophy into schools in West Yorkshire and Derbyshire with the aim of helping students to think about pursuing higher education in the future (Thinking Space, 2020). King's College Taunton run 'Philosothon' events in the South West of England where students are provided with a philosophical stimulus, and facilitated dialogue is encouraged in groups. This is modelled on the Philosothon P4C movement in Australia and New Zealand (philosothon. co.uk, 2020). It is not uncommon for secondary schools to run P4C inspired optional philosophy clubs for their students.

As outlined in the introduction, at secondary level, students often study philosophical content in the form of philosophy of religion and ethics components of Religious Studies courses. Until 2016, many Religious Studies General Certificate of Secondary Education (GCSE) specifications available were 'philosophy and ethics' courses, which used themes taken from applied ethics and philosophy to explore ideas from religions (e.g. OCR, 2012. Since 2016, GCSE specifications have become more focused on studying religion, and philosophical content has diminished. Between the ages of sixteen and eighteen, students in the UK have the option to study philosophy as an A-level course. The more popular Religious Studies A-level also covers philosophy in some detail. The course consists of three compulsory modules. For the exam board OCR the modules are: philosophy of religion, religion, and ethics and developments in religious thought (OCR, 2019).

Some schools in the UK teach the International Baccalaureate, which includes a compulsory 'Theory of Knowledge' (ToK) course. This is part of the core of the International Baccalaureate diploma and is designed to play 'a special role by providing an opportunity for students to reflect on how we know what we know. When done well, the course can have a huge impact on students, helping them to make connections between different disciplines, to be aware of multiple perspectives, and to be more aware of their own individual perspective and assumptions' (IBO, 2017b). ToK is not a philosophy course, but asks philosophical questions; 'the current ToK materials try to make clear that ToK is not intended to be a philosophy course, but a significant number of ToK teachers still approach the course in this way by, for example, basing their course around philosophical texts' (IBO, 2017a, p. 3).

Mirroring trends in philosophy teaching worldwide, there is a link between religion and philosophy as seen in the presence of philosophical content on religious studies courses in the UK. The idea that philosophy should be taught because it is an academic discipline is reflected in the philosophy A-level. The French approach that secondary education requires philosophical reflection is evident in ToK on the International Baccalaureate curriculum. P4C has also spread so that it is a popular addition to the curriculum or to extracurricular programmes at many schools.

While P4C has garnered positive press and seems to be growing in popularity, philosophy is not part of any compulsory school curriculum in the UK. Furthermore, the numbers of students taking a religious studies GCSE and A-level is dropping, the amount of philosophy on the Religious Studies GCSE and A-level has been reduced, and the number of students taking A-level philosophy remains small. ToK is only taught in a small minority of British schools. Like in many other countries, philosophy in schools is vulnerable to social, political and economic pressure. Currently, resources are being redirected to numeracy, literacy and the STEM subjects. This has led to difficulties for those making the case for teaching philosophy in secondary schools.

Philosophy for Children (P4C)

The majority of the debate about whether philosophy should be included on the curriculum comes from a large literature about P4C. This warrants spending some time setting out exactly what P4C is before moving on to a discussion of the different arguments for teaching philosophy in schools. A critical discussion of P4C, including its relationship to the academic discipline of philosophy will form part of Chapter 2.

Philosophy for children, or P4C, refers to a loosely related set of models for doing philosophy, which trace their roots back to Matthew Lipman's work to develop a pedagogy for teaching thinking skills through philosophy. The following excerpt from an interview provides Lipman's account of the origins of P4C:

> Back in the early '70s, when my own children were about 10 or 11 years old, the school they were attending did not give them the instruction in reasoning that I thought they needed. I was teaching logic at the college level at the time, and I felt that I wasn't accomplishing very much with my students because it was too late, they should have had instruction in reasoning much earlier (Lipman quoted in Brandt, 1988, p. 34)

Since its introduction by Lipman, P4C has spread across the world. Simultaneously, P4C has developed into a diversity of approaches. This makes providing a definitive account of P4C problematic. As such, I will restrict my exposition of P4C to approaches which emphasize use of the CoI or analogous pedagogies. I will refer to these as principled P4C approaches since they take the Deweyan principles behind Lipman's model of P4C seriously.

Lipman was influenced by Dewey's view that 'what should be happening in the classroom is thinking ... The route he [Dewey] proposed ... is that the educational process in the classroom should take as its model the process of scientific inquiry' (Lipman, 2003, p. 14). Following this approach, the focus of a principled P4C model is on inquiry with the aim of developing critical, creative and caring thinking amongst participants through open-ended philosophical dialogue (Lipman, 2003). Understanding the importance of Dewey's influence on Lipman is key to understanding the CoI. For Dewey, education aims to help children to develop. This entails 'continual reorganising, reconstructing [and] transforming of a child's experiences' (Dewey, 1916, p. 59). Since the CoI derives from this Deweyan understanding of education, in order to enact a CoI in a classroom it is important that 'a community of inquiry attempts to follow the inquiry where it leads rather than be penned in by the boundary lines of existing disciplines' (Lipman, 2003, p. 20). P4C is thus committed, in a principled way, to open-ended dialogue and minimal teacher-led exposition. It is worth noting that Dewey did not write about or propose the CoI, but that it is a Dewey-inspired approach which gives P4C a distinctive nature and value.

A useful distinction in coming to understand the CoI is Hand's distinction between directive and non-directive teaching. Directive teaching has 'the aim of persuading' while non-directive teaching 'has no persuasive aim' (Hand, 2018, p. 37). Directive teaching can include dialogue and does not imply didactic teaching. Hand gives the example of two teachers who each present children with a video debate about 'whether there is a justified moral requirement to vote in general elections' (p. 37). The non-directive teacher facilitates a class discussion whilst remaining neutral. The directive teacher 'ensures that (what he takes to be) the sound arguments for the requirement, and the sound objections to arguments against it, are thoroughly aired and understood, either by giving the floor to pupils able to articulate them or by feeding them into the discussion himself' (pp. 37–8). In both cases, students are engaged in dialogue, but in one case the teacher is neutral and in the other, the teacher is not. P4C is non-directive for principled reasons, meaning that teachers should facilitate without guiding the discussion and that any content must be presented in stimulus form rather than developed by the teacher. To directively engage in P4C would undermine the CoI's emphasis on child-centred inquiry.

The following account of P4C by Haynes is a fair representation of a typical principled P4C session: participants are asked to pause for thought, either through small group discussion or pair work or in silence. The next step involves questioning. In some sessions this is spontaneous and natural, but in others, children's questions are written on a board and grouped to allow children to vote on the questions they would like to start with. Group discussion is then facilitated with the aim of building on each other's ideas. The teacher should record the discussion and aim for closure at the end of the session with some form of review (Haynes, 2008, pp. 31–8). While the content of P4C sessions will vary depending on the desires of the participants, the structure of the session is prescribed and distinctive compared to other activities undertaken at school. It is this prescribed structure, based on the CoI, which I am referring to as the principled P4C model.

A principled P4C model is dominant in the UK. SAPERE is the largest UK-based organization offering training and guidance for those wishing to do philosophy in schools and communities. Their mission statement reads, 'We train teachers in Philosophy for Children which encourages children to think critically, creatively, collaboratively and caringly' (SAPERE, 2018). The SAPERE model of P4C is clearly CoI based: 'Children are taught how to create their own philosophical questions. They then choose one question that is the focus of a philosophical enquiry, or dialogue ... The teacher, as facilitator, supports the children in their thinking, reasoning and questioning, as well as the way the children speak and listen to each other in the dialogue' (SAPERE, 2018). SAPERE takes a principled stance against directive inquiry. The only guidance permitted by the facilitator is to encourage critical, caring and creative thinking.

The second largest P4C organization in the UK, the Philosophy Foundation takes a less principled approach and allows for some directive teaching, in particular to introduce philosophical ideas. Nonetheless, the Philosophy Foundation still emphasizes what it calls 'philosophical enquiry' and its own 'dialectical method of facilitation . . . with minimal interference from the facilitator' (Philosophy-Foundation, 2018). More broadly, P4C is not always principled, but many of the approaches to doing philosophy which associate themselves with P4C draw inspiration from the principled model and share a commitment to some form of non-directive dialogue-based group inquiry such as the CoI.

The idea of a CoI is central to almost all forms of P4C, but even so, there are large differences in approaches and in the theoretical groundings of different P4C models. *The Routledge International Handbook for Philosophy for Children* lists some of these differences and schisms in the field:

> Since the early 1970s there have been numerous and divergent approaches. Notable among these are Per Jespersen's approach that draws on the tradition of story-telling in Denmark; Catherine McCall's approach (Scotland) to the community of philosophical inquiry that emphasizes rigorous logical argumentation; Ekhart Martens' 'five finger model' (Germany) of incorporating phenomenology, hermeneutics, analysis, dialectics and speculation as phases of philosophical inquiry; the approach developed in the Netherlands by Karel van der Leeuw and Pieter Mostert, combining insights from Nelson, Lipman and Chinese philosophy; Michel Tozzi's 'democratic-philosophical method'

(France) in which students are assigned specific functions in the context of parliamentary discussion; and Oscar Brenifier's method of Socratic maieutics (France) that focuses on self-confrontation and the discipline of one's own thought and speech. In addition, Gareth Matthews' 1976 essay inaugurated the study of philosophy in children's literature, which was the topic of the column 'Thinking in Stories,' he wrote from 1979 to 2006 in the IAPC journal Thinking. This work opened the way for children's literature and picturebooks to become an important curricular resource, alternative to the IAPC curriculum. (Gregory et al. 2016, pp. xxvi–xxvii)

They conclude that despite these differences, P4C focuses on philosophical dialogue, rather than what they call 'text-based high school philosophy courses patterned on introductory college courses' (Gregory et al., 2016, p. xxvii).

P4C stands in contrast with traditional, disciplinary philosophy courses. These might focus on the history of philosophy such as those taught in secondary schools in Italy, or they might mirror university philosophy teaching such as the Philosophy A-level in the UK. In comparison, the P4C movement has a distinctive pedagogy. P4C sessions are not like traditional school lessons; they provide students with a different sort of experience. Since many of the existing arguments for teaching philosophy in schools derive from the P4C literature, setting out a clear understanding of what P4C is provides a starting point for a critical analysis of these reasons, which will be undertaken in Chapter 2. I argue that the sort of philosophy that should be taught in schools is at least somewhat directive and is more closely aligned to the academic discipline of philosophy than P4C is.

2

Existing Arguments for Teaching Philosophy in Schools

This chapter aims to do two things. The first is to introduce a set of criteria for judging claims about what should be included on the curriculum. The second is to show that existing claims about why philosophy should be taught in schools do not fully meet these criteria. This chapter is important because it demonstrates the need for the arguments put forward in Chapters 5 and 6, which aim to establish failsafe reasons for teaching philosophy in schools. By setting out two preliminary criteria as a basic framework for assessing existing reasons for including philosophy on the school curriculum, I conclude that as they stand, these existing reasons either do not meet the criteria, or require further development.

In brief, the two criteria that any adequate argument for teaching philosophy in schools needs to meet are that the argument should (1) demonstrate that teaching philosophy provides some specifiable educational good(s) and (2) that there is reason to hold that these educational goods are only, or best, delivered by teaching philosophy. These criteria are needed for any case for including a subject on the school curriculum.

With these criteria in mind, I examine the commonly cited reasons for teaching philosophy in schools. These are: those given by the P4C literature; reasons that link philosophy with moral and civic education; reasons based on the nature of philosophy as a discipline and reasons appealing to the idea that philosophy is central to education.

Following this evaluation, I set out the direction that my own arguments will take. My route to finding fail-safe reasons for teaching philosophy in schools involves first asking what it is that schools are hoping to achieve when they provide students with a broad theoretical education. I will argue that teaching philosophy is central to realizing the goals of providing children with a broad theoretical education. This approach ensures that the arguments I put forward specify the educational goods associated with teaching philosophy and can show that philosophy is best placed to provide those goods.

Criteria for Including a Subject on the Curriculum

In this section, I introduce and defend criteria for judging curriculum justifications. These criteria form the basis of a system for determining whether the reasons given for teaching philosophy in schools are good enough to justify its inclusion on the curriculum. There are two basic tests that these reasons can be subjected to. The first test asks whether the reason refers to some educational good and the second is whether the reason suggests that teaching philosophy is the best, or the only way of providing that good. Educational goods are the positive things that an education can contribute towards. Brighouse et al. list these as 'economic productivity, personal autonomy, democratic competence, healthy personal relationships, treating others as equals, and personal fulfilment' (Brighouse et al., 2018, p. 23). However, there is no reason to hold that this list of educational goods is definitive; a plurality can be proposed, in greater detail if needed.

Minimally, when making a case for the inclusion of an activity on the school curriculum, it is important to explain why the activity in question is a good use of students' time. This means explaining how it contributes to some educational good. School time is limited, and school timetables are pressed to deliver a range of different goods. Given the plurality of goods that schools could provide and the importance of ensuring basic goods such as literacy, numeracy and social goods such as preparing students for economic productivity are provided for, arguing for the addition of a new subject is no mean feat. Any argument for the inclusion of philosophy on the curriculum is going to need to make the case for its inclusion in competition with other possible activities.

Making a case for teaching philosophy in schools differs from giving reasons for teaching philosophy. Giving a reason for teaching philosophy in schools is less stringent than providing an argument for teaching philosophy in schools. When I was a teacher, one reason that I taught philosophy was that I enjoyed teaching it. Another reason was that I knew that many of my students enjoyed philosophy lessons. While these reasons might contribute to a case for teaching philosophy in schools, they do not amount to one. An argument, or a case, for teaching philosophy in schools needs to be valid; the reasons given need to lead to an inescapable conclusion. This means that listing the benefits of teaching philosophy is not sufficient to make a case for its provision in schools. A valid argument requires some account of what schools ought to teach, and reasons for teaching philosophy that inescapably contribute to this account.

In light of this, two basic considerations should guide decisions about the content of a curriculum. These are (1) that teaching philosophy provides some specifiable educational goods and (2) that there is reason to hold that these goods are only or best delivered by teaching philosophy. Ultimately, these criteria will require some account of the nature and aims of education in order to be able to establish what an educational good is, and also which educational goods ought to take priority over others when resources are limited (Hirst, 1974; White, 2012). This task will be undertaken in Chapters 3 and 4. In this section, I will explain the reasoning behind the two proposed criteria.

Hirst defines the curriculum as 'a programme of activities designed so that pupils will attain by learning certain specifiable aims or objectives' (Hirst, 1974, p. 2). For example, the English National Curriculum sets out the following aims:

> Every state-funded school must offer a curriculum which is balanced and broadly based and which: promotes the spiritual, moral, cultural, mental and physical development of pupils at the school and of society; prepares pupils at the school for the opportunities, responsibilities and experiences of later life. (Gov.co.uk, 2016)

A coherent curriculum is one which is based on well thought through educational objectives and aims which are realized via the prescribed content and programme of activities appropriate to those aims. In the case of the English National Curriculum, the aims given are expected to be met through the 'statutory programmes of study' of English, mathematics, science, art and design, citizenship, computing, design and technology, geography, history, language, music and physical education (Gov.co.uk, 2014). These subjects are held to contribute to the educational goods identified as aims by the English National Curriculum. Without well-thought-through aims and programmes of study to meet those aims, a curriculum can lack educational value. In order to assess the coherence of the English National Curriculum, both its aims and methods need to be subjected to scrutiny. This means that some account of educational goods, some account of which educational goods ought to take priority, and some account of how those educational goods might be provided for, all need to be thought through.

This sort of joined-up thinking about the curriculum is rare in practice. Writing in 1932, Whitehead describes a school curriculum which involves 'algebra, from which nothing follows; geometry, from which nothing follows; science, from which nothing follows; history, from which nothing follows; a couple of languages, never mastered; and lastly, most dreary of all, literature, represented by plays of Shakespeare, with philological notes and short analyses of plot and character to be in substance committed to memory' (Whitehead, 1932, p. 9). This caricature of education is still recognizable today. White thinks that the British curriculum is essentially Victorian; 'new patterns have been overlaid on old, but the old show through' (White, 2004, p. 179). The programme of study outlined by the English National Curriculum would be recognizable to Whitehead. It is also unclear why the programme of study outlined is the best means of fulfilling the aims set out by the English National Curriculum itself. White's view is that the curriculum is a mixture of ad hoc alterations to an arbitrary historical artefact.

Another consideration when planning the curriculum is that since during term time children spend up to one third of their waking life in school (Long, 2000, p. 131), this curtailment on their free time needs to be justifiable. White points out that the curriculum needs to at least provide them with something that is in their interests (White, 1973, pp. 6–7). A harmful, ill-thought through, incoherent or trivial curriculum would make the practice of schooling morally problematic. The question of what ought to go onto the curriculum is an important normative question because it concerns a mandated use of children's time. This infringement on liberty requires more attention than it is typically afforded in practice.

In *Ethics and Education*, Peters sets out a primary consideration for any curriculum subject. He defines education as 'the initiation of others into worthwhile activities' (Peters, 1966, p. 144). Since there are many competing worthwhile activities, planning a curriculum requires a 'choice between a range of activities which are thought to be worth passing on. Science, mathematics, history, art, cooking and carpentry feature on the curriculum, not bingo, bridge and billiards' (p. 144). There need to be guiding principles behind the selection of worthwhile activities for inclusion on the curriculum. Any argument for the inclusion of an activity onto the curriculum is going to need to be able to answer the question of 'why do this rather than that?' (p. 156). When it comes to arguing that philosophy ought to be included on the curriculum, it is essential to be able to justify its inclusion at the expense of some existing subject, or over other possible content which is not currently included. An argument for the inclusion of philosophy is going to need to be able to justify why philosophy should be included, rather than some other worthwhile activity. This holds even if a new curriculum is being planned from scratch; so long as resources are limited, some decision needs to be made about why one activity ought to be included over another.

Whatever reason is given for the inclusion of one worthwhile activity over another, if it is to serve as an adequate justification for placing a subject on the curriculum, it is going to need to appeal to some educational good. For example, some have argued that philosophy should be included on the curriculum because children enjoy it, and enjoyment is an educational good (Hobbs, 2018; Matthews, 1980). If this is going to provide the basis for a valid argument for the inclusion of philosophy, then reasons are needed for thinking that enjoyable activities are educationally valuable. It is uncontroversial that enjoyable activities are important outside of education, and it is uncontroversial that wherever possible, educational activities should strive to be enjoyable; however, the idea that enjoyment is an educational good does not necessarily follow. Furthermore, if enjoyment is an educational good, then a question arises about the relative importance of enjoyment. Excluding numeracy and literacy from the curriculum for those students who do not find them enjoyable, or in favour of more enjoyable activities, seems to raise enjoyment as an educational good above other educational goods that are often considered more important.

Hirst makes this point when he claims that the contents of the curriculum need to be guided by the aims and objectives of education: 'If curriculum planning is a matter of planning means to specified ends, and an educational curriculum therefore serves educational ends, the clearer we are about those ends and their nature the more adequate the planning can be' (Hirst, 1974, p. 16). Thinking about the curriculum requires thinking in terms of educational goods: the aims of education and the activities best suited to realizing those aims and bringing about the educational goods that accord with them.

There are many possible approaches to outlining the aims of education. Peters argues that the academic disciplines ought to be included in the curriculum because they aim at the pursuit of truth, which is the ultimate end of education. Hirst offers an account of education which links induction into 'forms of knowledge' to the development of 'mind' and claims that induction into the forms of knowledge is just what it means to be educated (Hirst, 1974, pp. 27–8). Alternatively, Dewey describes education as beginning 'unconsciously, almost at birth, and . . . continually shaping the individual's powers, saturating his consciousness, forming his habits, training his ideas and arousing his feelings and emotions' (Dewey, 1967, p. 19). The role of the curriculum is to allow students to engage in the 'continuing reconstruction of experience' which constitutes education (p. 27). This leads Dewey to suggest that the schools should be responsive to individuals' own interests rather than imposing a curriculum upon them. If the aims of education are taken to be vocational, a case could be made for designing the curriculum as a means of providing students with the skills and aptitudes that they are going to need once they start work. Or, if education aims to cultivate virtues, then the curriculum ought to be designed to bring about this end (Reiss & White, 2013).

Any discussion of the content of the curriculum supervenes on debates about the aims of education. This means that an argument for including philosophy on the curriculum is going to need rest on some account of the nature and aims of education. This is why White claims that 'we should not posit from the start that there should be a subject called "Philosophy" and then show what contribution it can make to school learning. This gets things round the wrong way. We should begin with fundamental aims [of education] and see what learning requirements these bring with them' (White, 2012, p. 457). An argument for including philosophy in the curriculum which does not appeal to the aims of education begs the question of whether the curriculum in question is itself educational, and whether the inclusion of philosophy has any educational value. Without answers to these questions, or if the answers are negative, there is no real justification for placing philosophy on the curriculum.

I will now go through some common reasons cited for teaching philosophy in schools and assess their potential to meet these two criteria: (1) that teaching philosophy provides some specifiable educational goods and it is the case (2) that there is reason to hold that these goods are only, or best delivered by teaching philosophy.

Reasons for Putting Philosophy on the School Curriculum

The primary sources of literature about why philosophy should be taught in schools relate to P4C. Here, several well-developed reasons are presented, grounded in both empirical and theoretical work on the subject. Other than P4C sources, few well-developed reasons are given for teaching philosophy. These include reasons for teaching philosophy as a part of religious, moral and civic education, reasons for teaching philosophy based on its status as a discipline, and some reasons based on the idea that philosophy is central to education. Each of these reasons will be evaluated in turn, and I will show why each falls short of providing a complete argument for teaching philosophy in schools.

Reasons Associated with Philosophy for Children

The P4C literature puts forward a variety of arguments for including philosophy in the school curriculum. These allude to improvements P4C interventions yield in students' academic skills (e.g. their critical thinking or cognitive test performance), ways in which P4C contributes to students' social skills (e.g. empathy, communication skills, teamwork), and the contribution P4C makes to students' attitudes or values (e.g. civic attitudes, moral or intellectual virtues). There are both empirical studies and theoretical works exploring each of these areas. It is worth bearing in mind that the relationship between P4C and a broader conception of philosophy is questionable. While P4C and philosophy overlap, they are not synonymous (Gatley, 2020, p. 548).

The first reason given for including P4C on the school curriculum is that it improves students' academic skills. Most often, this claim relates to critical thinking abilities, but it is also a claim about students' test results on cognitive ability tests and other tests such as reading, writing and mathematics. Lipman devised P4C as a fix for his own children's, and undergraduate students' lack of thinking skills. Cam claims that 'Lipman's main interest is in how best to promote critical, creative and complex thinking in the classroom. His view is that the richest resource at our disposal is philosophy' (Cam, 1995, p. 1).

There is empirical research addressing the relationship between P4C and academic skills in students. In 2006, Topping and Trickey published a systematic review of controlled outcome studies of P4C in primary and secondary schools. They point out that all show some positive outcome. Of the ten studies, six measure either critical thinking abilities or performance in mathematics and reading tests, which would indicate the acquisition of non-domain-specific thinking namely critical thinking (Topping & Trickey, 2006, p. 376).

Topping and Trickey also undertook their own empirical work into the relationship between P4C and cognitive ability test results. Their study 'investigated the long-term effects of experience of collaborative inquiry based on the principles of Philosophy for Children in primary school – and in particular, whether gains in cognitive ability were maintained when the pupils (students) were in secondary school 2 years later' (Topping & Trickey, 2007, p. 787). They found significant gains in cognitive ability test scores immediately after the intervention and also two years later, once students had moved to secondary school. Until March 2021, the most large-scale research into the cognitive benefits brought about by P4C was the original Educational Endowment Foundation (EEF) evaluation of P4C. Here, students who took part in P4C sessions were seen to make an additional two month's progress in reading and mathematics after a P4C intervention, and compared to their peers who did not do any P4C (Gorard et al., 2015). However, in March 2021, the EEF published a new study casting doubt on these findings (Lord et al., 2021). Initial findings were not replicated, and the EEF withdrew its support of philosophy in schools.

Following on from Gorard's 2015 research into the cognitive benefits of P4C, Siddiqui et al provided empirical evidence about the relationship between P4C and so called 'non-cognitive outcomes'. Using the control group from Gorard's research, they asked students about their '"social and communication skills", "team work and resilience" and "empathy"' (Siddiqui et al., 2017, p. 6). The study found small positive effect sizes for those participating in P4C sessions, suggesting that P4C does have the potential to contribute to these sorts of non-cognitive outcomes. In a 2020 case study, Gatley, Woodhouse and Forstenzer found that the same seemed to apply for secondary school students attending a philosophy conference; that the conference helped students to feel more confident in their social skills (Gatley et al., 2020).

Alongside this empirical work, there is theoretical literature about the effects of P4C on social skills. Lipman highlights the role of the Community of Inquiry (CoI), which is the pedagogy associated with P4C where the teacher facilitates group inquiry, as a means to developing caring thinking (Lipman, 2003, p. 197). The CoI, according to Lipman, fosters inclusiveness, participation, shared cognition, face-to-face relationships, social solidarity, deliberation, impartiality, modelling, thinking for oneself, challenging as a procedure, reasonableness, questioning and discussion (Lipman, 2003, p. 95). Some of these attributes can be cast as intellectual and moral virtues, others are improvements in social skills resulting from P4C sessions. Fisher describes P4C as helping 'to create a moral culture, a way of thinking and acting together that cultivates virtues such as respect for others, sincerity and open-mindedness' (Fisher, 2008, p. 57). Engaging in P4C is thus associated with students' social skills; often in relation to the CoI pedagogy.

Another prominent theme in the P4C literature is the role that P4C can play in engendering democratic values in children, schools and broader society. Haynes claims that when children learn through P4C to 'express their views with confidence, knowing that their voices are heard and they can raise questions of interest and concern to them' they are beginning to exercise their rights as citizens (Haynes, 2008, p. 57). Fisher points out that 'a fully participative democratic society requires autonomous citizenry that can think, judge and act for themselves', and views these abilities as outcomes of engaging in P4C sessions (Fisher, 2004, p. 10). The attitudes or virtues generated through participation in P4C sessions can be equated with the sorts of attitudes and virtues required by engaged citizens.

A slightly different, but parallel consideration is the idea that P4C can contribute to a politically engaged society through challenging power dynamics in schools. Haynes and Murris stress the importance of the role reversal between teacher and students in contributing to this. In a P4C session, the teacher facilitates the session, and it is the children's ideas which take the fore. This is important because it emphasises that 'a participatory democracy presupposes non-dualist epistemologies and implies that all voices in the classroom, including those of teachers, are viewed as partial and needing to be questioned' (Haynes & Murris, 2011, p. 287). Lyle takes a different angle and highlights the impact of P4C on teachers, such that 'the participatory practice of P4C has the power to shift teachers' narratives of childhood away from the deficit narratives of 'immature', 'incompetent', 'innocent', 'unruly', 'blank slate' or 'developing' (Lyle, 2014, p. 226). Furthermore, some have argued that P4C is the best approach to civic education since it allows for genuine engagement in dialogue, particularly between those from different social backgrounds (Makaiau, 2017 p. 19).

Evaluating P4C-Related Reasons

The literature promoting P4C points to educational goods brought about by teaching philosophy in schools. It provides a range of empirical, theoretical and anecdotal reasons for thinking that P4C brings about benefits which might justify including it on the curriculum. The P4C literature does not shy away from offering an account of the aims of education, and thus can provide some method of assessing which educational goods ought to be prioritised over others. P4C is aligned with Deweyan accounts of the aims of education, and the P4C literature argues that the pedagogy associated with P4C is central to these aims. As a result, the P4C literature meets the first criterion for arguing that philosophy ought to be included on the school curriculum: that (1) teaching philosophy provides some specifiable educational goods. However, the reasons given for bringing P4C into schools do not address the second criterion, of showing that (2) there is reason to hold that these goods are only or best delivered by teaching philosophy. The P4C literature does not fully establish that P4C is the only, or best method of bringing about the educational goods specified.

Academic Skills

Empirical evidence demonstrating the effect of P4C sessions on student attainment in cognitive ability tests (Topping & Trickey, 2006), on student attainment in mathematics, reading and writing tests (Gorard et al., 2015), and more generally, the often cited role of P4C in developing critical thinking skills and dispositions adds up to the claim that P4C sessions are worthwhile insofar as they develop students' academic skills. Since these academic skills are held to be educational goods, this constitutes a reason for putting P4C onto the school curriculum. In order to form the basis of an argument for teaching P4C, the second criterion of showing that P4C is the best or only way to develop academic skills in students must be addressed.

The most prominent claim about improvements in academic skills linked to P4C is that P4C improves critical thinking skills. I do not wish to dispute this. It seems clear that engaging in thoughtful dialogue about difficult questions, whilst responding to the views of others, would develop critical thinking abilities and dispositions. The empirical evidence is cumulatively convincing; many different investigations suggest some improvements in academic skills. I also do not wish to take issue with whether or not critical thinking ought to be encouraged in schools; this does not seem particularly contentious; it seems fair to say that the ability to engage in critical thinking is an educational good. However, it is not clear that P4C is the best or only way to improve these academic skills.

It is important to be able to say that P4C is either the only means of developing the cited academic skills or the best means of developing them. If this case cannot be made, then perhaps an existing subject on the curriculum could do the same work, or perhaps a different activity would be a more worthwhile addition to the curriculum. In the case of critical thinking, it seems that a course in critical thinking itself might be a more appropriate or effective means of developing students' critical thinking skills than P4C. Alternatively, critical thinking skills could be given greater emphasis in other subjects. The idea that only P4C can contribute to critical thinking skills, or even that it is the best way to develop critical thinking in students, seems to overlook the potential of many other ways of helping students to think critically.

There is the potential for an argument that could work. This would involve the claim that there is a certain sort of critical thinking, which is inherently philosophical, and which is a particular educational good that can only be brought about through philosophy teaching. If this could be shown to be the case, then some sort of philosophy course aimed at bringing about this sort of philosophical critical thinking would be a justified use of curriculum time. This is quite a demanding condition, and it is unclear what this philosophical critical thinking might be, or why it might be central to education. The existing literature does not offer this sort of case in any detail, although it is suggested by Worley's discussion of using philosophy to enhance students' metacognition (Worley, 2018). While I will not take this approach in my arguments, the argument that I present in Chapter 6 identifies how philosophical reasoning provides a distinctive educational good of solving conceptual confusions arising from broad theoretical curricula.

Research into the potential of P4C to contribute to other academic abilities faces similar problems. Gorard's research findings that P4C contributes to improvements in reading and mathematics do not explain why P4C makes these contributions to students' abilities. Since the research is quantitative, few hints are offered as to how or why P4C might help students to become better at, for instance, mathematics, which is not directly addressed during P4C sessions. The same can be said for reading. Whatever the reason, it seems plausible that devoting the time allocated for P4C sessions specifically to reading and mathematics might have a greater effect on test results. Similarly, research showing improved cognitive ability test scores does not tell us whether other interventions would have been more successful. No good reasons are given for thinking that P4C is the best way to bring about the academic skills listed.

Alongside falling short of making a case for teaching philosophy rather than other worthwhile activities, appealing to the role of P4C in developing academic skills does not meet White's stipulation that an argument for including philosophy on the curriculum cannot just appeal to the benefits associated with philosophy, it must also show that the benefits are a central to meeting some educational good. Further work is needed to explain why academic skills are educational goods, even if this seems uncontentious. The more difficult requirement is going to be explaining why the identified academic skills are more important educational goods than other educational goods, weighing up their place on the curriculum. This demonstrates the need for an account of the aims of education.

Social Skills, Attitudes and Virtues

Social skills, or what Siddiqui et al. label 'non-cognitive benefits' of P4C, relate to: team work, resilience and empathy (Siddiqui et al., 2017, p. 6); caring and creative thinking (Lipman, 2003, p. 197); inclusiveness, participation, social solidarity, impartiality and reasonableness (p. 95) and 'respect for others, sincerity and open-mindedness' (Fisher, 2008, p. 57). Cognitive benefits are those associated with belief-formation, whereas non-cognitive abilities are those associated with personal qualities and social interactions.

It seems plausible that P4C sessions contribute to students' social skills. Since a P4C session involves dialogue with peers, it is likely that students engaged in such dialogue develop personal qualities associated with social interaction. It also seems counter-productive to question whether these social skills are legitimate ends of schooling, although some account of their relative educational value would be helpful for comprehensive curriculum planning. It is straightforwardly the case that students ought to develop social skills during the time that they spend at school. Rather, the problem with this line of argument is similar to the problem with arguing that academic skills are furthered by P4C sessions: that P4C sessions might not be the only, or even best way of developing students' social skills.

Claims about the contribution of P4C to social skills do not establish that P4C is the best, or the only way to improve social skills. There are other possible methods of improving team work, resilience and empathy. Teamwork is often cited as an important outcome of playing sports at school, and spending time engaged in sport has the added benefit of contributing to students' fitness, so it could be argued that sports ought to be included over P4C, which has no such added benefit. Empathy might be better brought about through reading literature, spending time playing with peers or watching films. Similar points could be made about any social skill, since social skills can be developed in numerous different ways. There is no clear reason to think that P4C is the best or only way of developing students' social skills, and so there is no clear reason for including P4C on the curriculum instead of other activities, which could play a similar role.

This means that reasons based on improvements in social skills associated with P4C do not constitute a basis for an argument for teaching philosophy in schools since they do not establish that P4C is the only or best way of bringing about the educational goods identified. Similarly, no argument is currently offered to the effect that particular social skills, such as teamwork or communication skills, are educational goods which are central to the aims of education, although such a case could be made.

Another reason given for including P4C on the curriculum is that it contributes to students' civic education; 'a fully participative democratic society requires autonomous citizenry that can think, judge and act for themselves' (Fisher, 2008, p. 10). Bringing P4C into schools can help to bridge the divide between teacher and student, highlighting that children are members of society with rights as citizens so that schools become more virtuous environments (Haynes & Murris, 2011).

Like the other reasons given, this also falls short of meeting the second criterion for an argument for inclusion of P4C on the curriculum; it does not show that P4C is the only or best way of providing for this sort of civic education. This could involve teaching students about how democracy works, something which is not within the remit of P4C sessions, which are non-directive and focus on philosophical dialogue. If the focus is on civic virtues rather than teaching about civil society, then the case for P4C is going to rest on the extent to which P4C is the only or best means of bringing about civic virtues. Again, it is unclear whether P4C would be the best or only means; perhaps a course specifically designed to explore the nature of civic virtues, combined with activities such as volunteering in the community might be better placed.

Finally, it could be argued that the ability to engage in dialogue is necessary for members of a democratic society in order for a democracy to flourish. This would require an argument to the effect that the sort of dialogue required is necessarily philosophical. This sort of claim would need to give an account of the nature of philosophical dialogue, as opposed to other types of dialogue. This is an ambitious project, which I am not going to engage in, but in principle could work.

P4C and the Aims of Education

Apart from extensive literature about the benefits associated with P4C, the link between Dewey's philosophy of education and P4C presents a case for including P4C on the curriculum in light of specified aims of education. I will set out the influence of Dewey's philosophy of education on P4C, and then explain why this approach also fails to provide an argument for the inclusion of philosophy on the curriculum. In Chapter 1, I outlined the Deweyan grounding of P4C, and the distinctive non-directive, principled pedagogy, the CoI, which this has given rise to.

Based on the link between Deweyan aims of education and P4C, an argument can be constructed for its inclusion on the curriculum: if the aims of education are to encourage and allow for engaged communities of inquiry, then P4C ought to be included on the curriculum because the CoI meets this aim. The problem with this argument is that it does not take into account the possibility of using the CoI pedagogy elsewhere in the curriculum, without any emphasis on philosophy. Lipman proposed teaching philosophy as a means of bringing child-centred learning into schools because he thought that it had the most potential to allow for open-ended dialogue, however, he readily admits that other subjects could be used too (Lipman, 2003). If the aim of education is to allow students to shape their own learning, engage in a community of inquiry and develop critical, caring and creative thinking skills, then the CoI pedagogy could be implemented in existing lessons. Or the whole curriculum could adopt a CoI pedagogy, encouraging dialogue and non-directive, inquiry led teaching across the curriculum. This undermines the possibility of using Deweyan aims of education to argue for the inclusion of philosophy on the curriculum.

The distinctive nature of the P4C pedagogy makes it difficult to discern whether it is the CoI that is bringing about the benefits listed, or some attribute of P4C which is necessarily philosophical. The effects of P4C sessions could be associated with the benefits of engaging in dialogue, be it philosophical or non-philosophical. Any argument that education should involve a child-centred curriculum leads to the conclusion that this sort of inquiry should be included anywhere across the curriculum; not to an argument that philosophy should be brought into schools. The reasons provided by the P4C literature fall short of an argument that philosophy should be included on the curriculum. They also fall short of making the case that philosophy is a necessary component of the curriculum if certain aims of education are going to be met.

Nonetheless, the reasons given within the P4C literature for bringing P4C into schools hold some weight. Cumulatively, they show that P4C is beneficial to students in a range of different ways. This conclusion is important; however, it does not amount to a full argument for including P4C sessions on a coherent planned curriculum. This latter step would need a justification of why the educational goods brought about by P4C earn it a place on the curriculum, and whether P4C is best placed to bring about those goods. As it stands, this argument has not yet been fully presented. Finally, as was noted at the beginning of this section, an argument for teaching P4C in schools is not the same as an argument for teaching philosophy in schools because P4C has its own aims and pedagogy, which are not necessarily reflected in broader conceptions of philosophy.

Other Reasons for Putting Philosophy on the Curriculum

While the P4C literature provides explicit reasons for bringing P4C sessions into schools, other possible reasons for teaching philosophy in schools exist. I have classified non-P4C reasons under three headings: (1) reasons tied to the role of philosophy in religious, moral and civic education; (2) reasons tied to the disciplinary status of philosophy and (3) reasons tied to the idea that philosophy should sit at the heart of any curriculum. Each of these sets of reasons will be assessed according to the criteria introduced in this chapter. Unlike the P4C literature, which is well-developed, these reasons have not been discussed in great detail by existing literature.

Religious Reasons

The UNESCO surveys covered in Chapter 1 illuminate the historic relationship between religion and philosophy. In some countries, philosophy, religious belief and philosophical traditions are difficult to differentiate from one another, which means that they are taught in the same curriculum space. Catholicism is also linked closely to philosophy such that countries with an influential Catholic presence have traditionally seen philosophy as a part of education. For example, philosophy was taught as an advanced course in Jesuit education, since the 1590s (Carlsmith, 2002, p. 223).

The connection between philosophy and religion is exemplified by A-level courses in Religious Studies in British schools. One exam board summarizes its A-level course as 'designed to develop a greater understanding and appreciation of religious beliefs and teachings, as well as the disciplines of ethics and philosophy of religion' (OCR, 2018, p. 2). The philosophical content of the course begins with Plato and Aristotle, reflecting classical influences on Christianity. The work of the 'Church Fathers' and other early Catholic scholars is prominent on the specification. Aquinas' versions of the cosmological and teleological argument are covered, followed by Anselm's account of the ontological argument. Irenaeus and Augustine's responses to the problem of evil form a large component of the specification, as do the views of Boethius and Anselm on the nature of God. Similarly, the ethics module covers Aquinas' natural law, Fletcher's situation ethics and Aquinas' views on conscience. These are presented alongside the more secular Kantian and utilitarian approaches. The applied ethical topics are those which have recently concerned the Church such as euthanasia and sexual ethics (OCR, 2018, pp. 7–28).

Although exam boards do not labour their reasons for including philosophy and ethics on religious studies courses, it seems likely that it is due in part to the historical intertwining of religion and philosophy. Another possible reason is the need for a non-confessional Religious Studies course, where it is assumed that those taking the course are likely to come from secular backgrounds.

Philosophical approaches have the potential to provide a critical lens through which to study religion.

These approaches have been elaborated on in academic discussions. Hand thinks that one important reason to teach philosophy is to address problems regarding justifying students' religious standards (Hand, 2018, p. 4). A similar claim is made by van der Straten Waillet et al., who think that aspects of P4C ought to be included in religious education lessons to promote an 'evaluationist' attitude towards religious claims which 'better fulfils the individual need for meaning and the societal need for commitment and respect in a pluralist environment' (van der Straten Waillet et al., 2015, p. 287). They contrast evaluationism to absolutism and relativism, where absolutism rejects the possibility of learning from opposing views, and relativism rejects the possibility of disagreeing with opposing views, and of providing robust justifications for one's own views. Gaudin points to the importance of teaching philosophy in French schools as a means of framing how religious facts can be taught in a secular framework. He thinks that the teaching of philosophy in the final year of French education allows students to think well about their own beliefs, thus forming well-justified views on the religious facts they have been taught in the past (Gaudin, 2016). This provides a degree of neutrality to religious education in French schools because the onus is on the individual student to formulate their own response to what they have been taught.

These ideas ground some of the justification for including philosophy on Religious Studies courses at A-level and GCSE in British schools. For example, in the 2017 mark scheme for the philosophy of religion module at GCSE level, OCR stipulates that 'good' answers should 'reflect the significance of the issue(s) raised' and show 'clear evidence of an appropriate personal response, fully supported' (OCR, 2018, p. 7). There is the potential for using philosophical thinking and philosophical theories to help students to form these sorts of supported, appropriate personal responses.

A separate argument for the inclusion of philosophy on the curriculum is presented in Newman's account of Catholic university education. He claims that knowledge amounts to:

> One whole, because its subject-matter is one; for the universe in its length and breadth is so intimately knit together that we cannot separate off portion from portion, and operation from operation, except by mental abstraction; and then again as to its creator … He has so implicated Himself with it, taken it into His very bosom, by His presence in it, His providence over it, His impressions upon

it, His influences through it, that we cannot truly or fully contemplate it without in some main aspects contemplating Him. (Newman, 1902, p. 51)

To engage in knowledge acquisition is to engage in the study of God. Newman goes further, and says that studying individual disciplines gives only a limited understanding of God, and so education must include studying a range of different disciplines. Furthermore, studying philosophy is necessary because philosophy is a 'science of the sciences' which studies the 'bearings of one science on another and the use of each to each, and the location and limitation and adjustment and due appreciation of them all, one with another' (Newman, 1902, p. 51). To study philosophy is to facilitate the study of God in His entirety.

Another argument for teaching philosophy as part of Catholic education is presented by Whittle who thinks that 'a non-confessional Catholic school would want to introduce compulsory philosophy lessons in order to ensure that all pupils are given opportunities to think philosophically about their beliefs and values, both secular and religious. To safeguard against the tendency to catechise pupils . . . [and] to appeal to theological insights about the significance of the mystery of human existence' (Whittle, 2015, p. 604). Whittle reiterates the importance of being able to evaluate beliefs. His additional focus on engaging with mysteries is more akin to Newman's view that engaging in philosophy is a form of engaging with faith.

Religious reasons for teaching philosophy, either in the form of P4C, as a more traditional course, or as a specifically designed course, overlap with reasons given elsewhere. For example, Hand does not limit his claim about the importance of evaluating standards to religion, but broadens it to political and moral standards as well. Similarly, being able to evaluate competing views is a benefit cited by the P4C literature. If teaching philosophy can help students to evaluate competing, or controversial ideas within religious education, then it seems fair to say that philosophy should be taught as part of religious education. The same caveats apply as elsewhere, philosophy should be the best means of helping students to evaluate beliefs; and also, the ability to evaluate religious beliefs needs to be an educational good. A further question arises about the status of religious educational goods, particularly when set against their controversial social standing (see Clayton & Stevens, 2018). In some instances, for example in the United States, teaching religion in schools is rejected outright. It is for this reason that I will avoid resting a case for teaching philosophy in schools on its role in religious education; religious education itself is controversial and requires a convincing argument if it is to be made a compulsory part of any curriculum. Furthermore, the sort of philosophy course justified by this line of argument is a narrow one, focused on religion. I will present arguments for a broader philosophy course.

Newman's view that the aims of education are tied up with coming to know God provides both a justification for the inclusion of religious education on the curriculum and, in Newman's view, an argument for the inclusion of philosophy on the curriculum. Newman's case for philosophy as a curriculum subject is that it is necessary when attempting to establish how different subjects relate to one another. This in turn is important because of the unity of God, which is present in knowledge. If the aim of education is to strive towards knowledge of God through the study of God's creation, then it follows that attempts to piece together the unity of creation are part of the search for knowledge of God.

However, if Newman's assumptions are challenged, his view struggles to meet either criterion for selecting curriculum content. First, it is unclear how philosophy plays the role that Newman sets out for it. This means that the case for including philosophy rather than some other subject is unclear. Second, few people would want to claim that the aim of education is ultimately to come to know God. Nonetheless, there is space within Newman's account to develop a case, which does pass both criteria. If it can be shown that it is important to explore the unity of knowledge without appealing to God, and it is possible to demonstrate how philosophy achieves this, then a case could be made which meets both criteria. However, as it stands, Newman does not present such a case. Further, the idea that knowledge is unified is controversial and so preferably avoided.

Religious reasons for teaching philosophy raise two issues, the first is whether, as has been the case with other arguments for teaching philosophy in schools, teaching philosophy is best placed to bring about the goods promoted. The second is whether religious education itself has a justified place on the curriculum. A further thought is that many arguments for teaching philosophy in schools as part of religious education limit the scope of philosophy teaching to matters pertinent to religion. I would prefer to be able to present an argument for a broader conception of philosophy in which it contributes to a students' whole education, not just their religious education.

Moral and Civic Reasons

A similar case to the religious education case can be made about the relationship between philosophy and moral education, and philosophy and civic education. This is that there are fields of philosophy which deal with questions about morality and civic life, and so can help students to make progress in these areas. This is outlined by Hand, who argues that justifying subscription to moral, political and religious standards is important enough to include philosophy on the curriculum (Hand, 2018, p. 4). Hand claims that 'it is difficult to make much progress with them without access to distinctly philosophical forms of argument and analysis' (p. 14). Since philosophy has traditionally dealt with questions about moral, political and religious standards, it provides students with guidance about how to proceed with such questions (p. 15).

Aside from Hand's case for teaching philosophy based on its contribution to moral and political reasoning, there are cases taken from the P4C literature mentioned earlier in this Chapter. P4C is seen as an appropriate pedagogy for developing moral thinking through a CoI; it also develops civic virtues and ameliorates power dynamics, making schools more fair and democratic for children. The fact that ethics is present as a part of university courses such as medicine and business goes some way to suggest that there is a general consensus that teaching about morality using philosophical material is a good way to help people to deal with moral quandaries in practice.

My response to this approach is that it seems plausible that there is philosophical material that contributes to religious, moral and civic education. As it stands, the P4C literature does not show that teaching philosophy is the only or best way to do this. Hand's case is that philosophy has the best available material to support judgments about moral, political and religious standards. It seems that it is generally accepted that at least some content from philosophy is important in applied ethics courses, and that philosophy as a discipline often deals with how to justify moral, political and religious standards.

My stance on this possible direction of arguing for teaching philosophy is that there is some value to it. I believe that the arguments I will present in Chapters 5 and 6 provide a developed account of why philosophy is best placed to contribute to aspects of moral, civic and religious education. I argue that the discipline of philosophy is the discipline which most systematically studies ordinary concepts; some important moral, civic and religious concepts can be categorized as ordinary, and so it is philosophy which provides the best content and tools for dealing with questions based on these concepts. My argument is broader than just moral, political and civic concepts and gives reasons for including other areas of philosophy such as epistemology and metaphysics on the curriculum too.

Disciplinary Reasons for Putting Philosophy on the Curriculum

Another approach to justifying teaching philosophy in schools is that it is a well-established discipline, which has at least as much of a place on the curriculum as other similarly well-established disciplines. This sort of reasoning is behind the introduction of the A-level philosophy course, and other analogues such as the Pre-U course and the IB philosophy course. In these cases, course content is selected with the aim of presenting students with an accurate representation of the nature of the discipline. For example, the A-level in philosophy invites students to:

> Consider and develop an understanding of the ways in which philosophers have engaged with traditional philosophical issues and philosophical approaches to problems, through the detailed study of the arguments of philosophers in identified texts. Develop an understanding of the core concepts of philosophy and begin to develop their own skill of conceptual analysis, through the study of the ways in which philosophers have analysed concepts and have, through conceptual analysis, identified subtle differences which have a wider impact on philosophical arguments. (AQA, 2016)

Like subjects such as history, mathematics, literature, biology and so on, teaching philosophy in schools earns its place in virtue of being a legitimate area of academic study. Philosophy courses need only mirror the academic discipline of philosophy in order to meet this goal. The 1953 report on French philosophy from UNESCO illustrates a similar line of thinking: 'the teaching of philosophy is regarded as an introduction to the world of philosophic thought' (Monod in Canguilhem, 1953, p. 63).

There are reasons to be sympathetic towards this view; philosophy is a well-established academic discipline with a long history and a well-defined canon of work. Other school subjects get by on similar arguments, and so a parity argument could be presented: if other academic disciplines are taught in virtue of being well-established, then philosophy, as a well-established academic discipline ought to be taught as well.

The problem with this parity argument is that it provides parity with other poorly-justified subjects. Some additional reason about why being a well-established discipline qualifies something for inclusion onto the curriculum needs to be provided. This additional reason is going to need to answer to the two criteria set out earlier for curriculum inclusion. Is it the case that (1) teaching well-established disciplines provides specifiable educational goods and is it the case that (2) there is reason to hold that teaching well-established disciplines is only or best way to achieve these educational goods?

Cases for teaching well-established academic disciplines have been made. Newman, Peters, Hirst and White have all offered accounts of the aims of education, which provide some justification for placing a range of different disciplinary subjects on the curriculum. These will be examined in more detail in Chapter 3. To provide a brief illustration, Peters argues that those asking 'why do this rather than that' are implicitly engaging in the pursuit of truth; if they are engaged in the pursuit of truth, then they should study academic disciplines, which are the primary means by which truth is pursued because 'these sorts of inquiries are all, in their different ways, relevant to answering the sort of question he is asking' (Peters, 1966, p. 161). Newman argues that the different disciplines are different ways of coming to know God, which is the ultimate aim of education. Hirst presents an account of the aims of a liberal education based on the aim of the formation of mind, which takes place through induction into the six or seven different forms of knowledge (Hirst, 1974). White gives an argument for including philosophy as an academic discipline because it is within a class of activities which 'no understanding . . . is possible for those who have not come to engage in them' (White, 1973, p. 29).

Basing an argument for teaching philosophy in schools on its status as a well-established discipline is more complex than providing a parity argument. Some account of the value of teaching well-established disciplines is also needed. While philosophy might have parity with literature, history, mathematics, the natural sciences, and so on, reasons for teaching these other disciplines are also required. Their historical presence in schools does not in itself provide a justification for their inclusion on a coherent curriculum. In Chapter 3, I will also argue that appeals to the intrinsic value of disciplines fall short of providing an argument for the educational value of disciplines, essentially closing off this line of inquiry.

Core of the Curriculum Accounts of Philosophy

The final sort of reason given for including philosophy on the school curriculum is that it plays some sort of key role in education, and so should be at the core of the curriculum. This seems to be the rationale behind the inclusion of philosophy during the final year of secondary education in France. It also grounds the rationale for the inclusion of Theory of Knowledge on the IB curriculum. Newman's argument for the inclusion of philosophy in university education takes this form when he claims that studying philosophy is key to coming to a holistic understanding of other disciplines. This idea is underdeveloped in the literature, but I will outline a few existing instances of it.

The 1953 UNESCO report on philosophy teaching in French secondary schools touches on some reasons for its inclusion on the curriculum in the form of a list of quotes taken from the survey:

> In secondary education and in fact in higher education, the function of philosophical study is to provide a training of intellect and character, not to impart a specific body of knowledge. The study of philosophy should inculcate habits of thought, and train the student to investigate, reflect and express his thoughts and, in the best instances, to act. (Polin, University of Lille)
>
> In philosophy, there is nothing to learn, for the very good reason that there are no 'facts of philosophy'. Philosophy is born from reflection, i.e. from criticism, and dies when the critical faculty is no longer exercised. (Berger, University of Aix)
>
> In philosophy, instead of learning, they have to reflect on what they know, what they practise, what they love, what is familiar to them. (P. Lachièze-Rey, University of Lyons) (Canguilhem, 1953, p. 55)

Part of the justification for teaching philosophy in French schools is to provide space for reflection and to encourage critical thought. However, little is said about why reflection and critical thought are considered so central to education that they must occupy a compulsory place on the curriculum for final year students in France.

The International Baccalaureate takes a similar approach to France in placing philosophical content at the core of the curriculum with its ToK course. The International Baccalaureate is a little more explicit about why ToK is at the core of the curriculum:

> ToK aims to make students aware of the interpretative nature of knowledge, including personal ideological biases – whether these biases are retained, revised or rejected. It offers students and their teachers the opportunity to reflect critically on diverse ways of knowing and on areas of knowledge; [and to] consider the role and nature of knowledge in their own culture, in the cultures of others and in the wider world.
>
> In addition, TOK prompts students to be aware of themselves as thinkers, encouraging them to become more acquainted with the complexity of knowledge; [and to] recognize the need to act responsibly in an increasingly interconnected but uncertain world. TOK also provides coherence for the student, by linking academic subject areas as well as transcending them.

It therefore demonstrates the ways in which the student can apply their knowledge with greater awareness and credibility. (IBO, 2019)

Again, although the beginnings of a justification for the inclusion of philosophy are present in this statement, it is unclear exactly why this sort of course ought to be at the core of any secondary curriculum. Why is it important for students to be aware of the interpretative nature of knowledge? Is knowledge interpretative? Why should students be aware of themselves as thinkers or of the complexity of knowledge? Perhaps this would confuse them rather than help them in their education. Is coherence possible? Are academic subject areas linked? Can they be transcended? These are interesting questions, but they are open questions and require much more work to clarify and develop into a full justification.

The idea that philosophy plays the role of 'linking academic subject areas and transcending them' (IBO, 2019) is reflected by Suissa's account of the possible role of philosophy. She describes the place of philosophy on the secondary curriculum as part of a search for meaning in education. This role is particularly pertinent in secondary schools since 'adolescents already share a wealth of cultural and social knowledge; what they are curious about is what it all means, what it is for' (Suissa, 2006, p. 139). During secondary education, students are exposed to a curriculum which is 'fragmented into discrete units, each with its own internal logic, in which there is not much space to ask why bits of knowledge are there, what they are for, what they mean, and how they are related to each other' (p. 139). Suissa points to philosophy as a means of exploring the philosophical questions which arise from the nature of the curriculum.

Similarly, Lipman, Sharp and Oscanyan claim that 'all too often, students see no connection between what they are studying, what they do in their lives, and what society at large does' (Limpan, Sharp, & Oscanyan, 1980, p. 22). They continue that 'philosophy encourages the intellectual resourcefulness and flexibility that can enable children and teachers alike to cope with the disconnectedness and fragmentation of existing curricula' (p. 27). Phenix suggests this sort of role for philosophy on the curriculum; he describes philosophy as a synoptic subject which combines 'empirical, esthetic and synoetic meanings into coherent wholes' (Phenix, 1964, p. 7). Unlike the other disciplines, philosophy is 'concerned with every kind of human experience and not with any one domain' (p. 253).

Midgley also presents this sort of account of the role of philosophy. She asks:

> What is the aim, the proper object of philosophizing? What are we trying to do? . . . Often, we seem to be trying to resolve a complex jigsaw, one which has mistakenly brought together parts of several different pictures; trying to

give a single shape to a manifold vision. Indeed, we are bound to keep doing this, because our minds are never quite empty at the start. They always contain incomplete world-pictures, frameworks to which loose scraps of experience and of various studies, such as geology, history, mathematics, astronomy and so forth, can be attached. And these various frameworks do not fit together spontaneously. (Midgley, 2018, pp. 3–4)

According to Midgley, philosophy and philosophers attempt to piece together these different fields of study, and to make sense of them.

These arguments share an interest in the role of philosophy as a means of piecing together the rest of the curriculum. This line of thought holds potential because it appeals to an aim of education. This aim is something like meaningfulness or holistic understanding, but remains poorly defined. Furthermore, it is unclear that meeting this aim is easily achieved elsewhere in the curriculum. Other subjects are rarely outward looking, in that they are more concerned with their internal disciplinary consistency and students coming to know and understand the intricacies of the subject at hand, rather than being concerned with the relationships between that subject and the rest of the curriculum. However, the same problem holds true for philosophy: to what extent might it play this role? And importantly, how might it play this role, or is this role even possible?

I find these reasons based on the potential role of philosophy as a meaning-making, integrating or detangling subject compelling. This line of thought has the potential to make a case for the inclusion of philosophy which maintains that (1) teaching philosophy provides some specifiable educational goods and (2) there is reason to hold that these goods are only or best delivered by teaching philosophy. As it stands, however, much work is needed to establish a clear and rigorous argument to this effect. The argument presented in Chapter 6 offers an account of the educational value of philosophy that can accommodate these ideas about the centrality of philosophy to education. In Chapter 6, I argue that philosophy helps students to make sense of the different conceptual schemes employed by different subjects and that this helps to unify or at least untangle the curriculum.

Defining Philosophy and Deriving Reasons

So far, I have set out two criteria needed to make the case for the inclusion of philosophy in the curriculum. I have shown that as it stands, existing reasons for putting philosophy on the curriculum are either inadequate, or in need of development if these two criteria are going to be adequately met. Two tasks are going to be important going forwards. The first is to set out a clear account of the aims of education, and hence how to identify educational goods and how to weigh up the relative importance of different educational goods. The second task is to provide some clarity about the nature and aims of philosophy, so that more can be said about how philosophy contributes to educational goods, and whether it is best placed to do so.

The problem with defining the nature and aims of philosophy is that this itself is subject to philosophical disagreement. Demarcating philosophy from other disciplines is difficult. Likewise, drawing a coherent picture of what philosophy is poses difficulties. The diversity of philosophical traditions and the antagonism between these traditions makes the prospect of isolating a set of necessary and sufficient conditions to define philosophy a daunting one. Furthermore, even if a definitive account of philosophy could be agreed upon, the question of whether the content and skills falling under this account were educationally valuable would still be an open question.

Bialystok summarizes the difficulties with taking this approach when she points out that 'there is surprisingly little discussion in recent academic philosophy … about philosophy as a subject in relation to other conventional academic subjects. Philosophy departments tend to subdivide into predictable fields (ancient, ethics, Continental) and take their own borders as a discipline largely for granted, despite the expansive terrain it covers' (Bialystok, 2017 p. 819). This problem is exemplified by the contrast between Ryle, who holds that philosophy consists of conceptual analysis alone such that it is concerned with 'the unravelling of some complex tangle of interconnected ideas' (Ryle, 1971, p. 211), McGinn who views philosophy as a branch of the natural sciences (McGinn, 2015), and Rush who claims that 'philosophy coincides with genuine art, science, music, play, poetry, love, and the like' so that each of these can be philosophy, and philosophy can be each of these (Rush, 2016, p. 693). There is no agreement between philosophers about what it is that they are doing. There is some literature about the nature of philosophy; for example, in the journal *Metaphilosophy*, in monographs on the subject (e g. Glock, 2008; Williamson, 2007), and in the opening pages of introductory philosophy books (e.g. Hospers, 1990; Nozick, 1981), but there is little agreement amongst philosophers about the nature of their work, and the prospect of settling on an uncontroversial definition of what it is to do philosophy, and what constitutes philosophical content, seems distant.

Furthermore, many of the accounts of the nature of philosophy struggle to demarcate philosophy from other areas of study. Take the claim that

> philosophy asks, of even the most ordinary, everyday statements, 'what are your reasons for believing this?' and "how will you prove to me that what you said was true?" and 'if someone denied your claim, what could you say in defence of your claim against your opponent?' Philosophy is the study of 'how do you know' questions, applied to lots of different kinds of issues about the physical world, the mind, and scientific, religious and ethical theories. (Hospers, 1990, p. 3)

Hospers' account of philosophy could be an account of many disciplines, which are also concerned with "how do you know" questions. A physicist, artist or mathematician might equally ask all of the questions listed by Hospers without leaving their disciplinary boundaries. While it is intuitive and obvious to philosophers that what they are doing is distinct from what those working in other fields are doing, it is very difficult to articulate what this distinctive activity is. In relation to the previous paragraph, even if philosophers succeeded in doing this, it is unlikely that they would recognise or agree with others' accounts of philosophy.

This is important because a failure to agree on what philosophy is would make designing a philosophy course very difficult. Given the lack of time available to teach existing curriculum content, any additional philosophy course would have to leave out some content, which is deemed philosophical. It is possible that a school course with plenty of time allocated to it might be able to cover two different philosophical traditions whilst still being able to engage in an in depth study of how they work; but it is unlikely that time would permit covering any more without resorting to rote learning and over-simplification. An argument would still be needed to justify why some philosophical activity had been selected rather than some other.

Rather than starting with the task of defining philosophy, I am going to start with the task of setting out the aims of education. This will provide a more narrow focus on the sorts of educational goods to which philosophy might be able to contribute. An argument for teaching philosophy in schools does not need to hold that all aspects of the discipline of philosophy are educationally valuable, only that there are some educational goods which some aspects of philosophy are best placed to contribute towards.

The advantage of taking this approach is that it is guided by the central two questions behind including a subject on the curriculum. Defining the aims of education is necessary to make clear and defensible claims about the educational value of philosophy. This is in response to Hirst's point that 'if curriculum planning is a matter of planning means to specified ends, and an educational curriculum therefore serves educational ends, the clearer we are about those ends and their nature he more adequate the planning can be' (Hirst, 1974, p. 16).

Once the aims of education have been identified, philosophy will only earn a place on the curriculum if it is the only, or best available activity to meet those aims. Through seeking to present a coherent account of the aims of education, and identifying a necessary condition of meeting those aims which involves some philosophical activity, an argument for the inclusion of philosophy on the curriculum can be reached.

This is no simple task. I am going to narrow the scope somewhat. I will start my search for a justification for teaching philosophy in schools with an examination of the nature and aims of theoretical education. I will then identify two reasons why philosophy ought to be taught in schools as part of any theoretical education. The first reason is that including philosophical activities on a theoretical curriculum is consistent with reasons for including other activities. The second reason is that the aims of a theoretical education cannot be met without the inclusion of philosophy on the curriculum.

Conclusion

I have set out two principles for judging whether something ought to be included on the curriculum. These are: (1) that teaching philosophy provides some specifiable educational goods and (2) that there is reason to hold that these educational goods are only, or best delivered by teaching philosophy. After outlining and assessing the existing reasons and arguments given for teaching philosophy in schools, there remains a need for further work to provide a failsafe argument for including philosophy on school curricula.

Part 2
The Aims of Education

3

The Aims of Education

As I set out in the previous chapter, an argument for teaching philosophy in schools needs to appeal to educational aims. There are many possible aims of education, and I do not propose to reduce them all to a single aim. Instead, I will highlight one important educational aim associated with what I call the practice of 'theoretical education', and identify the goods associated with this practice. What I call a theoretical education is the practice of conveying ideas to students; it is something that takes place in schools across the world. Many of the subjects taught as part of traditional curricula are engaged in conveying ideas to students. For example, history, literature, science and geography are largely, although not exclusively engaged in communicating ideas to students.

Alongside outlining what I mean by theoretical education and its history, this chapter explores existing accounts of the aims and value of the practice of theoretical education. In Chapter 4, I will provide a coherent account of theoretical education which explains why it is a justifiable educational practice. In Chapters 5 and 6, I argue that any theoretical education ought to include aspects of the discipline of philosophy. This section of the book sets out the aims and value of theoretical education in order to provide a foundation for these conclusions by providing a framework for specifying the educational goods at stake.

Theoretical Education

A theoretical education is an educational practice which conveys ideas to students. Some examples of theoretical education seen in schools are liberal education models which primarily focus on communicating a broad range of ideas to students and curricula which focus on traditional school subjects. On a broad use of the term 'theoretical education', Western schooling has been dominated by some form of theoretical education since Classical times. This chapter and the next are interested in the justification for theoretical education. I ask what it is about theoretical education, or communicating ideas to students, that is educationally valuable. Another way of putting this is that I am asking about the aims and educational goods associated with theoretical education.

Examples of theoretical curricula include the following: (1) Athenian students over the age of fourteen were taught 'a voluntary course of higher studies, chiefly mathematics (i.e. arithmetic, geometry, and astronomy) and rhetoric, and sometimes including literature, art, dialectic, geography, prosody, logic, philosophy, and political science' (Attwater, 1927, p. 132); (2) Cicero's description of Roman education included geometry, music, knowledge of literature and poetry, of natural sciences; the study of peoples, the study of the State (Wolfe, 1994, p. 99); (3) after the fall of the Roman empire, the seven liberal arts consisting of grammar, rhetoric, logic, arithmetic, geometry, astronomy and music dominated schooling (Parker, 1890, p. 417) and (4) today, the English National Curriculum lists English, mathematics, science, art and design, citizenship, computing design and technology, geography, history, languages, music and physical education as requirements for secondary education (Gov.uk, 2014). These are all forms of theoretical education because they place a strong focus on communicating ideas to students. That is not to say that communicating ideas is the primary aim of these educational models, but in practice it is something that frequently takes place as a part of them.

The reason for listing these curricula is to draw attention to their similarities and to highlight the pervasiveness of theoretical education. They each cover a broad range of ideas, focus on theoretical rather than practical learning, are general rather than specific, contrast with training students for specific tasks and reflect something of the best available ideas of the time. They do not necessarily share the same aims or characterize themselves as theoretical, but they can be grouped together in this way. This sort of educational practice introduces students to a broad range of ideas.

Theoretical curricula remain widespread. Priestley and Biesta point to similarities between secondary curricula in Scotland, New Zealand, Australia, Northern Ireland, Wales, England and the United States; all of which fit the description of introducing students to a broad and balanced range of theoretical activities (2013, p. 149). Similarly, a 2004 UNESCO report covering OECD countries' secondary education trends identifies 'knowledge and skills in the more or less traditional subject areas of the national language, mathematics, natural and social sciences and foreign languages, among others' as one of three main objectives found in all of the curricula studied (Briseid & Caillods, 2004, p. 93). Theoretical education is widespread and deserves attention.

Having some account of why and how this sort of education might be worthwhile is important. If it is possible to identify justifiable aims of a broad theoretical education, then it is possible to make judgements about how much school time ought to be spent on it, and what a corresponding curriculum ought to look like. This is why a philosophical conception of theoretical education is needed. If the descriptive account of theoretical education is acknowledged, then a philosophical account of theoretical education is needed to account for its value and to identify its aims. In Chapters 5 and 6, I will argue that the nature of theoretical education implies that it ought to include some philosophical content.

All of this is not to say that there are no other educational practices that deserve attention. Educational practices such as teaching students skills, engaging in creative activities, building community, character education or engaging in physical activity are all important. However, I am focusing on theoretical education for a variety of reasons. First, during my time as a teacher in secondary schools in England, my students spent a large part of their day going from subject to subject, being taught ideas from each. It is in this theoretical-based context that teaching them philosophy seemed particularly important from my perspective as a practitioner. Another reason for focusing on theoretical education is that it is a practical way of educating people; communicating ideas is a cost effective and efficient method of preparing children for their adult lives (Kotzee, 2018). Regardless of the broader aims of education, theoretical education is likely to play at least some role.

Theoretical education itself is not an aim of education; it is a term I am using to describe the practice of conveying ideas to students. There are different possible aims and justifications of theoretical education. In the remainder of this chapter, I will discuss different possible aims for theoretical education: (1) providing students with intrinsically valuable educational goods; (2) providing students with cultural capital; (3) supporting a politically engaged liberal democratic state; and (4) developing students' rational autonomy. These aims emerge from the history of theoretical education, and the existing literature that seeks to justify it.

A History of Theoretical Education

Theoretical education has a long and distinguished place in the history of schooling. This history starts with the dominance of liberal education, which falls into the category of theoretical education because it has a heavy focus on conveying ideas to students.

Hirst claims that liberal education traces its roots to Classical Greece, he alludes to Plato's account of the nature and aims of education in his *Republic*. This provides an account of the perfect state within which the good life is possible. The 'good', according to Plato is an ideal which must be known and understood in order for people to live good lives, or to flourish. Knowledge of the concept of good, alongside other concepts, is central to flourishing for Plato; a theoretical education which focuses on providing knowledge, is essential to living a good life. This places a theoretical education at the centre of his perfect state and his understanding of what it is to flourish.

> When the vast Platonic educational machine consisting of mousike, gymnastike, the mathematical sciences, dialectic, and practical politics is fully successful, the result is someone possessed of each of the four virtues or excellences Socrates considers: wisdom, courage, temperance, and justice. The rational element in him knows and desires the good; the appetitive and spirited elements see and desire in harmony with reason. (Reeve, 2010, pp. 225–6)

This curriculum includes a theoretical education into the mathematical sciences, knowledge of the forms via the dialectic, and practical politics. Knowledge is part and parcel of living well, and so a theoretical education is a central part of the curriculum. It is justified on ethical grounds, as something which contributes to the intrinsically valuable state of flourishing.

Aristotle also emphasizes the importance of a theoretical education. Alongside Plato, 'they both agree that the training of character must come first and that it must have in view the practical requirements of the community. Its aim, in Plato's words, is to make us "spectators of reality" or, as it was put by Eudemos, a disciple of Aristotle, to enable us "to serve and contemplate God"' (Burnet, 1936, p. 136). According to Aristotle, a theoretical education is important because it enables someone to become 'a good judge ... Generally educated in medicine, for example, he is capable of judging whether someone has treated a disease correctly' (Reeve, 2008, p. 21). Someone who has come to know theoretical content 'is able to judge the works and advice of experts, a generally educated person is free from the sort of intellectual enslavement to them that would otherwise have been his lot' (p. 21). For Aristotle, theoretical education prepares people to be good epistemic agents.

Education in Classical Athens was the preserve of male citizens, who would lead privileged lives of leisure and play a role in the democratic governance of the state. Primary education consisted of studying 'grammar, music and gymnastics, and the foundation and inspiration of the whole of this education was the poetry of Homer' (Attwater, 1927, p. 133). From the age of fourteen, some students entered secondary education for four years where they studied 'a voluntary course of higher studies, chiefly mathematics (i.e. arithmetic, geometry and astronomy) and rhetoric, and sometimes including literature, art, dialectic, geography, prosody, logic, philosophy, and political science' (p. 135). Although this curriculum lacks the strong philosophical drive behind those suggested by Plato and Aristotle, it adheres to the same broadly theoretical model.

In Classical Greece, this sort of education was labelled a liberal education, and contrasted to artisan, mechanical or otherwise illiberal curricula. Here, the term 'liberal education' refers to the education of free men. Those without a liberal education were 'unleisured and unfit to rule because (1) they are "servile" labourers for hire, and (2) their minds/souls are made slavish by their lowly occupations' (Nightingale, 2001, p. 135). This distinction between liberal education and vocational education is one which persists today. Another persisting idea is that a liberal education is central to a functioning state. Athenian society was perceived to thrive and decline in line with the quality of education that the ruling classes received. Poor decision-making regarding Sicily marking the beginning of the downfall of the Athenian golden age and is blamed by Plato on poor teaching associated with the Sophists (Morgan, 1918, p. 274). Both Plato and Aristotle require their leaders to have received a liberal education. Finally, the connection between leisure and theoretical or liberal education persists through later accounts of education; a theoretical education is an education for people with leisure time to engage in the pursuit of truth, political debate, arts and literature, and so on. This idea is behind claims that theoretical education helps to prepare citizens to participate in liberal democratic state processes.

The Hellenistic model of education which emerged from Classical Greece was adopted by the Romans, who 'selectively fashioned Greek educational principles into a uniquely Roman form of citizen training' (Corbeill, 2001, p. 261). Greek tutors and teachers were brought in to teach Roman children, and Roman education continued to focus on the development of character and theoretical learning. The curriculum focused on 'linguistic capability and excellence in oratorical skills … the orator was the ideal of the educated man' (Pascal, 1984, p. 353). Cicero, one such educated man, lists the contents of the curriculum as *'geometria; musica; litterarrum; cognitionum et poetarum; de naturis rerum; de homimum moribus; de rebus pubicis'* (Wolfe, 1994, p. 99). This roughly translates as a theoretical curriculum covering geometry, music, literature and poetry, the natural world, human customs, and civic education. Nussbaum points to Seneca's exposition of this sort of liberal education:

> The world *liberalis* in the traditional sense meant 'suited for the freeborn gentleman'. Seneca begins by announcing that he will call that understanding of the term into question. For the only kind of education which really served the name *liberalis*, or 'freelike', is one that makes its pupils free, able to take charge of their own thought and to conduct a critical examination of their society's norms and traditions. (Nussbaum, 1997, p. 30)

The combination of character education and theoretical education of the liberal education ideal is seen as capable of meeting these aims. This idea is reflected in more contemporary ideas about the relationship between theoretical education and rational autonomy.

Roman liberal education, with its heavy focus on theoretical content was carried over into the so-called dark ages. The Roman Catholic Church took over many Roman schools as the empire fell, and so preserved a continuity between Roman education and post-Roman education (Lawton & Gordon, 2002, p. 38). Later, as Islamic scholars reintroduced Classical Greek texts, interest in classical models of education flourished. The resulting trend towards scholasticism combined an Aristotelian focus on logic with the faith-based liberal education of the Catholic Church (p. 54).

Over time, the seven liberal arts became the gold standard of education and the norm in universities and schools. These consisted of grammar, rhetoric, logic, arithmetic, astronomy and music (Parker, 1890, p. 417). Education was conducted primarily in Greek and Latin, and was the preserve of the leisured classes. A direct lineage was thus preserved between the liberal curricula of Classical Greece and Rome and liberal education in the Middle Ages. The mixture of character development and theoretical education was also preserved. The seven liberal arts can be thought of as encompassing a representative sample of the best theoretical content available to provide students with at the time. This continuity is described by Adler and Mayer as follows: The liberal arts were 'preserved through the dark ages in the monasteries … [and] they continued to dominate the medieval curriculum as they had the classical' (Adler & Mayer, 1958, p. 20). The Renaissance severed some of the links between liberal education and the Church, but 'accepted the education of antiquity' (p. 20). A move towards humanism 'present[s] a clear central theme: humanitas, the cultivation of the fullest possible extent of human creativity, modelled on the achievements of ancient Greece and Rome' (Kallendorf, 2003 p. 71). Schools remained within the sphere of influence of the Church, and so despite these alterations, a remarkable degree of continuity exists between the classical conception of liberal education and later education. This development of liberal education shifts the focus to an education into the disciplines. Disciplinary education is sometimes held as intrinsically valuable. The disciplines have also been justified as providing cultural capital. Here, being broadly educated in a recognized selection of disciplines is a marker of belonging to a particular social or economic class.

The next significant round of changes to education began during the industrial revolution, and led to present day curricula, in England at least. Here, liberal education had become synonymous with an education in the Classics: Latin and Greek, including the literature and history associated with Classical Greece and Rome. Secondary education remained the preserve of the upper classes, and primary schools were described as providing a jumbled mixture of reading and writing, some theology, Syrian geography, Jewish history, a little English history and geography and some moral education (Huxley, 1868, p. 87). The late 1860s appeared to mark a point of change for education in the UK. Male suffrage increased to include some renters alongside landowners; the idea that all people might eventually be allowed to vote leant weight to calls by people such as Arnold, writing in 1869, to make secondary education compulsory. At the same time, the rapid increase in knowledge which accompanied the industrial revolution led to calls for the inclusion of more than just the Classics in secondary education; Huxley argued that the sciences ought to be taught, others made the case that literature and English language ought to be included.

These pressures set the scene for the current National Curriculum to emerge. First, private schools began introducing the natural sciences, English literature and English language (see Ferrar, 1868). In 1904, a broad 'subject-based curriculum' was introduced in new local authority schools. This covered 'English language and literature, at least one language other than English, geography, history, mathematics, science, drawing, manual instruction (boys), domestic subjects (girls), physical exercise, and organised games' (White, 2005, p. 15). These secondary local authority schools were selective, educating around 25% of children, with the remaining 75% taught 'more manual subjects' (p. 16). Although selective, local authority schools brought theoretical education to a much wider subsection of society than the leisured classes, who previously had almost exclusive access to it. Furthermore, the theoretical education provided in these schools was broader, covering areas of study which had previously been left off the curricula.

These developments were continuous with the liberal education tradition. In the introduction to Arnold's work, Wilson comments that 'never in the history of the race was there greater demand for sweetness and light in human affairs, for a true Hellenic clarity of vision' (Arnold, 1869, p. xxxvii). Huxley says 'let us ask ourselves – what is education? Above all things, what is our ideal for a thoroughly liberal education? – of that education, which, if we were to begin life again, we would give ourselves – of that education which, if we could mould the fates to our own will, we would give our children?' (Huxley, 1868, p. 81). At the heart of the changes is an ongoing commitment to a Classical concept of liberal education. However, given the changes it has undergone over its history, I have chosen to refer to 'theoretical education' which is not committed to a particular educational ideal but rather describes any education which focuses on conveying ideas to students. This is true of previous incarnations of liberal education and of contemporary discipline based curricula.

Today's National Curriculum in England maintains a similar structure to the curriculum of the new local authority schools of the early twentieth century. In response to the introduction of the 1988 National Curriculum, Aldrich comments that it is essentially the same as previous curricula. Composed of English, mathematics, science, history, geography, modern foreign languages, art, physical education, technology and music, it reads like an updated version of the curricula from Classical Greece, the medieval liberal arts curriculum, and the revised curriculum of the industrial revolution. Aldrich was disappointed at the lack of change or vision behind the 1988 curriculum, saying that it mirrored 'the basic grammar school curriculum devised at the beginning of the twentieth century' (Aldrich, 1988, p. 22). White makes a similar point about the 2000 National Curriculum when he says that 'new patterns have been overlaid on old, but the old show through' (White, 2004, p. 179).

More recent curriculum changes introduced by Michael Gove appeal to a continuity with classical liberal education: 'What we desperately need is a department at the heart of government championing the cause of education, the value of liberal learning, the wider spread of knowledge as an uncontested good in its own right' (Gove, 2009, p. 2). In 2010, the centre-right Thinktank, *Civitas*, published a 150-page report into the relationship between liberal education and the English National Curriculum. This report politicizes the concept of a liberal education, maligning accounts of education which move away from liberal education, and endorsing a subject-based theoretical curriculum. The report concludes with the following statement which is reflected in Gove's curriculum reforms:

> In having to choose whether to extend or further contract the provision of liberal education, by either reverting to or moving further away from the National Curriculum in its original form, this country faces as momentous a decision as any that it has ever faced in terms of the effects that it will have on future generations. It is to be hoped that it has not yet come so servile and so ill-educated a nation as not to know how it must choose to ensure its children, and its children's children, receive the only form of education that is able to provide them with the best prospects for as good and fulfilled lives as they can possible enjoy – a liberal education. (Conway, 2010, p. 112)

Liberal education does not always clearly fall under the heading of theoretical education. Sometimes a liberal education is only partially theoretical and partially virtue or practice based. In the United States, liberal arts education is often discussed in terms of the sort of education fit for a liberal democracy. This is not necessarily theoretical, although in reality liberal arts curricula often are. Plato and Aristotle both emphasize the importance of education to the functioning of the state; Arnold was concerned with educating new voting classes to play their role in a democracy. Furthermore, there remains an assumption that a broad theoretical education is well placed to educate for a liberal democracy. In the United States, a liberal arts course at university level 'would include several classes each in social sciences, natural sciences, and humanities, as well as one or two courses in math and quantitative reasoning, one or two writing and/or communication requirements, and several courses in a foreign language' (Brighouse, 2019, p. 5). Thus, although its aims appeal to personal flourishing and civic involvement, in practice a liberal arts course in the United States often provides a straightforwardly broad theoretical education.

On the other hand, liberal education as discussed in the United States is commonly thought of in terms of aims and objectives rather than content. Brighouse describes Derek Bok's account of the aims of liberal education as 'teaching students to communicate, to think, building their character, preparing them for citizenship, for a career, and for living in a global society, teaching them to live with diversity, and facilitating the acquiring of broader interests' (Brighouse, 2019, p. 5). This could be done without much use of theoretical education. For example, many of these aims could be achieved by setting up political structures for students to participate in while at school such as student councils or community service. This liberal democratic account of liberal education does not straightforwardly track theoretical education because it is a hybrid of theoretical content and non-theoretical aims and goods.

Nussbaum describes liberal education in terms of the Socratic ideal of 'cultivation of humanity' combined with the requirements liberal democracies place on their citizenry (Nussbaum, 1997). Nussbaum is not alone in emphasizing the connection between liberal education and liberal democracy. Sometimes the two concepts are run into one another such that a liberal education is equated with an education suitable for a liberal democracy: 'Many liberal political theorists believe that democratic societies require rationally autonomous citizens. A primary aim of schooling in liberal democracies, in this view, is to promote the rational autonomy of students' (Alexander, 2007, p. 609). It is worth bearing in mind that an education fit for a liberal democracy is not necessarily a theoretical education; the two concepts are distinct.

Since theoretical education has played such a dominant role at least in the history of Western education, and since it continues to be held by some as an educational ideal, some account of its aims and value is called for. This is not a trivial question since so much of education around the world has at least some theoretical strand. Making a case for teaching philosophy as part of a theoretical education subsequently amounts to making a case for teaching philosophy in many secondary schools across the world.

The Nature and Aims of Theoretical Education

In this section, I explore the possible aims of theoretical education and its associated educational goods. I ask why a broad theoretical education into a range of different ideas might be considered worthwhile.

One source of answers to these questions comes from the literature about liberal education. Liberal education is loosely defined, and its associated literature provides several different accounts of the value of a broad theoretical education. I am going to outline these accounts whilst simultaneously assessing how well they explain the value of the sort of broad theoretical education often provided by schools. My aim is to identify good reasons for providing students with a theoretical education. If there are good reasons for a theoretical education, then the reasons for providing it can be used to guide what it ought to look like. The vision of theoretical education that I posit in Chapter 4 incorporates a requirement for including philosophy on the theoretical curriculum. The reasons for this are given in Chapters 5 and 6.

In this section, I will review four possible accounts of the value of a theoretical education: (1) an intrinsic value account; (2) a cultural capital account; (3) a political account and (4) a rational autonomy account. It is worth bearing in mind that different conceptions of the value of theoretical education overlap, so that for example, Hirst's account of liberal education combines an intrinsic value account with a rational autonomy account. In evaluating these accounts, I identify difficulties with each of them, and these difficulties motivate setting out my own account of the value of theoretical education presented in Chapter 4.

The Intrinsic Value Account

One common account of the value of theoretical education rests on an appeal to the intrinsic value of knowledge. A theoretical education focuses on communicating ideas to students. One way of thinking about this task is that it involves the transmission of knowledge about the world; and one rationale for this sort of education is that knowledge is intrinsically valuable, making a theoretical education intrinsically worthwhile.

O'Hear appeals to the intrinsic value of disciplines; he says that 'the disciplines are taught and engaged in for their own sake, because they are recognised to be valuable in their own right and part of any fully civilised existence' (O'Hear, 1981, p. 4). The idea that the pursuit of truth or knowledge, is intrinsically valuable relates to Plato's view that the pursuit of the truth is part of the good life, or a constitutive part of flourishing, itself intrinsically valuable.

Both Hirst and Peters endorse this line of reasoning when justifying a liberal or theoretical education. Hirst cites the Classical Greek conception of liberal education as the basis for his work. Here, 'the pursuit of knowledge is … the pursuit of the good of the mind and, therefore, an essential element in the good life' (Hirst, 1974, p. 30). Hirst's revised account of liberal education attempts to draw a relationship between knowledge and intrinsic value without recourse to Plato's views about flourishing. Hirst sets out to provide a more minimal account of the relationship between the value of knowledge and the value of a theoretical education. The result is an endorsement of Peters's transcendental argument.

The transcendental argument for the value of the pursuit of truth starts with a claim that people are generally interested in the question 'why do this rather than that?' (Peters, 1966, p. 161). Once a commitment to this question is taken for granted, it follows that people are generally committed to pursuing the truth:

> Why then, must a person who asks seriously the question 'why do this rather than that?' be more committed to these sorts of activities which have this special sort of cognitive concern built into them? The answer is obvious enough, namely that these sorts of inquiries are all, in their different ways, relevant to answering

the sort of question he is asking. If his question is concerned, as has been shown, with the nature and quality of possible activities which he can pursue, he has already embarked upon a difficult and almost endless quest. (p. 161)

He is 'committed to those enquiries which are defined by their serious concern with these aspects of reality which give context to the question he is asking' (Peters, 1966, p. 164). Implied within the question of 'why do this rather than that' is a pre-existing commitment to pursuing truth, and the pursuit of truth is best engaged in via theoretical activities such as 'science, history, literary appreciation, philosophy, and other such cultural activities' (p. 160). The pursuit of truth is intrinsically worthwhile, and people are already committed to it; this grounds the value of a theoretical education.

Another example of the intrinsic value account of theoretical education is Newman's view of liberal education. Newman says that 'knowledge is capable of being its own end. Such is the constitution of the human mind, that any kind of knowledge, if it really be such, is its own reward' (Newman, 1931, p. 27). Newman adds a distinctly theistic slant, claiming that a broad theoretical education acquaints students with 'the eternal order of things' (p. 63). Here, 'the physical and moral world, sciences, arts, pursuits, ranks, offices, events, opinions, individualities, are all viewed as one with correlative functions, and as gradually by successive combinations converging, one and all, to the true centre' (p. 63). The value of a theoretical education rests on the intrinsic value of coming to know God.

These appeals to intrinsic value raise some puzzles which demonstrate that if there is a relationship between intrinsic and educational value, it demands some scrutiny. First, there are activities which hold intrinsic value, but are not ready contenders for inclusion on the curriculum. While there is general agreement that viewing original works of art is intrinsically worthwhile to the extent that this motivates the provision of free art galleries in the UK, there is no such consensus that viewing original works of art ought to take up curriculum time. Schools might be obliged to introduce students to the possibility of viewing original art works, but it does not seem particularly educational to spend much school time engaged in this activity. Since intrinsic value is either present or not present, and if viewing an original piece of art is intrinsically valuable, it seems that a curriculum entirely composed of viewing original pieces of art is just as valuable as a broad curriculum covering a range of different intrinsically valuable activities. Similarly, romantic love is, if anything, intrinsically worthwhile, but encouraging romantic love in schools does not seem like an educational activity. Teaching theoretical material about relationships and love is worthwhile, but the experience of romantic love itself, although intrinsically worthwhile, does not seem educationally valuable. In these cases, intrinsic value does not seem to correspond to educational value.

A second puzzle is given by White in his criticism of Peters's transcendental argument. He claims that Peters fails to countenance the idea that the pursuit of truth is not the only intrinsically or educationally valuable pursuit. Asking 'why do this rather than that' may not amount to a commitment to truth; 'suppose a man with a knowledge of the arts and sciences decides to jettison any interest he had in them in favour of a life of idleness and comfort: can it be proved to him that he is somehow irrational, that rationality demands that in his own interests he takes the other course?' (White, 1973, p. 14). Spending time in idleness and comfort is not instrumentally valuable; if it holds any value at all, which it clearly does for some people, then that value is surely intrinsic. If there are intrinsically valuable pursuits other than the pursuit of knowledge, then why isn't a liberal education also an education into idleness? White concludes that there are no valid arguments to this end. The intrinsic value of truth does not explain why activities centred on the pursuit of truth ought to be the focus of the curriculum, rather than other intrinsically valuable activities.

Intrinsic, Extrinsic, Final and Instrumental Value

The most common construal of intrinsic value is that it sits in opposition to instrumental value. Something is intrinsically valuable if it is valuable for its own sake; it is instrumentally valuable if it is valuable as a tool to achieve something else. However, Korsgaard argues that this misconstrues intrinsic value through a series of conflations between two different sets of distinctions (Korsgaard, 1996, p. 249). She sums up the misconstrued account as follows: 'objects, activities, or whatever, have an instrumental value if they are valued for the sake of something else – tools, money, and chores would be standard examples. A common explanation of the supposedly contrasting kind, intrinsic goodness, is to say that a thing is intrinsically good if it is valued for its own sake' (p. 250). Rather than contrasting intrinsic value with instrumental value, Korsgaard argues that there are two distinctions at play when it comes to value: a distinction between intrinsic and extrinsic value, and a distinction between final and instrumental value.

The distinction between intrinsic value and extrinsic value is a distinction between the different sources of value of an activity, state of affairs or object. This distinction is 'between things which have their value in themselves and things which derive value from some other source' (Korsgaard, 1996, p. 250).

One way of understanding this account of intrinsic value is that intrinsic value is contained within an object or state of affairs itself, and so it holds regardless of the context; 'if you find that a certain kind of thing is not good in any and all circumstances, that it is good in some cases and not others, its goodness is extrinsic – it is derived from or dependent upon the circumstances' (p. 251). It could be argued that beauty is intrinsically valuable, that a world with beauty is better than a world without beauty, regardless of other circumstances. Alternatively, it could be argued that beauty is extrinsically valuable, resting on the experiences it elicits in people, and that a world with beauty but no people would be no better than such a world without beauty. This account of intrinsic value, as value residing within an object can be traced back to Moore, as 'very roughly speaking, something's intrinsic properties are the properties it would have in isolation' (Bradley, 2002, p. 23). Something is intrinsically valuable if, even in isolation, it holds its value within itself. Something is extrinsically valuable if its value derives from some external source.

Korsgaard's second distinction is between instrumental value and final value. This distinction is not about the properties of an object or state of affairs, but about whether it is desirable for its own sake, or for the sake of something else. Money is instrumentally valuable; it is valuable insofar as it allows people to achieve other ends. If money was not capable of serving as an instrument for meeting other ends, it would hold no value. On the other hand, pleasure can be seen as an end in itself, it has final value. Someone might justify going to an art gallery because it is a pleasurable experience for them. However, it would seem strange to ask them to justify seeking a pleasurable experience, because pleasure is valued for its own sake. Something is instrumentally valuable if it is valued as a means to an end; it is finally valuable if it is valuable as an end in itself. Korsgaard thinks that the term intrinsic value is ambiguous as it is used to refer to both final value (as opposed to instrumental value) and intrinsic value (as opposed to extrinsic value).

Korsgaard points out that attempting to argue that states of affairs with intrinsic value are necessarily states of affairs with final value requires a theoretical link between the two different distinctions;

> If intrinsic is taken to be the opposite of instrumental, then it is under the influence of a theory: a theory according to which the two distinctions in goodness are the same, or amount to the same thing. According to such a theory, final goods or things valuable as ends will be the same as intrinsic goods, and instrumental goods, or things valuable as means will be the same as extrinsic goods. (Korsgaard, 1996, p. 250)

If it is assumed that something which is valuable as a final end has intrinsic value, then 'the significance of the former [intrinsic/extrinsic] distinction drops out' (Korsgaard, 1996, p. 251). If, instead, we 'equate ends and intrinsically good things ... by claiming that those things which have intrinsic value are or ought to be treated as ends', the significance of the final/instrumental distinction is undermined (p. 251). Korsgaard holds that this conflation of the two distinctions rests on an unjustified claim that we ought to act on 'the attribute of intrinsic goodness' (p. 251). For example, spending time with a loved one can, under certain circumstances, be difficult and lack properties which would afford it intrinsic value, but it could still be held as a final end for someone. Conversely, extrinsic and instrumental value do not always go together; viewing a sunset might only be good under certain conditions, and so not intrinsically valuable, but if viewing the sunset is extrinsically valuable, it is not necessarily instrumentally valuable (p. 252).

To summarize, in spite of the commonly held distinction between intrinsic and instrumental value, Korsgaard suggests that there are in fact two distinctions. There is a distinction between intrinsic value, which rests on properties of an object or state of affairs, and extrinsic value, which rests on external conditions. There is a second distinction between instrumental value, where an object or state of affairs is valuable insofar as it serves as a means of reaching another state of affairs, and final value, where an object or state of affairs is valued for its own sake. This means that something might be both intrinsically and instrumentally valuable or extrinsically valuable and hold final value, or any other combination of the two sets of distinctions. For example, a work of art might be considered intrinsically valuable because of properties inherent to it, and instrumentally valuable if an artist earns a living from it. Or someone might collect artwork for the enjoyment their collection brings to others, but at the same time this could hold final value to them.

Importantly, Korsgaard holds that the assumption that final value derives from intrinsic value only works if 'a mysterious ontological attribute' links the two (Korsgaard, 1996, p. 273). There is no clear reason why the intrinsic value of an artwork grounds its final value. The two are logically distinct. The significance of drawing these two different distinctions for Korsgaard is that 'the things that are important to us can be good: good because of our desires and interests and loves and because of the physiological, psychological, economic, historical, symbolic and other conditions under which human beings live' (p. 273). On Korsgaard's account, final value can ground normative claims, thus widening the sorts of activities, states of affairs or objects which can be taken into consideration to more than those with intrinsic (as opposed to extrinsic) value.

Peters's Transcendental Argument and Intrinsic Value

Peters rests the value of theoretical activities on the intrinsic value of the pursuit of truth. This can either be read as the idea that the pursuit of truth is valuable because of some properties internal to it, or that the pursuit of truth is an end in itself. If the pursuit of truth is intrinsically, as opposed to extrinsically valuable, then its intrinsic value has little bearing on educational value since something is educationally valuable in virtue of the effect it has on students, which would be extrinsic to the pursuit of truth itself. If the pursuit of truth is valuable as a final end, then White's criticism holds: Why should we expect students to value truth as an end in itself? What is wrong with the student who is disinterested in the question 'why do this rather than that' and who spends their days fishing for trout rather than engaged in theoretical activities? Final value is determined by each individual, rather than by the nature of the activity valued. This is because final value is distinct from intrinsic value: it is not about the properties of the object or activity itself. Since there is no clear relationship between intrinsic and final value, there is no reason to stipulate that students ought to value the pursuit of truth as an end in itself. This is because the final value of truth does not derive from the intrinsic properties of pursuing truth; the only other place final value might come from is the person it is valuable to. I might find painting finally valuable, but someone else might not. If I was to say that painting is finally valuable, the most that I might reasonably mean is that painting is finally valuable to some people. The pursuit of truth, on this view, is only educationally valuable to those who value it as a final end. This is where the force of Peters's transcendental argument lies; Peters tries to argue that students already value the pursuit of truth as a final end, but this is not clearly true; and Peters cannot recourse to the stronger claim that students ought to value the pursuit of truth as a final end. Some people do not value the pursuit of truth as an end in itself.

Although Peters argues that it is the activity of pursuing truth, which is valuable, a slightly different argument could be presented based on the value of truth itself, as an object or educational good. If truth itself is intrinsically valuable, then spending school time on the pursuit of truth is worthwhile. This sort of argument is presented by Newman. This approach does not have any clear advantages over arguments for the intrinsic value of activities. If truth is intrinsically, as opposed to extrinsically valuable, then its value is independent of its effect on students. This leaves open the question of why students should be provided with truths. The fact that a truth is independently valuable does not mean that people have an obligation to value that truth. Alternatively, if truth is valuable as a final end, it is still only educationally valuable to those students who hold that it is finally valuable to them. This does not mean that truth or knowledge are not educationally valuable, just that the educational value of truth or knowledge does not derive from its intrinsic value. For example, in Chapter 4, I will argue that truth is valuable insofar as it facilitates effective interaction with the world, making it instrumentally and extrinsically valuable, as opposed to intrinsically valuable. The educational value of truth could rest on its extrinsic and instrumental value.

In summary, Korsgaard suggests that the commonly held distinction between intrinsic and instrumental value is a conflation of two separate distinctions: a distinction between intrinsic and extrinsic value, and a distinction between final and instrumental value. Furthermore, Korsgaard claims that there is no relationship between these two distinctions, so that the intrinsic value of an activity does not imply that it ought to be valued as an end in itself. These distinctions suggest that intrinsic and educational value are unrelated; that intrinsic value does not determine educational value. The intrinsic (as opposed to extrinsic) value of an activity has no bearing on educational value because educational value requires some relationship between an activity and its effect on a student; educational value requires extrinsic value. The final (as opposed to instrumental) value of an activity has some bearing on educational value, but fails to support some of the stronger claims made about the educational value of activities. If an activity holds final value to someone, then that activity is educationally valuable to that person; however, there is no reason to think that all people ought to hold that activity as valuable, and so no reason to say that one activity is more educationally worthwhile than another. Whether a student values something for its own sake is up to them, there is no moral imperative to value some things rather than others. Claiming that something is intrinsically valuable, whichever way intrinsic value is understood, struggles to account for the value of theoretical education.

Cultural Accounts

An alternative to placing the value of a theoretical education on the intrinsic value of the ideas transmitted is to appeal to the social value of a theoretical education. The cultural account claims that the body of ideas transmitted by, for example, a liberal education, is a determinant of social class and that possessing it provides students with the ability to access high-status social goods.

There are several instances of theoretical education being associated with transmission of culture. For example, Oakeshott's account of liberal education describes liberal education as initiation into 'an inheritance of human achievements: an inheritance of feelings, emotions, images, visions, thoughts, beliefs, ideas, understandings, intellectual and practical enterprises, languages, religions, organisations, canons and maxims of conduct, procedures, rituals, skills, works of art, books, musical compositions, tools, artefacts and utensils' (Oakeshott, 1989, p. 45). One way that we attribute the label of 'educated' on someone is in light of how well acquainted they are with a particular body of culture. This sort of understanding of the value of a liberal education harks to the idea that it is an education for the leisured, elite classes.

In *Culture and Anarchy*, a book which marked the policy behind reformations to the British education system in the late 1800s, Arnold appeals to the value of cultural capital when he explains the value of a theoretical education. On his view, initiating students into cultural goods is important for the unity of the country, and for the functioning of democracy. Arnold makes a case for

> culture as the great help out of our present difficulties; culture being a pursuit of our total perfection by means of getting to know, on the matters which most concern us, the best which has been thought and said in the world; and through this knowledge, turning a stream of fresh and free thought upon our stock notions and habits, which we now follow staunchly but mechanically. (Arnold, 1962, p. 7)

Arnold's view is that a shared cultural awareness draws a nation together and that theoretical education is instrumentally worthwhile when it comes to technological and other progress.

Neither Arnold nor Oakeshott develop the relationship between culture and social status, but they do seem to rest something of the value of a theoretical education on the value of having an awareness of the best cultural goods that humankind has to offer. Oakeshott's list of everything from utensils to intellectual enterprises suggests that liberal education needs to encompass everything that has been said or done. If we add to his list things that presumably he did not consider, but which seem important today, the list expands further. The idea that education needs to be so broad as to cover everything that has been thought and said seems untenable. Secondly, neither Oakeshott nor Arnold give more than a vague suggestion as to the value of being introduced to human culture in such a broad sense.

To Oakeshott, a liberal education liberates people 'from the distracting business of satisfying contingent wants' (Oakeshott, 1989, p. 28); or 'it is acquiring in some measure an understanding of a human condition in which the "fact of life" is continuously illuminated by a "quality of life". It is learning how to be at once an autonomous and a civilised subscriber to human life' (p. 70). Neither of these seem particularly important when weighed up against the importance of the 'distracting business of satisfying contingent wants', or when the value of being a so-called *civilised* subscriber to human life is questioned. It is difficult not to notice the elitist undertones of Oakeshott's account. Going back to the Classical origins of liberal education, an education which shuns contingent needs seems to be the sort of education suitable for people of leisure, rather than those to whom making a living is a pressing, if contingent, concern.

In Arnold's case, he seems motivated by more worthwhile aims. There is the suggestion that people need a broad and balanced education for democracy to work. Wilson's introduction to *Culture and Anarchy* points out the importance of widening suffrage at the time of Arnold's writing and the subsequent importance of improving access to a suitable education. Arnold also points to the superior technological acumen of Prussia, which he attributes to their broad and balanced school curriculum. However, Arnold does not present a fully developed account of the value of a liberal education based on induction into culture.

More explicit cultural accounts are presented by theorists such as Adler, Hirsch, and current developments in education such as the 'knowledge rich curriculum' idea in the UK, and some Charter Schools in the United States.

Adler advocates an education based on reading 'great books'. He picks out this particular element of human culture as central to helping people 'to think for themselves. To do this, they must first be able to think, and have a body of ideas to think with. They must be able to communicate clearly with one another and receive communications of all sorts critically. It is for such ends that skill in reading and reading the great books are obviously only means' (Adler, 1940, p. 367). Adler contrasts this account of education with Deweyan discovery learning, which he thinks fails to make the most of 'what others already know and therefore can teach' (p. 45). Being acquainted with 'culture' in the form of having engaged with reading 'great books' is central to a functioning society on Adler's account.

Hirsch takes the idea further and advocates a core curriculum which aims to provide students with cultural literacy. Cultural literacy involves a body of knowledge required to properly access and partake in national debates. Cultural literacy 'demands more than mere linguistic skills; it demands participation in, and knowledge about a shared body of knowledge, a knowledge of national culture of the nation. Knowledge of this body of ideas and history is assumed by writers of everything from training manuals to newspapers, yet many adults do not possess this knowledge' (Hirsch, 1984, p. 1). This model of education introduces students to a body of 'core knowledge', which is instrumental to their ability to interact with society, and instrumental to a well-functioning society. Hirsch's core knowledge foundation claims that its resources are used in 12,000 classrooms in 2016, and 'purchased by schools serving 500,000 students' (Core Knowledge, 2016, p. 5).

Hirsch and Adler also appeal to the idea that cultural capital is needed for individuals to play an active and effective role in society. Without a good foundation of cultural knowledge, it is not possible to properly understand, converse with or interact with the contemporary cultured world. The second justification they appeal to is the value of a culture-based education to individual's social standing: 'Students who possess this knowledge are prepared to participate in civic life, move up career ladders, succeed in college, converse confidently with a wide variety of Americans with whom they work or socialize, and generally have the esteem that comes with being regarded as an educated person' (Hirsch, 2020).

This relationship between education and culture has been developed by an appeal to cultural capital. The phrase 'cultural capital' can be traced to Bourdieu where it is taken as 'a broad array of linguistic competences, manners, preferences, and orientations' (Reay, 2004, p. 74). These include 'the embodied state incorporated in mind and body … cultural capital in the institutionalised state, that is existing in institutionalised forms such as educational qualifications, and third, in the objectified state, simply existing as cultural goods such as books, artefacts, dictionaries and paintings' (p. 75 citing Bourdieu, 1986). Oakeshott's list of cultural goods, if provided to students, would give them cultural capital.

This line of thought brings considerations about social justice to bear on the theoretical curriculum. If an expensive independent school inducts its students into culturally valuable practices, for example, it teaches them Latin in a world where knowledge of Latin is seen as a mark of being well educated, then those students have a social advantage over students who have not been taught Latin. Some charter schools in the United States, and certain academy schools in the UK take up this idea and adopt curricula which mirror the sort of education provided by prestigious independent schools. Brighouse and Schouten describe 'high commitment charter schools', which 'often embrace intense curricular and cultural regimes that are characterized by long school days and stringent disciplinary protocols' (Brighouse & Schouten, 2014, p. 346). The commitment of these schools to a theoretical education is visible in their names, for example the 'Knowledge is Power Program' (p. 346). The Michaela Community School in London takes a similar approach with a curriculum which prioritises 'rigorous, traditional academic subjects' providing 'an education that will rival what many of their counterparts receive in the private sector' (mcsbrent.co.uk, 2020).

Michael Young grapples with this tension between the role of the curriculum when it comes to social justice and social mobility, and the value of knowledge independent of this social role. In his earlier work, he criticizes the idea that students should be taught socially powerful knowledge. Later, Young endorses the view that powerful knowledge ought to be taught, but he is unclear whether it is socially powerful knowledge, or knowledge which is practically useful or powerful which ought to take precedence. Young traces his thinking, explaining that 'sociological critiques of school knowledge have equated school knowledge and the curriculum with 'knowledge of the powerful'. However, the fact that some knowledge is 'knowledge of the powerful', or high status knowledge as I once expressed it … tells us nothing about the knowledge itself' (Young, 2009, p. 14). Young's current approach provides an account of 'powerful knowledge', which 'refers to what the knowledge can do – for example, whether it provides reliable explanations or new ways of thinking about the world' (p. 14). This is a different account of the value of knowledge, independent of the cultural capital account. Cultural capital accounts of the value of a theoretical curriculum place a theoretical education's value on the social value of the theoretical content taught.

There are thus three culture-based reasons for claiming that a theoretical education is worthwhile. The first is Oakeshott's view that the existence of a cultural heritage justifies its place on the curriculum. The second is the view expressed by Arnold, Adler and Hirsch that a shared cultural awareness unites a nation and strengthens democracy. The third is the idea that a theoretical education provides students with cultural capital, and that the fair distribution of cultural capital is a matter of social justice; it contributes to social mobility by making sure that all students have the same level of socially valuable theoretical content.

I have already mentioned that Oakeshott's account of the value of a theoretical education based on the existence of culture is unhelpful: it gives little curriculum guidance, merely suggesting that every existing cultural achievement ought to be taught. It is likely that Oakeshott attached an intrinsic value account of theoretical education to this idea. If culture is intrinsically valuable, then it makes sense to say that it ought to be taught in schools. The problems with intrinsic value accounts of theoretical education have already been covered.

Arnold, Adler, and Hirsch's claims that induction into a shared cultural heritage is good for the health of society has been appealing to policymakers, for example, the ex-minister for education Gove makes reference to it, claiming that cultural literacy 'helps bind society together' (Gove, 2009, p. 4). There are two reasons to be cautious about this justification of theoretical education. The first is that the idea that cultural literacy binds society together is unsubstantiated, or if it is true, the binding of society attributed to a shared cultural heritage needs to be weighed up against the value of the rich spectrum of cultures and ideas, which, for example, Mill thinks are needed for social progress (Mill, 1924). The second reason for caution is that this justification for a theoretical education appeals to the value of somebody's education to the state, rather than the value of their education to themselves. A curriculum which moulds obedient citizens for the state who are ill equipped to live flourishing lives, particularly outside of the state they were educated for, is valuable to the state, but not to the individual.

The third culture-based account of the value of a theoretical education is that it provides students with cultural capital, which contributes to social mobility and works towards a more just society. Insofar as it is true that being well-read, or having a basic grasp of Latin are seen as markers of social class, and insofar as these markers of social class can advantage people in their search for jobs, further education, or other goods, this consideration should not be overlooked. If teaching state school students the sort of curriculum taught to independent school students helps to level the playing field, then schools have a duty to seriously consider the sort of traditional, elitist curriculum proposed. However, there are also reasons to be uneasy with this idea.

One problem for culture-based accounts is that the sort of theoretical education advocated for is arbitrary, the content is picked out according to social fashions of the time. In 1868, Parker described education in the Middle Ages, which focused on Greek and Latin. He says

> In the middles ages Latin was made the ground work of education; not for the beauty of its classical literature, nor because the study of a dead language was the best mental gymnastic, or the only means of acquiring a masterly freedom in the use of living tongues, but because it was the language of educated men throughout Western Europe, employed for public business, literature, philosophy, and science, above all in God's providence, essential to the unity, and therefore enforced by the authority, of the Western Church. (Parker, 1890, p. 4)

This account of a transparently culture-based curriculum is disquieting for several reasons. First, it is clearly true that someone in the Middle Ages who did not know Latin and Greek was at a social disadvantage. However, the social importance of Latin and Greek is likely to have pushed out other potentially valuable pursuits from the curriculum. Their social value led to an arbitrary curriculum which was only worthwhile because of the fashion for Latin and Greek in the upper classes. Advocating a curriculum based on culturally valuable theoretical content risks creating a similar arbitrary curriculum of, for example, a selection of 'great books'. What we understand by 'great books' changes over time. This can be seen in discussions about race and gender in the contents of the English Literature school curriculum in the UK (e.g. Elliott, 2021).

Another problem with the view that a theoretical education is worthwhile because it provides students with cultural capital is that cultural capital is only valuable if it helps someone to access social goods. It is easy to imagine a world in which every student was taught the same curriculum, regardless of their social background, yet there was still social injustice. Other markers of belonging to a social elite might easily take the place of the cultural markers which were being taught for in schools; for example, club membership, music preference or yacht ownership. Social classes are differentiated by arbitrary markers indicating membership of different groups; the curriculum would need to be constantly altered to reflect this and it is unlikely that it would continue to be an entirely theoretical education.

A final consideration for this sort of account of the value of a theoretical education is that induction into socially valuable cultural content is only valuable if it leads to certain social goods which are in high demand and low supply. A theoretical education based on cultural capital is only going to benefit a minority of students; those who gain access to well-paid or high-status jobs. The students who do not end up in these positions might have little to show for their education. If Latin and Greek had been taught to everyone in the Middle Ages, it would not have increased the number of high status positions available to people. As a result, many students would have continued to live lives which made no use of Latin and Greek. These students would have gained nothing from their education other than the right to take part in the competition for high status jobs. It is also likely that in such a society, the markers of society's elite would have shifted, so that knowledge of Greek and Latin was not sufficient. A justification of theoretical education ought to appeal to something valuable about theoretical education itself, not to its social value, as this can be subject to arbitrary change.

This is not to say that there is no real value to culturally valuable activities; going to the theatre, visiting an art gallery, reading a classic novel are all culturally valuable, and have the potential to enrich people's lives. This, however, does not justify a broad theoretical education. It does not answer the question of 'why do this rather than that?': why should a curriculum focus on valuable cultural activities rather than vocational training, for example?

Political Accounts

Liberal education is sometimes taken as synonymous with the sort of education best suited to liberal democratic societies. This might suggest that an education motivated by liberal democratic ideals overlaps with theoretical education, since liberal education is often theoretical in nature. Some justifications of liberal education make the case that such an education is suited for a liberal democracy. In a sense, this conflates two different ideas: first, that a liberal education is any education which fits with liberal democratic societies and second, that a liberal education is a theoretical education. These two historical uses of the term 'liberal education' should, preferably, be kept conceptually distinct. However, there are some reasons for thinking that a theoretical education can be justified in terms of the contribution it makes to liberal democracy.

This idea has already been briefly covered in the previous section where Arnold, Hirsch, Adler and Gove made the case that a shared cultural awareness contributes towards preparing citizens for liberal democratic life. This is particularly the case for Arnold, who was directly concerned with newly franchised voters. The same idea is present in Classical accounts of liberal education. In Greece and Rome, a liberal education was an education for free men who were responsible for governing the state. Aristotle described an educated man as someone who 'is free from the sort of intellectual enslavement to them that would otherwise be his lot. He knows who is and is not worth listening to on any matter, and so can get good advice when he needs it' (Reeve, 2008, p. 23). Plato saw liberal education as a political good, since his Republic required an educated leader who was acquainted with the truth (Plato and Waterfield, 1998).

More recently, Meira Levison has described a liberal education as one which is guided by the values of autonomy, choice, cultural coherence, citizenship, economic competitiveness, democratic self-reflection and equality (Levison, 2002, p. 134). These values are also central to liberal democratic societies. Similarly, Nussbaum casts the value of liberal education in terms of liberal democratic values; 'becoming an educated citizen means learning a lot of facts and mastering techniques of reasoning. But it also means something more. It means learning how to be a human being capable of love and imagination'

(Nussbaum, 1997, p. 14). Nussbaum sees a central role for the humanities alongside a general broad theoretical education as a way of developing students' imagination alongside their knowledge about the world. Simultaneously, she emphasises the value of independent and critical thought.

In accounts linking liberal education with education for liberal democracies, the role of theoretical education is unclear. It is unclear whether Nussbaum and Levison think that the sort of theoretical education that has traditionally been taught in schools meets the political concept of liberal education they have in mind. In Nussbaum's case, she emphasizes the importance of educating for human flourishing and developing students' intellectual and moral virtues. A purely theoretical education would fall short of meeting these aims. Levison's list of values is also perhaps better met through non-theoretical practices. Plausibly, educating for liberal democracies ought to include spending school time on democratic practices such as dialogue, voting and community service. Dewey's view that education for citizenship ought to draw together home and public life, and enact democratic practices, offers a compelling alternative to a purely theoretical education. While it seems fair to say that theoretical education plays some role in educating for liberal democracy, the accounts of liberal education relating to liberal democracy blur lines between theoretical activities and non-theoretical activities. This leaves how much students need to know to be good citizens as an open question. Perhaps they do not need to know much at all, but can instead possess civic virtues, or be fully involved in their local communities.

Another concern with associating liberal education with liberal democracy is that it implies that the value of a theoretical education is limited to its value within a liberal democratic society. However, this seems to underplay its value; even if someone lived in a non-democratic society, it seems that they would still benefit from a broad theoretical education. This suggests that there is something worthwhile about a theoretical education, which is not entirely political in its scope. A theoretical education is not, by itself, a sufficient education for liberal democratic citizenship; at the same time, a theoretical education's value is not fully captured by the aims of educating for democracy.

For the sake of clarity, it is better not to confuse the idea of a theoretical education with the idea of an education for liberal democratic societies. This means that accounts of liberal education that are closely tied to liberal democracy do not clearly illuminate the value of theoretical education in a way that differentiates theoretical education from other sorts of education, such as virtues education, which contribute to healthy democratic societies. However, given the relationship between education and the functioning of the state, it is important to provide an account of the value of theoretical education which is at least in harmony with liberal democratic commitments. There are good reasons why a theoretical education is good for democracy; it provides citizens with knowledge, understanding and a shared cultural inheritance. However, a theoretical education ought not be entirely determined by the requirements of liberal democracies on their citizens, nor limited in value to its value to the state. It should be good for the individual, regardless of their political status.

Rational Autonomy Accounts

The final account of theoretical education that I will cover is that it is an education for rational autonomy. Winch and Gingell claim that rational autonomy 'has been a declared aim of liberal education at least since the time of Plato' and that 'in the works of Peters and his immediate successors, rational autonomy has become the main aim of liberal education' (Winch & Gingell, 1999, p. 199). Carr describes what he calls 'liberal rationalism' as an idea that 'locates the development of reason, and therefore of personal autonomy, in a liberal education consisting of initiation into and mastery of putatively locally necessary forms of knowledge' (Carr, 2005, p. 76). Bonnet and Cuypers state that 'educational philosophers in this "rationalist tradition" … have tended to see autonomy as making rationally informed choices, and to maintain that its development therefore requires a broad and compulsory curriculum that would initiate the student into the relevant forms of rationality and provide the necessary knowledge base' (Bonnet & Cuypers, 1998, p. 327).

Given the prevalence of this view, it will require a developed explication and response. I will argue that although this is a promising account of the value of a theoretical education, it still falls short of giving a full account of its value. First, I will outline different versions of rational-autonomy accounts of the value of theoretical education. Then, I will give a more detailed insight into Hirst's account of liberal education, which has been described as 'the high-water mark of liberal traditionalist curriculum theorizing' (Carr, 2009, p. 286). I conclude with the problems faced by rational-autonomy accounts. Chapter 4 will present a reconstructed view of the value of theoretical education which draws on the strengths of rational autonomy accounts whilst ameliorating for their short comings.

Peters and Hirst offer a developed account of theoretical education in relation to rational autonomy. They speak in terms of a liberal education, Peters traces the term to a 'plea for education rather than vocational training or training of hand and brain for utilitarian purposes' (Peters, 1966, p. 43). A liberal education is freeing for Peters because it allows someone 'to do what he wants freely' (p. 43), whereas vocational training limits someone to certain roles or circumstances. Part of Peters's analysis of the concept of education is that it necessarily includes 'cognitive perspective', which means that the mind is not 'confined by or restricted to one mode of thought. No scientist should emerge, for instance, without a good understanding of other ways of looking at the world, historically, for instance, or aesthetically' (p. 44). Peters is talking about a broad, theoretical education, which he describes as freeing.

When it comes to curriculum guidance, Peters turns to Hirst's account of liberal education. This is the view that liberal education is an induction into different forms of knowledge. These forms of knowledge are 'the complex ways of understanding experience which man has achieved, which are publicly specifiable and which are formed through learning' (Hirst, 1974, p. 37). Together, the logically distinct forms of knowledge fully develop mind: 'Whatever else is implied in the phrase, to have 'a rational mind' certainly implied experience structured under some form of conceptual scheme' (p. 38). Hirst concludes that 'a liberal education is, then, one that, determined in scope and content by knowledge itself, is thereby concerned with the development of mind' (p. 39). The justification for this kind of education is that it results in rationality, and that rational mind 'remains basic to freeing human conduct from wrong' (p. 41). The emphasis is on the role that a broad theoretical education can play in developing a person's rational autonomy.

White's 1973 account of a rational-autonomy-based liberal education is also worth mentioning. He takes the view that a liberal education ought to introduce students to different ways of living and give them the skills to decide which they ought to pursue. Here, autonomy consists of the ability and inclination to live a good life. The view that White presents in *Towards a Compulsory Curriculum* is that in order to live autonomous lives, an educated person should 'know of all the possible things he may want to choose for their own sake, and he must be ready to consider what to choose from the point of view not only of the present moment but of his life as a whole' (p. 22).

On this account, the curriculum ought to cover knowledge of activities and knowledge of ways of life. This lends it a theoretical focus. White makes a distinction between two types of activities: those which can be understood without engaging in the activity and those which cannot be understood without engaging in the activity (White, 1973, p. 26). Schools should teach the latter, because without doing so, students will not be aware of a set of activities that they might choose to pursue. White reaches the conclusion that 'if children were left free not to have to … study mathematics, physics, philosophy or contemplate works of art, then this might well harm them, since they might never come to know of whole areas of possible wants' (p. 35). Students should also be introduced to ways of life such as 'a way of life devoted to the pursuit of truth … [or] a way of life devoted to artistic creativity' (p. 44) because these widen their understanding of different ways of living a good life.

One problem with White's account is that it attributes little value to providing a theoretical education to students who will have no choice about the sort of life they want to lead. This echoes the fact that liberal education used to be seen as an education for the leisured classes. If a liberal education is to be a justified use of all students' time, not just those who will have the possibility of making significant decisions about how to live their lives, then some other justification is going to be needed. Schools impose a compulsory liberal curriculum on their students, and White's account does not fully justify that. Hand makes a similar point when he talks about the problem of identifying an educatable concept of autonomy. He describes the first sense of autonomy alluded to by White as 'circumstantial' since it '[pertains] to the circumstances in which one lives' (Hand, 2006a, p. 537). He points out that this is not a legitimate aim of education, because the circumstances in which one lives cannot be taught.

Another concern with White's account is that it does not imply the sort of curriculum taught in secondary schools at all. An alternative curriculum, which is more in line with White's account would be to introduce students very briefly to the full range of activities they might choose to pursue, and then to allow them to specialize as soon as they felt ready to make a commitment. In later work, White advocates this sort of curriculum and it would meet his aims equally well, but students would only spend a very small amount of their schooling being taught a theoretical curriculum. White might reply that to fully understand and appreciate an activity, students will need to be inducted into it in some detail; however, I do not think that learning mathematics, history or literature requires anywhere near the amount of time spent on them at school. There are, then, doubts about the extent to which White is able to account for the value of the sort of theoretical education provided in secondary schools. Instead, White could reasonably argue for an education which does not focus much on providing students with theoretical content. Most recently, White and Reiss have argued that flourishing ought to guide educational practices, drawing attention away from theoretical education (Reiss & White, 2013).

Bailey claims that what a liberal education 'liberates the person from is the limitations of the present and the particular. The liberally educated person is capable of responding to the stimuli of his present and particular environment in a way that stands in the starkest possible contrast to animal reaction' (Bailey, 1984, p. 19). Given this aim of liberal education, Bailey thinks that what should be taught is whatever is the most fundamental and general aspects of knowledge and understanding: 'The intuitive idea here is that the more fundamental is an aspect of knowledge and understanding ... the more general are its applications and the more liberated I am in terms of choices I can make and perspectives I can bring to bear' (Bailey, 1984, p. 20). Bailey also ties in the idea of reason, so that a liberal education is 'concerned with a life of reason' (p. 20). The sort of education Bailey is describing as liberal is a broad theoretical education.

For Bailey, a theoretical education is justified in so far as it is useful. It is not useful in a single sense, but 'it is precisely its general and fundamental utility that provides part of the justification for a liberal general education' (Bailey, 1984, p. 28). This gives Bailey an inroad into making claims about what should go onto the curriculum. He states that education requires knowledge and understanding of 'those frameworks of interrelated ideas and activities that have stood the test of time in terms of fundamentality, non-arbitrariness and coherence and ... the initiation and engagement of pupils in frameworks of interrelated evidentially held beliefs where ideas of justifiable correctness are significant' (pp. 66–7).

This account of what should go on the curriculum draws inspiration from Hirst's forms of knowledge thesis because Bailey thinks that 'to be rational is ... to become initiated into public bodies of knowledge in which statements gain meaning by their location within clusters of other statements related in publicly organised ways' (Bailey, 1984, p. 25). As such, there are parts of Bailey's account of liberal education which face the same criticisms as Hirst's, which will be outlined in the next section. However, Bailey can get away with an account of theoretical education without Hirst's theoretical commitments. Simply to claim that a broad and balanced theoretical curriculum can provide students with a useful understanding of the world around them should suffice as a justification for such an education. This is the route that I will take in Chapter 4. What is lacking in Bailey's work is an account of what ought to go onto a curriculum in order to provide this maximally useful education. What should we teach if we want to maximise the utility of schooling? This might turn out to be something very different from the traditional account of liberal education. Bailey's work makes the important point that a theoretical education could be justified instrumentally.

As is stands, Bailey could be seen as providing a utility account of liberal education, but instead he blocks this interpretation with the claim that the instrumental value of liberal education is a consequence of its intrinsic value: 'The argument would be that we involve pupils in what is fundamental because fundamental understanding of human experience is intrinsically worthwhile, but in doing this we are necessarily providing pupils with the knowledge and understanding that has the most general relevance and utility for anything they are likely to want to do' (Bailey, 1984, p. 15). This appeal to intrinsic value is mixed up with a rational autonomy justification. Thus, Bailey's account falls into three different categories: intrinsic value, rational-autonomy and utility. I will come back to the utility account in Chapter 4.

Returning to rational-autonomy, this account of the value of theoretical education raises questions which need to be cleared up for it to fully justify the sort of theoretical education often taught in schools. On the other hand, the idea that education should aim to instil rationality and enable autonomy in people is appealing, it is hard to argue that these are not legitimate educational goods. The first problem raised by rational autonomy accounts is that it is unclear how a broad theoretical education might help to develop rational autonomy. Hirst provides an account of the connection between rational autonomy and theoretical education in his forms of knowledge thesis. This will be examined in more detail shortly, and I will argue that this runs into problems of its own. Peters does not provide a justification of the connection between theoretical activities and rational autonomy, beyond occasional discussions that seem to take the connection for granted (Peters, 1966). Bailey hints that a broad utility account of the value of a theoretical education might be more fruitful, but falls back on Hirst's forms of knowledge thesis without fully developing his utility account (Hirst, 1974). White's attempt to link theoretical education to rational autonomy leads to a circumstantial account of rational autonomy (White, 1973). It also draws attention away from the value of theoretical education, focusing it on the best sort of education at helping students to live a flourishing life. This may or may not be theoretical.

A further problem is the lack of clarity about what exactly rational autonomy is. Hirst defines rationality in terms of 'mind' and being able to think according to all of the different forms of knowledge. He then asserts that this is freeing with little explanation. Peters describes being able to see the world with cognitive perspective, leading to the freeing of the student through their broad and balanced education. Peters does not address how this broad theoretical education leads to rationality, even if it might lead to a form of autonomy. Bailey focuses on freedom or autonomy, but not rationality. All of this is to say that more work needs to be done to clarify what might be meant by the idea that a theoretical education aims at developing rational autonomy in students.

Hirst's account of theoretical education is a developed and influential example of a rational autonomy account of the value of theoretical education. In this section, I will examine Hirst's account in more detail to show why even this well-developed account leaves important questions about the value of theoretical education unanswered. This section illustrates some of the aforementioned problems with rational-autonomy accounts, and demonstrates that they fall short of providing a clear account of the value of theoretical education. In summary, Hirst's account of liberal education can be set out like this:

(1) There are a determinate number of logically distinct ways of understanding experience. Call these 'forms of knowledge';
(2) To be able to understand the world in these ways is to have developed rational mind;
(3) Rational mind 'frees human conduct from wrong', which is the aim of a liberal education;
(4) Therefore, a liberal education consists of teaching students the forms of knowledge.

Premise 1: Forms of Knowledge

The most influential part of Hirst's account of liberal education is his forms of knowledge thesis. He says that it is 'a basic philosophical truth about the nature of knowledge that, whether we like it or not, all knowledge is differentiated into a limited number of logically distinct forms or disciplines' (Hirst, 1974, p. 5). These are 'the complex ways of understanding experience which man has achieved, which are publicly specifiable and which are gained through learning' (p. 38). Once identified, the forms of knowledge can guide what ought to be included on the curriculum. The basic idea is that there exist a number of distinct ways of understanding the world around us. A liberal education is whatever it takes to help students to develop these ways of understanding the world.

Hirst identifies four methods by which the forms of knowledge can be distinguished. They 'involve certain central concepts that are peculiar in character to the form'; they have developed a 'distinctive logical structure'; they 'are testable against experience'; and they have their own methods of 'exploring experience and testing their distinctive expressions' (Hirst, 1974, p. 44). The forms which Hirst identifies are 'mathematics, physical sciences, human sciences, history, religion, literature and the fine arts, philosophy' and classified as a 'field of knowledge', he adds morality (p. 46). In later work, Hirst lists: formal logic and mathematics, physical sciences, interpersonal knowledge, religion, aesthetics, philosophy and morality (Hirst & Peters, 1970, pp. 63–4). In a much later paper, Hirst changes his focus 'from seeing education as primarily concerned with knowledge to seeing it as primarily concerned with social practices' (Hirst, 1993, p. 184).

There is a lot of literature pointing to difficulties with the forms of knowledge thesis. Some have targeted the difficulties defining the forms of knowledge; a difficulty which Hirst grapples with himself. For example, Hand sees no reason why Hirst settles on his six or seven forms of knowledge, instead identifying three forms of knowledge which can reasonably be said to exist (Hand, 2006b). Others have cast doubt on the existence of the forms of knowledge. A Deweyan perspective would see all knowledge as continuous, with both experience and with other fields of knowledge. The burden is on Hirst to show that forms of knowledge really exist, or are important conceptually for thinking about education.

The conceptual importance of the forms of knowledge thesis is questionable. Arguably, the forms of knowledge thesis can lead to counter-intuitive conclusions. For example, Pring uses the forms of knowledge thesis to argue that the idea of curriculum integration is incoherent because different subjects, like forms of knowledge, are logically distinct (Pring, 1973). McPeck uses the forms of knowledge thesis to argue that critical thinking cannot be a general capacity, but instead it only makes sense to think about specific types of critical thinking which are tied to forms of knowledge. This means that there is mathematical critical thinking, religious critical thinking and moral critical thinking, but there is not a general critical thinking ability which works across the different forms of knowledge (McPeck, 1990). There does not seem to be much merit in denying the possibility of a general capacity for critical thinking, or of the possibility of integrating disciplinary content. Admittedly, conceptual work is needed to figure out what either of these ideas precisely means, but denying their possibility seems an unwelcome conclusion of Hirst's forms of knowledge thesis.

Further, Hirst and Peters's insights about the importance of different sorts of theoretical activities can be maintained without appealing to logically distinct forms of knowledge. One alternative is to take Collingwood's account of disciplinary sciences. Collingwood says that a disciplinary science 'in its ordinary sense … means a body of systematic or orderly thinking about a determinate subject-matter' (Collingwood, 1940, p. 4). Rather than being logically distinct, disciplines are contingently distinct, having diverged over time, but all being part of the broader endeavour of human inquiry. He elaborates that 'history, then, is a science, but a science of a special kind. It is a science whose business is to study events not accessible to our observation, and to study these events inferentially, arguing to them from something else which is accessible to our observation, and which the historian calls 'evidence' for the events in which he is interested' (Collingwood, 1999, p. 6). Differences exist between theoretical activities, but they can be explained adequately without appealing to forms of knowledge. This sort of account avoids some of the less intuitive consequences of Hirst's account; interdisciplinarity and general critical thinking are both possibilities.

In light of the difficulties identifying the forms of knowledge, the arguably counter-intuitive consequences of holding a forms of knowledge thesis, and a viable alternative which avoids these problems, on balance there are better reasons for moving away from the forms of knowledge thesis than for holding onto it.

Premise 2: Forms of Knowledge and Rational Mind

Next, Hirst claims that grasping the forms of knowledge equates to developing rational mind:

> To acquire knowledge is to become aware of experience as structured, organized and made meaningful in some quite specific way, and the varieties of human knowledge constitute the highly developed forms in which man has found this possible. To acquire knowledge is to learn to see, to experience the world in a way otherwise unknown, and thereby to come to have mind in a fuller sense … to have a mind basically involves coming to have experience articulated by means of various conceptual schemata. (Hirst, 1974, p. 41)

Hirst cautions against interpreting this move as positing some metaphysical claim about the nature of mind, instead he says that:

> What is being suggested, rather, is that the 'harmony' is a matter of the logical relationship between the concept of 'mind' and the concept of 'knowledge', from which it follows that the achievement of knowledge is necessarily the development of mind – that is, the self-conscious rational mind of man – in its most fundamental aspect. (Hirst, 1974, p. 39)

Hirst defines rational mind in terms of the forms of knowledge such that to acquire knowledge, or to learn to understand experience via the full set of forms of knowledge, is to come to have a rational mind.

Hirst's use of terminology requires some clarification. The term 'mind' has become strongly associated with the field of philosophy of mind, and Hirst is not making philosophy of mind type claims. The rational mind is Hirst's terminology for what might better be termed rationality, although rationality and rational mind are not synonymous. This links to Hirst's claims about the forms of knowledge, which can be described as ways of thinking or forms of inquiry combined with theoretical content. Hirst thinks that a fully developed mind is one which has mastered all of the forms of knowledge. Someone who has developed rational mind might be described as someone who is good at thinking in many different ways.

A problem with this part of Hirst's account is that it is unclear that coming to know the forms of knowledge leads to rationality. There are two possibilities here; the first is that acquiring a broad range of propositional content is necessary and sufficient for rationality. The second is that being able to think in a broad range of different ways is necessary and sufficient for rationality. Neither of these is convincing. If acquiring propositional content is necessary and sufficient for rationality, then someone who has not come to know a large enough amount of content from formal logic and mathematics, physical sciences, interpersonal knowledge, religion, aesthetics, philosophy and morality, cannot be rational. This seems too high a bar to set; we would want to attribute rationality to a much broader set of people than just those who have paid good attention to, understood and remembered the contents of such a curriculum.

The second option, that learning to think in a variety of different ways is necessary and sufficient for rationality, is also problematic. It seems possible that someone could be rational without being able to think in all of the ways captured by the forms of knowledge thesis. Most people are not adept at thinking in all of the ways outlined by Hirst, yet there are many people we would want to say are rational regardless of their grasp of the forms of knowledge. It also seems possible that someone could have a good grasp of all the forms of knowledge, and yet act irrationally in matters of everyday, or non-disciplinary thinking. The image of the absent-minded professor comes to mind. Or the fact that regardless of how broadly educated people are, they still face the same problems when navigating personal relationships. The charge of irrationality within this sphere does not seem to discriminate between people's adeptness at thinking according to the forms of knowledge. Combining both theoretical content and disciplinary ways of thinking runs into the same problems. It seems that someone without a broad theoretical education could be rational or that a theoretically educated person could be irrational.

Finally, it is worth noting that Hirst was keen to present an account of liberal education which was free from the metaphysical commitments of classical accounts. He claims that he has presented a non-metaphysical account of liberal education and is keen to stress that his concept of mind is not metaphysical. However, it seems that the forms of knowledge thesis is a metaphysical thesis; particularly since he claims that the forms of knowledge are logically distinct, and that he is offering an account of education based on 'the nature of knowledge itself' (Hirst, 1974, p. 30). If the forms of knowledge thesis amounts to a claim about the nature of knowledge, then Hirst's concept of mind is also laden with metaphysics, since his concept of mind is defined directly in terms of the forms of knowledge. This makes Hirst's account almost as contentious as the classical accounts which he was aiming to simplify, particularly since his forms of knowledge thesis is troublesome in its own right.

Premise 3: Rationality and Rational Autonomy

As a rational autonomy account, Hirst aims to explain how a broad theoretical education leads to autonomy. Hirst makes the following claims to draw this connection: 'It is a form of education knowing no limits other than those necessarily imposed by the nature of rational knowledge and thereby itself developing in man the final court of appeal in all human affairs' (Hirst, 1974, p. 41); and 'liberal education remains basic to the freeing of human conduct from wrong' (p. 41). The view presented is that a curriculum consisting of the forms of knowledge develops rationality, and that rationality leads to this freeing of human conduct from wrong.

Since there are two possible interpretations of Hirst's account of rationality, there are two possible things that he might mean by autonomy. If Hirst thinks that rationality is the same as possessing knowledge, then he might be referring to the idea that knowing more facilitates freedom from error. If Hirst thinks that rationality is a matter of being able to think in a variety of different ways, then it is a set of critical thinking abilities which frees people from error. It is likely that Hirst had a combination of both accounts in mind so that a theoretical education frees people by both informing them, and by helping them to think critically about the world. Either way, Hirst's account lacks an explicit link between having a rational mind and freeing conduct from error since he does not elaborate how his proposed curriculum imparts freedom from error. Instead, he asserts that it develops rationality.

Furthermore, the problems linking the forms of knowledge thesis with rationality mean that the more fundamental link between an education into a broad and balanced set of theoretical activities and some sense of autonomy is undermined. According to Hirst, being taught the forms of knowledge leads to rationality, which frees human conduct from wrong. But it is unclear how the forms of knowledge lead to rationality, what Hirst means by rationality, and whether the sort of rational mind that Hirst thinks the forms of knowledge develop does in fact result in freedom from error.

The account of liberal education presented by Hirst attempts to draw all of the connections needed for a coherent account, but faces difficulties. What follows is my own attempt to give a coherent account of a liberal education where there are clear connections between a broad and balanced education, and a sense of liberal which is potentially justifiable. The project is the same as Hirst's, but the reconstruction attempts to avoid the problems presented by his account.

Rational-autonomy accounts of the value of theoretical education are faced with three questions which require further work: (1) what exactly is meant by rational autonomy? (2) how does a theoretical education contribute towards rational autonomy? and (3) how should a curriculum designed to bring about rational autonomy look?

Conclusion

There is a long history of providing students with a theoretical education; an education which focuses on communicating ideas about the world to students. This history translates into contemporary curricula, such as the National Curriculum in England, which takes inspiration from the liberal education tradition and is heavily theoretical in its content. This theoretical education is prevalent around the world, and demands some sort of justification if it is to be held as a legitimate use of students' time. Existing accounts of the value of theoretical education remain underdeveloped. Many take the form of a discussion about the value of liberal education. Different accounts of the value of liberal education appeal to a range of reasons for its value, which often overlap. There are problems or outstanding questions with each account.

4

A Utility Account of Education

So far in this book, I have outlined the history of philosophy in schools, explored the different reasons given for including philosophy on the school curriculum, explained what I mean by a theoretical education and set out the different reasons it might be valuable. At the same time, I have argued that any argument for teaching philosophy in schools requires a clear account of the nature and aims of education. This is because an argument for teaching philosophy in schools needs to appeal to some specified educational good(s) that teaching philosophy is best placed to provide students with.

This chapter focuses on providing an account of the aims of theoretical education and its resulting educational goods. This will ground the two arguments in Chapters 5 and 6 for the necessity of teaching philosophy. Here, I argue for a utility account of theoretical education. Theoretically educating people is valuable because it is broadly useful to them. The educational good that it provides is the ability to interact effectively with the world in virtue of the insights into the world provided by theoretical content.

I call the positive account proposed in this chapter a utility account of theoretical education. I argue that it is the utility to an individual student of receiving a broad theoretical education that justifies it. The account borrows from Hirst and Peters's claims about the capacity of theoretical activities to shape how people see the world. I develop this to show how being able to see the world in different ways directly contributes to people's freedom or liberty, an idea which is frequently appealed to in existing accounts of the value of theoretical education. Despite using Hirst and Peters's work as a starting point, I part ways with them when it comes to the forms of knowledge thesis, their emphasis on logically distinct disciplines and claims about rational mind. Instead, I focus on the idea that a theoretical education provides theoretical content about the world that helps students to effectively interact with it. By this, I mean that students are better able to make decisions and act on them because they are well-informed about the nature of the world they are acting in. Someone who can interact more effectively with the world is, all things considered, more free than someone who cannot. In a minimal sense, a theoretical education frees students to achieve their aims through providing them with knowledge and understanding about the world that they live in. This is a clear, achievable and justifiable aim for theoretical education and for education in general.

In the context of this book, the utility account of education that I put forward plays a central role. From it, I derive guidelines about the curriculum which provide a foundation for two arguments for teaching philosophy in schools. The first argument, presented in Chapter 5, is that content from the discipline of philosophy provides the best available answers to a class of prominent and pressing questions that a utility-aimed curriculum ought to address. The second argument, presented in Chapter 6, is that any theoretical education faces a problem when it comes to how students understand and make sense of the broad array of ideas they are taught. The discipline of philosophy, in particular its attention to concepts and conceptual schemes, is uniquely placed to help students to make sense of a broad theoretical curriculum.

Rational Autonomy Accounts and the Utility of Theoretical Education

In Chapter 3, I outlined the shortcomings of traditional rational-autonomy accounts of the value of theoretical education. In summary, these are that they do not fully explain (1) what exactly is meant by rational autonomy; (2) how a theoretical education contributes towards rational autonomy and (3) how a curriculum designed to bring about rational autonomy should look. Despite these shortcomings, they provide appealing accounts of the value of theoretical education, because ultimately rational autonomy, in one form or another, seems like a justifiable aim of education. Another appeal of rational-autonomy accounts is that they are well-developed accounts, which have been systematically set out by a number of philosophers of education. Although I will diverge from these accounts, there are aspects of them that I will adopt; in particular there is a strand of thought in the works of Peters, Hirst, Bailey and Hand (all rational autonomy advocates) which alludes to a simpler and more fundamental benefit to a theoretical education; this is its general utility.

Hirst and Peters talk about education in terms of coming to see the world in new and different ways. Neither present a developed exposition of this idea, preferring to focus on the development of rational mind and the forms of knowledge. However, it is this idea that theoretical content provides ways of understanding the world that links in a straightforward way to freedom from error. Hirst says that 'to acquire knowledge is to learn to see, to experience the world in a way otherwise unknown, and thereby to come to have mind in a fuller sense' (Hirst, 1974, p. 4).

Peters goes into slightly more detail and states that theoretical activities 'illuminate other areas of life and contribute much to the quality of living ... there is an immense amount to know and if it is properly assimilated, it constantly throws light on, widens and deepens one's view of countless other things' (Peters, 1966, p. 159). According to Peters, theoretical activities such as science, history and literary appreciation 'consist largely in the exploration, assessment and illumination of the different facts of life. They thus insensibly change a man's view of the world ... a person who has pursued them systematically develops conceptual schemes and forms of appraisal which transforms everything else that he does' (p. 160).

These claims stand independent from the forms of knowledge thesis or reference to the development of mind. They amount to the claim that when a teacher tells a student something, they are hoping that the student will acquire some new way of making sense of the world around them. The practice of teaching aims to provide students with something that illuminates the world around them. If a student memorizes what they are told but avoids or fails to see the world around them differently, it seems that the aim of the interaction has failed. This is true of theoretical activities, but not necessarily true of more skills-centred activities such as language teaching. This suggests a simple and minimal role for theoretical education: coming to know and understand something can provide a new way of seeing and understanding the world.

To tease theoretical education apart from other sorts of education a little more, a theoretical education provides students with ideas that have some effect on their broader understanding of the world. Reading a novel provides a theoretical education because it asks someone to see the world through the eyes of the novelist or the characters in the novel. Learning about the history of a building helps the learner to see that building in its historical context and lends it new significance in the learner's eyes. Studying the theory of gravity changes how a student understands common phenomena around them and helps them to make sense of more complex phenomena. In all of these cases, merely memorizing the content taught without seeing the world any differently falls short of learning what was intended to be taught.

Theoretical education contrasts with skills-based education, such as becoming numerate, where being able to do sums does not require any change in how a student sees the world. Similarly, literacy is non-theoretical because it is sufficient to memorize the content and rules of written language without changing ones' view of the world. Learning a language is the same. This is not to say that language learning, numeracy or literacy cannot lead to changes in how someone sees the world, but on their own they are not theoretical. The sort of vocational training referred to frequently as opposed to liberal education is the same. To learn how to touch-type or to grasp the basics of accountancy does not require any change in how someone sees the world. However, it undermines the complexity of vocational education to say that none of these are theoretical in any way. I imagine that the best touch-typists would be influenced by their training and skills to see the world in a way that enhances their work.

The idea that a theoretical education changes how people understand or see the world is explored by Bailey, who offers a parallel strand of through. He says that a liberal education 'liberates the person from is the limitations of the present and the particular. The liberally educated person is capable of responding to the stimuli of his present and particular environment in a way that stands in the starkest possible contrast to animal reaction' (Bailey, 1984, p. 19). Bailey thinks that the most fundamental and general aspects of knowledge and understanding should be taught as part of a liberal education: 'The intuitive idea here is that the more fundamental an aspect of knowledge and understanding ... the more general are its applications and the more liberated I am in terms of choices I can make and perspectives I can bring to bear' (p. 20). For Bailey, a liberal education is justified insofar as it is useful. It is not useful in a limited sense, but 'it is precisely its general and fundamental utility that provides part of the justification for a liberal general education' (p. 28).

It is worth bearing in mind that Bailey's use of the term 'liberal education' is synonymous with theoretical education as it is being used here. Further, despite Bailey's endorsement of Hirst's forms of knowledge thesis, he offers a different connection between the forms of knowledge and the value of knowledge. Bailey brings up the possibility that a broad theoretical education is instrumentally valuable, that it holds broad utility.

This broad or general utility is a distinct concept from more traditional uses of the term 'utility'. Bailey does not think that a liberal education is useful because it prepares people for specific tasks or roles but that it frees people in a broader sense. He does not think that a liberal education is useful for getting a job or for a better functioning state. Instead, a broad theoretical education provides an arsenal of ideas that allows people to think about their situation, their options and their actions. This might be what Bailey means when he says that a liberal education allows people to act in a way that contrasts with 'animal reaction'. They can think about the world around them in an informed and careful way.

This focus on the general usefulness of a theoretical education is discussed by Hand who suggests that Peters lays out the basis for an instrumental account of the value of theoretical activities. Drawing on the idea that knowledge and understanding of theoretical activities shed light on and transform many aspects of experience, Hand proposes that 'we should give curriculum priority to those worthwhile activities that enhance, enter into or shed light on all others' (Hand, 2010, p. 118). His rationale for this is that

> our task as educators is to prepare children for adult life. We cannot do this by initiating them into the activities that will occupy their time as adults because we do not yet know what those activities will be. Instead, we must try to prepare them in some general way, so their education will be useful to them whatever they choose to do with their lives. (Hand, 2010, p. 118)

Hand appeals to Bailey's 'general utility justification' of liberal education (Hand, 2010, p. 120).

Combining Hirst's claim that 'to acquire knowledge is to learn to see, to experience the world in a way otherwise unknown, and thereby to come to have a mind in a fuller sense' (Hirst, 1974, p. 40) with Peters's view that theoretical activities 'illuminate other areas of life and contribute much to the quality of living ... [liberal education] constantly throws light on, widens, and deepens one's view of countless other things' (Peters, 1966, p. 159) and Bailey's point that 'it is precisely its general and fundamental utility that provides part of the justification for a liberal general education' (Bailey, 1984, p. 28) does not provide a fully worked out justification for a theoretical education, but does provide a grounding for an account of the aims of a theoretical education that has the potential to coherently link a broad and balanced curriculum with something of educational value.

A final basis for such an account can be extrapolated from utilitarian-inspired accounts of liberal education dating back to the time of the industrial revolution. Pring explains that 'there are many versions of the liberal ideal. And indeed it is dangerous to assume that all versions were averse to some form of utility. The arguments were rehearsed, and the different versions clearly exposed, in a nineteenth-century debate which tried to accommodate a liberal tradition to the different conditions of an industrial society' (Pring, 2005, p. 49). For example, Mill talks about the 'utility of knowledge' such that useful knowledge

> teaches us how to seek what is good and avoid what is evil; in short, how to increase the sum of human happiness. This is the great end: it may be well or ill pursued, but to say that knowledge can be an enemy to happiness is to say that men will enjoy less happiness when they know how to see it, than when they do not. (Mill, 1924, p. 268)

Knowledge is a condition of achieving our ends, and when happiness is seen as 'the great end', knowledge of how to reach happiness is going to be useful. Applied to education, this account of the utility of knowledge overlaps with Bailey's 'general utility'; it is useful in a broad sense rather than for limited, pre-defined purposes.

One of the clearest accounts of a liberal education premised on utility is presented by Thomas Huxley. He uses an analogy to explain the general utility of acquiring knowledge:

> Suppose it were perfectly certain that the life and fortune of every one of us would, one day or other, depend upon his winning or losing a game at chess. Don't you think that we should all consider it to be a primary duty to learn at least the names and the moves of the pieces; to have a notion of a gambit, and a keen eye for all the means of giving and getting out of check? Do you not think that we should look with disapprobation amounting to scorn, upon the father who allowed his son, or the state which allowed its members, to grow up without knowing a pawn from a knight?
>
> Yet it is a very plain and elementary truth, that the life, the fortune, and the happiness of everyone one of us, and, more or less, of those who are connected with us, do depend upon our knowing something of the rules of a game infinitely more difficult and complicated than chess. It is a game which has been played for untold ages, every man and woman of us being one of the two players in a game of his or her own. The chess-board is the world, the pieces are the phenomena of the universe, the rules of the game are what we call the Laws of Nature. The player on the other side is hidden from us. We know that his play is always fair, just and patient. But also we know to our own cost, that he never overlooks a mistake, or makes the smallest allowance for our ignorance. (Huxley, 1868, pp. 81–2)

Huxley continues that to be educated is to learn the rules of the game of life. In this sense, there is clearly a body of knowledge which falls under the category of theoretical education and has straightforward utility. Without appealing to happiness, or to forms of knowledge, Huxley makes the case that the more we know about the world, the better able we are to act effectively within it.

The idea that a theoretical education has general utility overlaps with rational autonomy accounts of the value of theoretical education. Using what you know to solve problems with the aim of living a good life could be taken as an articulation of what it is to be rational. The advantage of focusing on the general utility of a theoretical education is that general utility is a clearer concept than rationality, it is also easier to identify and link to education.

A Utility Account of Theoretical Education

On the back of these ideas, I present the following account of the aims and value of a broad theoretical education. This account specifies the aim of theoretical education. It is also possible to derive guidance from it about the shape of the curriculum. These two points are essential for an argument for teaching philosophy in schools. Another way of understanding this account is that it is a clearer, better-justified version of the rational-autonomy accounts of theoretical education explored in Chapter 3.

In summary, the utility account of liberal education looks like this:

(1) Acquiring a broad array of theoretical content amounts of acquiring different ways of understanding the world;
(2) Different ways of understanding the world contribute to a person's ability to act effectively within the world;
(3) Providing students with the ability to act effectively within the world is a justifiable aim of education.

Each of these points will be explored in detail.

Premise 1: Theoretical Content and Understanding the World

In this section, I will explain what I mean by the idea that theoretical content provides ways of understanding the world. In particular, I will focus on the term 'theoretical content' and explain why it is the best unit for thinking about the building blocks of the curriculum. This may seem laboured at times, but it is central to being able to make the arguments presented in Chapters 5 and 6. In particular, I will draw a distinction with typical uses of the term 'knowledge' and theoretical content. The former is understood as justified, true belief and often equated with facts. Theoretical content provides a softer stance on the epistemic standards needed for something to be taught in schools, but also embeds a requirement for understanding into learning.

Hirst and Peters talk about curriculum content using two different sets of terms. Peters uses 'theoretical activities', and Hirst talks about knowledge and forms of knowledge. They share in common an emphasis on grasping disciplinary ways of thinking, alongside the importance of propositional content. This makes sense because grasping a disciplinary way of thinking, such as historical thinking, without acquiring propositional content about history seems nonsensical – what is there to think historically about without having some content about historical events? Acquiring propositional content alone, without learning about its disciplinary provenance and significance, faces the problem of reducing educational practices to memorizing inert facts – consider a history course which merely required memorisation of dates with no further elaboration. The balancing act between empty disciplinary thinking and inert fact acquisition motivates Hirst and Peters's attempts to set out the nature and aims of the education and curriculum. I will explain the problems that Hirst's and Peters's accounts pose and explain why I think drawing on the term 'theoretical content' helps.

Both Hirst and Peters are attempting to pin down something about the curriculum that helps students to come to see the world in new ways. Hirst chooses the route of talking about different ways of thinking; this is evident in his forms of knowledge thesis. The problem with this way of talking about the curriculum is that being able to see according to different forms of knowledge does not clearly make sense. This can be illustrated by considering whether inducting someone into a form of knowledge helps them to see phenomena in a new way. For example, someone might be taught how to think scientifically, but it is unclear how thinking scientifically would lead them to see a tomato plant in a new way. This is on the assumption that thinking scientifically is separable from propositional content (which Hirst does not assume). In this case, it is unclear what seeing a tomato plant scientifically might mean. While there is a wealth of propositional content about tomato plants, thinking scientifically about them does not mean that someone is taking that knowledge on board. Perhaps it means asking scientific questions about the plant and using scientific methods to inquire about it. Similarly, thinking historically about tomato plants suggests a starting point for finding something new out about the plants, rather than providing a new way of seeing them. It might involve investigating and researching the history of tomato plants whilst adhering to the standards of the discipline of history, but until something has been discovered about the history of the plants, it is unclear how this would help someone to see them differently. Disciplinary thinking, without content, is not transformative in the way described by Peters.

On the other hand, propositional content about tomato plants does seem more transformative. However, it will only be transformative if it has been taught well and they understand the propositional content, and see its relevance to tomato plants. Learning that tomato plants have green leaves because leaves contain chlorophyll that allows chloroplasts to absorb red light and transform it into usable energy provides a student with a new way of seeing or understanding the plant. This new way of seeing the plant is accompanied by a set of platitudes about how to interact with it. In this case, it can be surmised that the plant would benefit from being placed on a sunny windowsill. The more propositional content someone acquires about tomato plants, the better able they will be to use what they have learned to interact with it effectively. Historical propositional content such as the fact that tomatoes are native to South America, that they were cultivated from wild plants, and that they were introduced to Europe by Spanish conquistadors, casts the sort of transformative light over a common object that Peters says education ought to, where a theoretical activity 'throws light on, widens, and deepens one's view' (Peters, 1966, p. 159). While some of this content seems mundane, generally the more someone knows about tomato plants, the better able they are to successfully interact with them under a broad range of circumstances. This would be true even if the person did not have a good grasp of the disciplinary ways of thinking from which the content originated.

Propositional content, then, seems better suited for talking about curriculum content because it has greater potential to be transformative. However, it faces problems. First, it runs the danger of promoting a form of education that lapses into the transmission of inert ideas. Peters rightly stresses that it is not sufficient for a person to acquire facts that are inert 'either in the sense that they make no difference to his general view of the world, his actions within it, and reactions to it, or in the sense that they involve no concern for the standards immanent in the forms of thought and awareness, as well as the ability to attain them' (Peters, 1966, p. 9). Memorizing propositional content about tomato plants is compatible with not understanding the content, not knowing what it means, how it should be applied or how to evaluate its trustworthiness. Propositional content on its own does not necessarily transform how someone sees the world.

To solve the problem faced by the apparent choice between empty ways of thinking and inert facts without resorting to Hirst's forms of knowledge, which has problems of its own, I propose talking about theoretical content. By theoretical content, I mean content that is theoretically significant, alongside the theories the content is a part of. This contrasts with focusing on knowledge and an account of education as the pursuit of truth, which risks overemphasising the value of empty facts. It also contrasts with relying on disciplinary ways of thinking, and thinking more generally which underemphasises the value of propositional content.

The idea that theories and theoretical content are important follows the lead of philosophers of science who face similar issues about the value of scientific propositions, theories and methods. Epistemological debates within philosophy of science about the nature of scientific knowledge range from accounts which hold that it correctly captures the external world, to those that hold that scientific knowledge merely provides us with a model for understanding the external world without necessarily accurately representing it. As Papineau puts it,

> Nearly all contemporary philosophers of science accept that science aims literally to describe an unobservable world of microscopic particles and intangible waves. And a significant number draw the sceptical conclusion that science cannot succeed in this aim: since the world which science aims to describe is beyond the reach of human perception, we have no reason to think that its theories are true. (Papineau, 1996, p. 4)

The same can be said for much of what is taught in schools; it is quite possible that the best that humankind has to offer is not a complete body of justified, true belief. This does not mean that education is futile, but that curriculum content should be drawn from our best theories, which aim to capture the external world but may not accurately represent something that is not fully accessible to even the most acute experts. Anti-realist philosophers of science do not dismiss scientific theories as untrue, rather they focus on what makes a good theory, including the practical value of theories when employed in the world.

Where Peters and Hirst argue that education is about the pursuit of truth, I argue that education is about the pursuit of useful ways of understanding the world. This works in the same way as when scientists are described as searching for fruitful models of the world. Whether or not these fruitful models of the world are true is a separate question. It would be wrong to teach ways of understanding the world that are clearly misleading or false, such as outdated scientific theories or holocaust denialism, but where theoretical content is not clearly true or not clearly well-justified, it might nevertheless be appropriate to include on the curriculum if it provides a useful way of seeing the world. This is the case when important questions do not have well-established answers. Here, providing students with a range of ways of seeing the issue at hand is sometimes the best that educators can do. If the question is important enough, then the curriculum ought to do this.

Talking about theoretical content rather than knowledge illuminates several further ideas. First, theoretical content is only intelligible when situated as part of a broader theory. This is consistent with Hirst's idea that education ought to pay attention to different ways of thinking. Rather than casting these ways of thinking at a disciplinary level, they can instead be seen at a theory level. To apply a distinct theory to a problem is to think according to that theory.

Second, talking about theoretical content does not deny the value of propositional content: to apply a theory to a problem or to think about a phenomenon using a theory uses both theoretical ways of thinking and propositional content. When someone thinks about a tomato plant with theories about photosynthesis in mind, they think in terms of the logical relations proposed by the theory, and they see the tomato plant in a new light based on the propositional content tied up within the theory.

Third, talking about theoretical content avoids the possibility that being educated is the same as having memorized a broad and balanced selection of propositional knowledge. Theoretical content cannot be reduced to propositional knowledge because theoretical propositions are meaningless without some understanding of the theory which they are a part of. A history course which asked students to memorize dates would not be sufficient for a student to be theoretically educated. The student would need to grasp some way of seeing how those dates fit together into a coherent theory. This theory need not, and probably should not, encompass the whole of history. Theories can be limited in their scope, dealing with only small pieces of the world. But theoretical content always needs to be connected to some theory that is trying to communicate some way of seeing the world.

Talking about the curriculum in terms of theoretical content adds clarity to Hirst and Peters's accounts of liberal education. It solves some of the problems associated with the forms of knowledge thesis and it avoids describing education in terms of inert ideas. Theoretical content also captures the idea that grasping content changes how someone sees the world. Borrowing from philosophy of science, Kuhn describes the strength of the effect of theory change such that 'the historian of science might be tempted to exclaim that when paradigms change the world itself changes with them' (Kuhn, 1962, p. 111). A simple example is that when we are presented with an image, our understanding of it changes according to whether we are told that it was created using a microscope or a telescope. The theoretical content associated with microscopic or telescopic images alters how we see the image. When someone learns a theory, they become equipped with a new way of understanding their experiences and a new way of weaving experiences together into a meaningful viewpoint. This parallels the language Hirst and Peters's use when they describe the transformative effect of forms of knowledge.

Finally, talking about the curriculum in terms of theoretical content helps to clarify the relationship between knowledge and understanding, because to come to know a theory implies coming to understand it; its propositional content is inert without understanding the broader theory. Elgin differentiates between knowing individual truths and understanding them (Elgin, 2007, p. 35). The example she uses is the difference between saying 'I understand that Athens defeated Persia in the battle of Marathon' and 'I understand the Athenian victory over Persia in the battle of Marathon'. If understanding is just a case of grasping propositional knowledge, then there is no difference between the two claims. However, Elgin holds that understanding involves grasping 'a suitable unified, integrated, coherent body of information' (p. 36). She continues, 'I understand that Athens defeated Persia in the battle of Marathon, because I grasp how the proposition stating the facts fits into, contributes to, and is justified by reference to a more comprehensive understanding that embeds it' (p. 36).

What I mean by theoretical content is akin to what Elgin talks about when she says that understanding rests on grasping the broader body of information in which a proposition is embedded. Regardless of whether propositions coincide with justified, true beliefs, they are part of broader bodies of information that explain and describe the world around us. These are what I want to call theories, and all of the content associated with these theories is what I call theoretical content. This includes propositional content, but it also includes ways of thinking about the world that are inherent in the structure of a theory and the skills required to implement the theory. Drawing on Elgin's non-factive account of understanding, I propose that we can understand the world around us without necessarily being sure that we hold justified, true beliefs about it. Elgin points to the example of Copernican astronomy, which wrongly claimed that the earth's orbit was circular rather than elliptical, but still constituted a major improvement on Ptolemaic astronomy. She says that 'so long as (1) the theory or system as a whole is suitably connected to the phenomena, (2) the requisite epistemic standards are met, and (3) the felicitous falsehoods perform their epistemic functions, the system affords an understanding of the domain' (Elgin, 2012, p. 8). These conditions also apply to curriculum content.

Talking about theoretical content allows us to focus on teaching humankind's best available theories and prioritizes understanding over memorization, whilst preserving the importance of aiming to capture and explain reality. It also clearly provides students with new ways of seeing and understanding the world. For these reasons, I will refer to the content of a theoretical education as theoretical content. Theoretical content captures what it is that a theoretical education aims to transmit – different ways of seeing the world.

This is different from Hirst and Peters's forms of knowledge. The forms of knowledge place the focus of the curriculum on learning to think in disciplinary ways. Another way of thinking about this is that students are inducted into different forms of inquiry. I argued earlier that focusing on forms of inquiry sidelines the role of the content learned. However, Hirst and Peter's might reply that focusing on theoretical content sidelines the role of inquiry. My response to this is that induction into disciplinary ways of thinking is still important to place theories in their correct context and to teach students how to properly understand them. This is something that I will expand on later in this chapter. However, my account avoids the need to claim that disciplines are logically distinct from one another, and this in turn allows me to be able to talk about cross-curricular thinking in a way that Hirst and Peters struggle to do. In practice, the sort of curriculum I am advocating is only subtly different from Hirst and Peters's. In principle, the focus is on theoretical content rather than methods of inquiry. This is important because it more accurately illuminates the part of a theoretical education doing the work for students, better highlights the aims of theoretical education, and allows for thinking across and between different disciplines on the curriculum – something that is needed for my argument in Chapter 6.

Premise 2: Acting Effectively in the World

In this account, theoretical content rather than forms of knowledge or ways of thinking is prioritized. This means that prior accounts of the value of a theoretical education, such as the claim that induction into forms of knowledge leads to rationality, do not hold. As a replacement, I propose that the value of a theoretical curriculum is that theoretical content helps students to interact effectively with the world.

When someone sees a tomato plant through the lens of photosynthetic theory, they come to understand how to grow tomatoes better. When someone comes to see the Battle of Marathon through the unified, integrated and coherent body of information constituting theoretical content about it, they are better able to make predictions about or respond effectively to similar situations. Grasping Copernican astronomy similarly allows someone to interact effectively with the night sky, and grasping modern astronomical theoretical content allows the ability to place satellites into orbit or land spacecraft on Mars.

In a simple and basic way, theoretical content frees people to effectively interact with the world around them. This is something that holds fairly readily of knowledge, with Olsson summarizing that

> everyone agrees that knowledge is a good thing to have. If you know which horse will win the race, you can bet on that horse and make a fortune; if you know all the answers to the teacher's questions, you will pass the exam; and so on. Knowledge is clearly valuable in the sense of being conducive to successful practical action. Even philosophers, who disagree about many thing other things, do not normally debate the proposition that knowledge is valuable. (Olsson, 2011, p. 874)

In the absence of knowledge about which horse will win the race, theoretical content about the race, the horses involved, horse racing and so on, is the next best thing to have. It will provide a competitive advantage over others who do not have it, and it will provide a basis for making accurate predictions about the world. Theoretical content is useful for interacting with the world, even if it is not always strictly knowledge.

This account, although different from Hirst and Peters's emphasis on the relationship between forms of knowledge and rationality, is consistent with their understanding of the link between education and educational goods. Hirst claims that 'to acquire knowledge is to learn to see, to experience the world in a way otherwise unknown' (Hirst, 1974, p. 40); that 'it is the distinct disciplines that basically constitute the range of unique ways we have of understanding experience' (Hirst, 1973, p. 104); and that 'liberal education remains basic to the freeing of human conduct from wrong' (p. 101). When isolated from claims about the importance of the forms of knowledge in relation to the rational mind, the sense of freeing that Hirst seems to have in mind is the freedom to interact effectively with the world in light of being well informed by the different ways of understanding it that humanity has developed. On my account, the material playing this role is theoretical content.

If a theoretical education informs people about many different ways of understanding the world taken from the best theoretical content available to humankind, then it is valuable because it helps students to interact effectively with the world. This account of the value of theoretical education draws on the strengths of the rational-autonomy account presented by Hirst and Peters, but avoids unnecessary epistemological commitments. My proposed account of theoretical education is that a broad theory-based curriculum is valuable because being well informed by theoretical content helps people to interact effectively with the world.

Premise 3: Justifying Theoretical Education

The task for this chapter is to identify and explicate an account of the value of a broad theoretical education with the potential to be a justifiable use of children's time in school. Since I claim that a theoretical education helps people to interact effectively with the world, I need to show that the ability to interact effectively with the world is an educational good which ought to be given curriculum time. The justificatory basis of this account of the value of a theoretical education rests on its utility. Since other educational goods are also valuable in terms of their utility, this account provides no reason to think that a theoretical education is the only sort of education which ought to be provided by schools. However, it does mean that the utility of a theoretical education can be assessed against the utility of other forms of education. This task will be taken up in the final section of this chapter.

A theoretical education provides students with theoretical content amounting to ways of understanding the world. These ways of understanding the world, which are valuable insofar as they are useful to students. Bailey's account of the instrumental value of theoretical education focuses on its broad utility. It is the broad and balanced nature of a theoretical education that means that students are able to deal with a broad range of different issues they might face in life. On my account, it is the utility of individual theories that I want to focus on. Following Huxley's claims, acquiring theoretical content holds utility if it provides people with an understanding of the problems that they are likely to encounter as they navigate the world around them. A theoretical education is valuable if it helps people to deal with the issues that they are likely to encounter as they live their lives. It is justified if it is broadly useful in this way. Later in this chapter I will weigh up the educational goods provided by a theoretical education against other possible goods to further explore the extent to which theoretical education is justified.

Curriculum Content

Hirst's account of liberal education provides clear guidelines about what ought to be included on the curriculum. Since the aim of education is rational autonomy, and rational autonomy is defined in terms of induction into the forms of knowledge, a curriculum need only induct students into the forms of knowledge in order to constitute a complete liberal education. My revised account of theoretical education does not yield this conclusion. Rational autonomy is no longer the aim, rather the general utility of theoretical content is. A new set of curriculum guidance is needed, but this is not too difficult to derive from the utility account of the value of theoretical education set out above.

Why Do This Rather Than That?

This revised account of theoretical education focuses on theoretical content. Patently, there is a vast quantity of theoretical content which could be included on the curriculum. This means that work is needed to answer Peters's 'why do this rather than that?' question and identify which theoretical content ought to be included on a limited curriculum. The question that I will address here is how to select theoretical content from the large quantity available.

Since theoretical content is valuable if it improves people's ability to effectively interact with the world, it is important that the content on a theoretical curriculum meets the needs of the people that it is being taught to. Theoretical content is instrumentally valuable, it is a tool for interacting with the world. This means that theoretical content, as a tool or instrument, ought to be selected with regard to its utility. Since the aim is to be able to navigate the world that students will come to inhabit more effectively, a theoretical education ought to provide students with theoretical content which arms them to do this. The selection or curation of theoretical content needs to be centred on the aim of helping people to interact effectively with the world. This is at odds with the emphasis of Hirst and Peters on the forms of knowledge or theoretical activities understood broadly in line with academic disciplines. On Hirst and Peters's account, curriculum content is selected in terms of forms of knowledge, rather than usefulness.

To make a case for focusing on usefulness, spending excessive amounts of time teaching students details from academic disciplines without providing them with the theoretical content that might guide them to navigate the world might fail to meet the aim I have identified. Someone who has been educated about obscure aspects of theoretical physics because it is part of an established academic discipline, but has not been given any guidance about personal relationships, has not been properly theoretically educated because they will remain uninformed about theoretical content, which might help them to navigate their personal relationships more effectively. It is unlikely that they will use the content from theoretical physics, and it is highly likely that they will need guidance about relationships. A theoretical curriculum should primarily be guided by the aim of providing theoretical content to help people to understand salient parts of the world around them, so that they can interact with these parts of the world more effectively. It should not be primarily guided by the nature of knowledge or by disciplinary boundaries; although, it might be the case that disciplinary boundaries track salient parts of the world.

This stands in contrast with accounts of theoretical education that focus on truth or on academic disciplines. On these accounts, curriculum content is selected either based on how fundamental it is to an academic discipline, or based on how well established it is. This might be why content from theoretical physics could be selected over content about relationships. By changing the focus to questions that students are likely to face in their lives, sometimes content that does not easily fit within an academic discipline, or content that is poorly established, will be prioritized to at least give students some guidance about the questions they might face.

Hand makes this point when he talks about the importance of addressing prominent and pressing questions. The claim is that 'children should be equipped by their education to deal effectively with at least those problems that feature prominently and pressingly in ordinary human lives ... whatever else we put on the core curriculum, inescapable problems and the means of tackling them surely belong there' (Hand, 2018, p. 7). Whatever else it is that education is about, it is also about dealing with the sorts of questions that people are likely to encounter in the future. Not to do so would be remiss. This idea can be repurposed to suit my account of theoretical education: a theoretical education aiming to bring about the capacity for effective interaction with the world ought to address prominent and pressing questions that people are likely to encounter over the course of their lifetime, because these are the areas where the capacity to act effectively is going to be important.

This is not to say that the content of the curriculum needs to constitute direct answers to specific questions. This would be an inefficient use of curriculum time. Theoretical content is more abstract than the answers to individual questions.

A theory is often applicable to a broad range of questions. The picture is further complicated by the fact that often there are many theories that answer a single question about the world in different ways. This is most often the case when the best that humankind has to offer in response to a question is unclear. In the case of personal relationships, we do not have a single sure-fire answer to many of the questions. Instead, we have a body of theories about love, relationships, family and so on, often expressed in literary form or through media such as films. There are also theories about our psychology, biology and chemistry which pertain. Or studying the history and anthropology of relationships might bring to light new ways of understanding them.

There are bound to be too many questions to answer in the curriculum time available. However, it ought to be possible to rank questions by how prominent and pressing they are likely to be in a student's life, and to try to answer as many of the most prominent and pressing questions as possible. This requires some judgement from educators about what students might need to know. Some theoretical content is going to be multipurpose, in that it plays a role in addressing a range of questions. This should be taken into account too. Picking out how to answer prominent and pressing questions using theoretical content is not straightforward and does not imply a simplistic question-based curriculum. It is worth bearing in mind the idea of general utility introduced by Bailey. Here, curriculum content can be broadly valuable if it sheds light on a larger rather than narrower part of the world. This broad value ought to be taken into account when selecting content alongside the more narrow or applied utility of theories. Curriculum content ought to be prioritized according to its broad utility to students, but also in such a way that the most prominent and pressing questions they are likely to face are addressed, regardless of the quality or quantity of the theoretical content available in response to them.

Disciplinary Sciences

Not all theoretical content has utility, in fact much may be trivial, ineffective or even harmful. It is not hard to develop theoretical content to answer questions. Someone might hold that tomato plants grow best when the gods are happy, and so sacrifices ought to be made to improve harvest. This is a theory that explains the phenomenon at hand, but it is not a useful theory. It provides some guidance about how to interact with the world, but this guidance is ineffective.

To ensure that curriculum content tracks the best that humankind has to offer, rather than superstition, prejudice, fabrications or guess work, the theoretical content taught should be taken from some systematic area of study. Here, Collingwood's account of disciplinary sciences is helpful.

Collingwood sets out an account of what we might mean by a systematic area of study when he talks about sciences. A science 'in its ordinary sense … means a body of systematic or orderly thinking about a determinate subject-matter' (Collingwood, 1940, p. 4). It is a contingent, historical fact that human knowledge can be divided up into sciences. These seem to arise from attempts to address particular aspects of the world or to answer particular questions. Over time, they become specialized into sciences. Collingwood elaborates that a science or discipline is 'of some definite subject-matter, having special problems of its own that arise out of the special peculiarities of the subject-matter, and special methods of its own that arise out of the special problems' (Collingwood, 1940, pp. 14–15). He contrasts these disciplinary sciences with ordinary thinking where 'our thoughts are coagulated into knots and tangles …' whereas 'thinking scientifically means disentangling all this mess, and reducing a knot of thought in which everything sticks together anyhow into a system or series of thoughts in which thinking the thoughts it at the same time thinking the connections between them' (p. 22). Scientific thinking deals with things in their logical order (p. 39) so that each claim's significance is transparent, and its standards of assessment are clear.

The advantage of Collingwood's account of sciences (I will call them disciplinary sciences) is that there is nothing fundamental or necessary about them. Wherever people have happened upon areas of the world which have puzzled them, or which have required further investigation, they have developed disciplinary sciences. Over time, many of these areas of interest have become specialized such that there is a systematic body of theoretical content which has been built up over time in response to the initial puzzle. Collingwood's account does not sharply divide disciplinary sciences or limit them to only a certain number of logically distinct forms. It is also possible, on Collingwood's account, for there to be several different disciplinary sciences offering theories in response to a single puzzle. All of this seems to be a reasonable way of describing the trajectory and results of human inquiry.

Based on this account, ensuring that theories are part of established disciplinary sciences confers advantages. The first is that theoretical content has been critically analysed over time by experts. This means that the content is less likely to be misleading, obviously false or harmful; it has been vetted. Taking content from established disciplinary sciences links the curriculum with the best that humankind has to offer since disciplinary sciences track the course of human inquiry, developing and discarding theories as they go.

The second advantage is that each disciplinary science has explicit standards of theory assessment built into it. For example, the physical sciences require reproducibility of results and empirical data to back up their theories. History requires testimonial and archaeological evidence alongside skilled interpretation. Learning theories whilst coming to understand the sciences from which they have been developed is important because it clarifies the sort of theoretical content that is being learned. A theological theory is very different from a theory from the natural sciences, and someone who learned content as part of the study of theology as a discipline and content as part of the study of natural sciences as disciplines would be aware of the differences. This is because coming to understand disciplinary sciences involves coming to understand the standards of assessment used within the different sciences. Furthermore, disciplinary sciences provide an inbuilt structure for learning since they have their own logical structure that can be adopted for schemes of work, lessons and curriculum progression. There are skills, facts and theoretical content that are prior to further learning.

So, although disciplinary sciences should not determine the content of the curriculum (it should be determined by prominent and pressing questions), they play an important role in communicating the nature of the theoretical content being taught. Knowing that one theory is theological, another historical and another biological is important because it clarifies how each theory has been established. This provides a value judgement about the nature of the theoretical content provided, and it also provides the means for assessing whether content is good by the standards of its own disciplinary science. A basic induction into the most relevant disciplinary sciences is also going to be an important prerequisite to learning more complex theoretical content from each disciplinary science.

While the curriculum should be determined by the sorts of questions its students are likely to face, the answers to those questions should be taken from disciplinary sciences wherever possible. These disciplinary sciences can guide content selection in response to questions. They help to determine what the best available material to respond to questions is. Learning about theoretical content within its originating disciplinary science helps students to understand how the content was developed and provides them with tools that might allow them to engage in inquiry themselves. This is similar to Peters and Hirst's use of forms of knowledge to determine the content of the curriculum. It differs because it is not induction into disciplines which is itself valuable, it is the ways of understanding the world provided by theoretical content that is valuable. Disciplinary sciences are convenient structural vectors for selecting the best available content and transmitting it well.

The Theoretical Curriculum: Identifying Prominent and Pressing Questions and Selecting Theoretical Content

A theoretical curriculum is not subject-driven. Instead, it is driven by prominent and pressing questions. While disciplinary sciences play the role of selecting answers to those questions, structuring how answers are presented, and arranging theoretical content into accessible units of study, they should not determine what ought to be taught – rather how it is taught. This is because subjects do not necessarily track the questions students will be faced with as they live their lives. This means that the English National Curriculum is not an ideal theoretical curriculum since it focuses too heavily on induction into subjects, at the expense of prominent and pressing questions. This is important because an education focusing on disciplines might fail to prepare students for parts of their lives that do not fall into the disciplinary sciences. To solve this problem, the driving force behind curriculum choices needs to be the questions that students are likely to face. Another way of thinking about this is that a theoretical education ought to prepare students for their present and future lives. In their lives, students will face a range of difficult situations about which they will have questions. At the minimum, a theoretical education ought to address those questions, helping people to navigate their lives in an informed and effective manner. Disciplines are only important to help select the best theoretical content in response to those questions, and to present that content well. Disciplines or subjects should not determine the questions themselves.

At this point, some further elucidation of what I mean by 'prominent and pressing' is needed. Since the aim of a theoretical education is to provide students with theoretical content which provides them with the resources to interact effectively with the world, a prominent and pressing question is one that facilitates effective interaction. In order to capture the most useful theoretical content to students, we can think about the sorts of questions they are likely to encounter. Without some guidance, certain aspects of the world are difficult to navigate or can easily lead to muddled or even dangerous action. What to eat is a good example of this. Without some grasp of basic theories about nutrition, someone could easily eat unhealthily and cause themselves harm without intending to.

As students progress through school, there is scope to introduce them to more abstract theoretical content that has more wide-reaching applicability than straightforward answers to straightforward questions. This is theoretical content with general utility. Grasping the basics of the natural sciences provides students with theoretical frameworks for answering a host of questions about the natural world. Even if they do not end up answering questions, they will see the world around them with some transparency; they will see the potential to answer questions which arise. For example, most people who had studied some basic science in secondary school had some insight into the science of Covid-19 as a result of this, although work was needed to relate that understanding to the situation at hand.

This introduces the idea that there is no limit to the prominent and pressing questions that a curriculum could address, other than the time limit imposed by compulsory education rules and the pressure to fit other aims of education into school time. This is a difficulty, and means that educators need to use their judgement to select content. There are always going to be cases where a school curriculum covers content that is, in fact, trivial to students; or something which would have been prominent and pressing at the time of teaching becomes redundant due to changes in the world. The other problem is that, given the limited time available for schooling, many prominent and pressing questions are bound to be left off the curriculum. My response to these problems is that, rather than defining a definitive set of questions which need to be answered in order to have had a theoretical education, it makes more sense to say that a theoretical education is unlimited; it can be as long or as short as there is time for. Schooling in the UK provides a vast amount of time for theoretically educating students. They are in school between the ages of four and eighteen, and the part of their education between the ages of eleven and sixteen already focuses heavily on theoretical content. Within this time, once basic prominent and pressing questions have been addressed, there is scope to move on to less obvious and more abstract questions where answers have more general utility.

It is also worth noting that different questions will be more or less prominent and pressing to different students, and so a theoretical education ought to be responsive to its students' needs, tailoring theoretical content to their concerns. This is something that is overlooked by traditional accounts of theoretical education that focus on disciplines and the pursuit of truth. Educators ought to be able to adjust the curriculum if they judge that their students are facing a particular body of prominent and pressing questions that are not being covered in school. Furthermore, the indeterminate nature of the future is going to cause problems for selecting content for a theoretical curriculum, as the prominence of questions may wax and wane. Here, taking care to present generally applicable theoretical content rather than presenting piecemeal answers to specific questions will arm students with a more flexible toolkit for facing the questions they will run into. Aside from that, careful thought and reasonable judgement for content selection is the best that curriculum planners can hope for.

I can also say more about the sorts of answers given to prominent and pressing questions, and some basic pedagogical rules that follow. When it comes to some prominent and pressing questions such as those to do with healthy eating, there are clear, uncontroversial disciplines to turn to for relevant theoretical content. In the case of healthy eating, primarily theories arising from the broad heading of biology, and within biology, physiology and medicine. Since the discipline of biology has a long and successful history of systematically studying the human organism and the impact of what people eat on their health, theoretical content from biology is well-placed to answer questions about healthy eating. The sorts of answers available from biology are also fairly complete; biology is able to answer many of the prominent and pressing questions we might have regarding what we should eat. If answers do not exist, the disciplinary science of biology is in a position to provide guidance about how to find answers. Since the disciplinary science of biology is a systematized, formal discipline within which questions about healthy eating have been studied, it is well placed for answering questions about healthy eating.

There are, however, a host of prominent and pressing questions which do not link to a single disciplinary science. A good example of this is questions about relationships. These are prominent and pressing in that they are the sorts of questions that worry young people, and which as young people enter adulthood they are going to have to navigate. Making choices about whether to enter into a romantic relationship, the boundaries of relationships, relationships with siblings and parents, whether to start a family and whether to dissolve a relationship are mainstays of human life and cause a lot of problems for people. Given this, a theoretical education ought to provide theoretical content to help answer these questions. The problem is that there is no clear disciplinary science which studies questions about relationships. Furthermore, casting the net further and finding theoretical content from a range of disciplinary sciences still leaves uncertainty and gaps when it comes to answering questions. Human inquiry has just not settled on really useful theoretical content regarding this set of prominent and pressing questions. However, since a theoretical education needs to be driven by questions rather than disciplines, it is not acceptable to ignore questions where theoretical resources are limited. Instead, the curriculum is obliged to provide students with the best available theoretical content to help them to make progress with these questions. This is one key advantage to an account driven by prominent and pressing questions. At present, many of the most prominent and pressing everyday questions are excluded from the English National Curriculum in favour of established disciplinary content. This has the potential to leave its students unable to interact effectively with pressing aspects of their lives ahead of them.

In practice, where there is little systematic inquiry into a prominent and pressing question, lessons will need to be dialogical. Relationships education might involve airing prominent and pressing questions, talking about possible answers and providing theoretical content which is potentially illuminating whilst discussing its limitations. Personal relationships, being prominent aspects of human existence, are widely addressed across many disciplines, but rarely systematically. There is a vast body of literature, films and other artwork which provide loose theoretical content to illuminate questions about relationships. There is some theoretical content from the natural sciences regarding the evolutionary function of relationships or the chemical and hormonal bases of attraction. There is also historical content about relationships, which provides ways of reimagining them and serves to distinguish between nature and cultural norms. Finally, there is theoretical content about toxicity, consent, wellbeing and so on taken from sociology, psychology and other disciplinary sciences. In the case of relationships, the curriculum is going to need to be pluralistic, drawing from a range of disciplines and building in time for careful discussion of how much weight to place on each idea. The messy nature of human inquiry into relationships does not excuse leaving relationships education off the curriculum, nor inhibit meaningful theoretical education about relationships.

From questions about healthy eating and questions about relationships, an idea of what a theoretical curriculum ought to look like emerges. First, it needs to address prominent and pressing questions, regardless of whether they are associated with disciplinary sciences. Secondly, as many prominent and pressing questions need to be addressed as there is time to do well. Since schooling in the UK is extensive, there will be time to address immediate questions (such as healthy eating and relationships), and also more abstract questions that may or may not arise but that having theoretical content about will facilitate easier interactions with. Lastly, some prominent and pressing questions are straightforwardly answered by clear disciplinary content. In contrast, other questions are not straightforwardly addressed by a single disciplinary science and so will need a broader, more pluralistic pedagogical approach. Such an approach to curriculum planning is not simplistic and rule-based, but the principles of addressing prominent and pressing questions using the best available theoretical content (to be determined by disciplinary sciences) does provide a workable method of making curriculum decisions.

I suspect that the proposed theoretical curriculum will not look very different from the current school curricula, but that it will be better suited to its purpose of aiding effective interaction with the world. The secondary school curriculum in England is already heavily based on theoretical content. Examples of theoretical content taken from GCSE specifications include: literature: Orwell's theory of human nature advanced in *Animal Farm* (OCR, 2015, p. 6), chemistry: the theory of atomic structure (OCR, 2016, p. 6), history: 'the link between social structure and army command' from c.1250–c.1500 (Edexcel, 2015, p. 14) or religious studies: 'Biblical accounts of creation' (p. 8). It is likely that a carefully crafted theoretical education will maintain some structure from the disciplinary sciences. This is because learning theoretical content from a disciplinary science makes more sense if the formalities of that disciplinary science are understood. It is also because disciplinary sciences, as systematic areas of study, are cumulative. Grasping basic theoretical content is a prerequisite to grasping more complex theoretical content, and so grouping theoretical content together is going to make learning it more straightforward and the curriculum more efficient.

The key difference between existing theoretical curricula and the proposed curriculum is that the rationale behind this conception of theoretical education means that content ought to be guided by questions rather than induction into disciplines, or factivity or truth. The curriculum ought not to go into too much detail within a discipline at the expense of other more prominent and pressing questions. A discipline-based curriculum is likely to side line prominent and pressing questions and so fail to fully prepare students for their lives. On my proposals, arts and humanities subjects will be on the curriculum because they provide answers to prominent and pressing questions, for example, about identity, relationships, emotions, morality; the sciences clearly address many questions about the natural world. Numeracy and literacy do not directly provide theoretical content, but are prerequisites to accessing theoretical content and to continuing education outside of school and so are clearly a part of any theoretical education. Neglected prominent and pressing questions need to be better addressed, either discretely or across other subjects. And, as I will argue in Chapters 5 and 6, philosophical theoretical content ought to be included on the curriculum to deal with two different sorts of prominent and pressing questions: ordinary prominent and pressing questions, and conceptual prominent and pressing questions raised by the pluralistic nature of a theoretical curriculum. In both cases, the discipline of philosophy offers resources drawn from the systematic study of these sorts of questions.

My utility account of theoretical education allows an appraisal of what it is that contemporary educational practices are aiming to achieve, and so speaks directly to school teachers and curriculum planners. The account presents a rationale for the sort of education that they are delivering, with the potential to adjust the curriculum to better fit the rationale.

The Relative Importance of Theoretical Education

So far, I have chosen to focus on the value of theoretical education. Descriptively, theoretical education is the part of education that communicates ideas to students. As I demonstrated in Chapter 3, this is a historically pervasive form of education. I also argued that existing justifications of theoretical education fall short of clearly accounting for the value of theoretical education. In response, the focus of this chapter has been on introducing a utility account of the value of a theoretical education. I argued that a theoretical education is valuable because it provides students with theoretical content that helps them to interact effectively with the world. I then discussed the curriculum implications of this account of the value of theoretical education.

In this section, I will explain the role of theoretical education in schooling when considered more holistically. While theoretical education is a common feature of schooling around the world, both historically and today, it is not the only sort of education that does or should take place in schools. I will argue that a theoretical education is a worthwhile use of school time and ought to be provided to all students. My main line of argument here is that a theoretical education that facilitates effective interaction with the world is a primary educational good. This means that it contributes to many other possible educational goods.

This is an important step towards arguing that philosophy should be taught in all schools. Without examining the relative importance of theoretical education, it could be held that although philosophy is central to theoretical education, theoretical education itself is not worthwhile compared to other educational practices. I will explain why a theoretical education, understood on my utility account, is worthwhile as a primary educational good, even in the face of a plurality of other possible educational aims and associated goods.

Other Aims of Education

In Chapter 3, I outlined different possible aims for theoretical education, but there also are aims of education which fall outside of theoretical education. These different possible aims are captured by Brighouse et al.'s list of educational goods: 'Economic productivity, personal autonomy, democratic competence, healthy personal relationships, treating others as equals, and personal fulfilment' (Brighouse et al., 2018, p. 23). These are not necessarily theoretical. For example, economic productivity can be educated for using work-experience schemes, training in practical skills or enforcing a professional dress code. If there are possible aims of education that do not require a primarily theoretical education, then what makes a theoretical education worthy of curriculum time in comparison to them? I will argue that the broad utility a theoretical education contributes towards these other educational goods. So, while economic productivity can be educated for non-theoretically, a broad theoretical education will also help students to become economically productive. This justifies teaching a theoretical curriculum regardless of the overall aims of education being pursued.

I do not think that non-theoretical educational goods are unimportant. Rather, I want to show how a theoretical education can contribute towards them. While I hold that the aim of education is to facilitate students' effective interaction with the world, I also hold that the ability to interact effectively with the world contributes towards economic productivity, personal autonomy, democratic competence, healthy personal relationships, treating others as equals, personal fulfilment, and whatever else might be identified as an educational good. A theoretical education is not sufficient for educating for economic productivity, but it does make economic productivity easier to achieve. The same goes for other goods. Effective interaction with the world is useful towards any end of education. Furthermore, a utility-based theoretical education can stand alone, without further specific or more complex educational aims. Educating people to help them to interact effectively with the world is worthwhile in itself.

One advantage of a utility account of theoretical education over other accounts of education is that facilitating effective interaction with the world is an aim with little theoretical baggage. There is no need to advocate for flourishing as an aim of education, nor to enumerate what constitutes flourishing. There is no need to explain why economic productivity, personal autonomy, democratic competence or healthy personal relationships ought to take up school time. These are all at least somewhat controversial. Parents might disagree with the idea that their children should be taught about personal relationships in schools, or they might object to their children being taught about certain vocational options. However, it is harder to disagree with the idea that someone who is able to interact with the world in an informed way is better off than someone who is not.

Unlike other proposed educational aims, providing students with the ability to interact effectively with the world through a utility focused theoretical education is worthwhile at a very basic level. It avoids commitment to more complex goals with potentially controversial ideas about the good life and society.

Educational Goods

One way of assessing different educational aims against each other is to move away from talking about the aims of education, to talking about educational goods. There are many different things that educational institutions and educators could provide people with. Furthermore, many of these are valuable. There are a plurality of educational goods that can be provided to students. Talking about goods allows their importance relative to one another to be explored and assessed. In talking about economic activity, personal autonomy, democratic competence, healthy personal relationships, treating others as equals and personal fulfilment as educational goods, they can be assessed against each other and the educational good of effective interaction with the world.

In their 2018 book *Educational Goods*, Brighouse et al. present a framework which recognizes a plurality of considerations that policymakers need to take into account when thinking about education. They divide the values relevant to education into three groups: 'educational goods, distributive values, and independent values' (Brighouse et al., 2018, p. 19). Educational goods are: 'knowledge, skills, dispositions, and attitudes' (p. 19). Educational goods 'help people's lives to go well' (p. 21). An educational good is whatever it is that educators can provide students with that is good for those students. Living well is not something that itself can be educated for. This is because 'luck – serious injury or illness, for example – is also bound to play a role in determining the extent of people's flourishing however well equipped they are and however well they choose' (p. 21). Education can only do so much work; alongside education, luck and the material conditions for flourishing outside of school also need to be in place.

The use of the term 'goods' echoes Rawls's *Theory of Justice*. Rawls is concerned with how and which 'goods' should be distributed in a just society. In order to do this, he thinks that it is sufficient to consider what someone would want for themselves, regardless of their position in life. These are primary goods:

> Primary goods ... are things which it is supposed a rational man wants whatever else he wants. Regardless of what an individual's rational plans are in detail, it is assumed that there are various things which he would prefer more of rather than less. With more of these goods men can generally be assured of greater success

in carrying out their intentions and in advancing their ends, whatever these ends may be. (Rawls, 1971, p. 92)

Primary goods are resources with general utility; they are the conditions for achieving further desires. As Buchanan explains,

> Primary goods are perhaps best thought of as (a) maximally flexible means for the pursuit of one's goals, as (b) conditions of the effective pursuit of one's goals, or as (c) conditions of the critical and informed formulation of one's plans. Wealth, in the broadest sense, is a maximally flexible means in that it is generally useful for achieving one's goals, regardless of what one's goals are. (Buchanan, 1980, p. 8)

Rawls does not present an in-depth account of the sorts of goods that education can provide.

Theoretical Education and Primary Educational Goods

It is possible to describe theoretical content as an educational good that brings about the capacity to interact effectively with the world. As such, it can be assessed against other educational goods to establish how far it ought to play a role in schooling. I turn to Rawls's account of primary goods to argue that theoretical content is a primary good as it is a good with which 'men can generally be assured of greater success in carrying out their intentions and in advancing their ends, whatever these ends may be' (Rawls, 1971, p. 92). This means that regardless of other aims of education, or other educational goods, theoretical education is worthwhile as it contributes towards them.

Unlike the primary goods outlined by Rawls, the goods supplied by a theoretical education are not only, or primarily social goods. They are goods that each individual can acquire themselves, and that serve the individual first, and society second. Hypothetically, someone who existed outside of society would still benefit from theoretical content. For example, they might be able to grow their own food more easily. Nor is theoretical content a limited resource that requires careful distribution. Unlike wealth, there are few limits to the amount of theoretical content we can provide people with; the only limit comes from a person's available time and motivation. A suitably motivated person could spend their free time acquiring theoretical content using online resources, libraries or other knowledgeable people. Since children are already required to spend their free time in school, it is not costly to distribute theoretical content. In many ways, theoretical content is probably the most straightforward resource for schools to provide. Teachers teach classes of between twenty and thirty students theoretical content for many hours a week in British schools. Universities can achieve the same effect sometimes with hundreds of students at a time.

A theoretical education provides the educational good of being able to interact effectively with the world. This good works in combination with external political, social and economic resources to support students to live a good life. Being well informed about how the world works via the best theoretical content available has utility in that it helps people to interact effectively with the world. A well-informed person has a better understanding of what is happening in any given situation than an ill-informed person, and having a better understanding of a situation opens up options and choices about how to act and makes it more likely that those choices will lead to effectively navigating a situation.

Theoretical content, and the associated ability to interact effectively with the world, fits the description of a primary good, where having more of the primary good is clearly a good thing, and having less of it is a bad thing. This is because theoretical content is instrumental to realizing desires. Someone who is well-informed by theoretical content will be more able to interact effectively with the world, and so will be more able to realize their desires. Like wealth, it is something that we would want for ourselves, and so it makes sense to say that schools ought to provide students with it.

Theoretical content leads to the educational good of effective interaction with the world, which in turn contributes to other educational goods and aims. Effective interaction with the world plays a role in the other goods listed by Brighouse et al.: 'economic productivity, personal autonomy, democratic competence, healthy personal relationships, treating others as equals, and personal fulfilment' (Brighouse et al., 2018, p. 23). In each of these cases, being well informed about the world confers an advantage. In the language of Rawls, theoretical content provides a primary educational good because it helps to achieve other aims and goods. This means that regardless of the overall aims of schooling as determined by the state, policymakers, schools, parents or children, theoretical content is always going to play a role. A case for the place of theoretical education in schools can be made on the back of this analysis.

Theoretical Education and Other Aims of Education

The idea that theoretical content contributes to other aims of education is relatively commonplace. White and Reiss, who argue that flourishing is the proper aim of education, acknowledge the role of theoretical content in meeting this aim. They claim that studying history gives students 'a background understanding of the human world' (Reiss & White, 2013, p. 40); studying the natural sciences, mathematics and technology 'help us to situate ourselves both temporally and spatially in the world in which we live' (p. 42) and can contribute to education for work (p. 45). Brighouse makes a similar point when he talks about the aims of education. He points out that if autonomy is an aim of education, then 'an autonomous life cannot be led without the information about the world in which it is led' (Brighouse, 2006, p. 23). The same can be said for the broader aim of flourishing of which autonomy is a component. Similarly, Gutmann argues that democratic education includes a commitment to a broad theoretical education because theoretical content helps 'children to learn how to live a good life in the nonmoral sense' (Gutmann, 1987, p. 51). As I have already mentioned, theoretical education is worthwhile on its own terms. Effective interaction with the world is a worthwhile aim of education. However, it is also compatible with more theoretically-laden aims, such as flourishing, democratic education and economic productivity.

To illustrate this relationship between broader aims of education and theoretical content as an educational good, I will consider how theoretical content can contribute to two different educational goods: economic productivity and democratic competence.

Economic productivity is supported by a broad theoretical education. There are two reasons; the first is that education for economic productivity involves helping students to make informed choices about the sort of work they wish to pursue. On my account of theoretical education, this is within the realm of theoretical education. Questions about economic productivity are prominent and pressing and ought to be addressed using the best available theoretical content. The second reason that economic productivity is underpinned by a theoretical education is that economic participation is enhanced, or made more effective, by being able to interact effectively with the world. Someone who is well informed about the world around them will be a more effective employee. Even menial jobs are made easier and more enjoyable through having a grasp of how they work, what they are for and how they might be improved; this can be provided by theoretical content. Finally, if someone did take such a job, a liberal education would allow them to see opportunities to leave the job if they wanted to. Being broadly informed about the world is a good outcome for employees to come out of school with: both for them and for their employers.

Theoretical content can contribute to democratic competence because a good citizen is a well-informed citizen. People who have been taught broad theoretical content about the world are better able to exercise effective judgement, which is essential to a functioning state. Being acquainted with the best theoretical content about justice, legislature, political institutions, the history of citizenship, war, democracy, human-interactions, injustice, poverty, tolerance and so on, is instrumental to developing the ability to making good democratic decisions and take part in fruitful dialogue. There is much more that could and should be done to educate for democratic participation than to provide a theoretical education. However, without some theoretical education, students are unlikely to develop the dispositions or have the requisite knowledge and understanding of the world to be competent democratic participants.

Since my account of theoretical education holds that a theoretical education is one that provides students with content that will serve them when they are faced with prominent and pressing questions, it makes sense that a theoretical education will contribute to a range of more specific and complex aims of education and educational goods. Regardless of whether schools are primarily aiming to prepare students for economic productivity, personal autonomy, democratic competence, healthy personal relationships, treating others as equals or personal fulfilment, being well-informed about the world is going to be helpful. This means that even if we are undecided on, unclear about or endorse a plurality of aims for education, there is always going to be a case for providing at least some amount of theoretical education.

This is not to say that theoretical education ought to take up all, or even the majority of school time. This will depend on the needs of students: if they cannot read or write, then teaching them to read and write will take priority. If they are going to be joining the workforce in the immediate future, then it makes sense to focus on training for a particular job. If students need immediate care, as I imagine children in refugee camps might, then schools should focus on that. However, given that in many cases children are in schools for a long period of time; enough time to teach them how to read and write, train them for jobs and support them to feel safe and cared for in their immediate environment, it is often going to be the case that there will be time to provide a theoretical education. Since a theoretical education provides a primary educational good, and the capacity to interact effectively with the world helps to achieve other educational aims, schools ought to provide students with theoretical education. In the next chapters, I will argue that wherever students are being provided with a theoretical education, they ought to be taught philosophy.

Conclusion

In this chapter, I presented a utility account of the value of theoretical education and explored the curriculum implications of such an account. I then discussed the place of theoretical education in schooling, and concluded that in many cases, it ought to play at least some role in a student's schooling. Two curriculum guidelines emerge: that students should be provided with answers to prominent and pressing questions that they are likely to face and that those answers should be derived from the best available resources. The best available resources are those from disciplinary sciences which systematically study the sorts of questions at hand. Finally, although theoretical education is not the sole concern of schooling, theoretical content is an educational good, and ought to be provided by schools as a primary educational good.

Part 3

Two Arguments for Teaching Philosophy

5

Teaching Philosophy to Clarify Ordinary Concepts

This chapter and the next present two separate but related arguments for teaching philosophy in schools. Both chapters draw on the conclusions reached in Chapter 4 about the nature, aims and value of a theoretical education. Together, Chapters 5 and 6 develop the claim that any theoretical education ought to involve some philosophical education. In this chapter, I argue that a theoretical education which excludes philosophy is failing to address an important set of prominent and pressing questions in a way that draws on the best available content. In Chapter 6, I argue that a theoretical education excluding philosophy risks failing to provide students with useful ways of seeing the world by failing to help them to make sense of the plurality of theoretical content they have learned. My conclusion is not that all students need to be taught all of philosophy, but only that any theoretical education needs to include some specific and purposeful philosophical content. In both cases, I identify prominent and pressing questions where the discipline of philosophy is best placed to provide theoretical content in response.

Before introducing the first argument, I will discuss a distinction which plays a role in both arguments; this is the distinction between theoretical and ordinary concepts. Both arguments rest on the idea that a theoretical education provides students with a range of theoretical concepts – concepts that play roles in theories. The first argument claims that ordinary concepts (as opposed to theoretical concepts) need to play a role in theoretical education too. The second, that the range of theoretical concepts presented as part of a theoretical education requires students to be able to figure out how different theoretical and conceptual schemes relate to one another, including how theoretical concepts relate to ordinary concepts.

Ordinary and Theoretical Concepts

In Chapter 4, I explained why theoretical content is appropriate as the basic unit of a theoretical curriculum. Any theoretical content is content that is tied into a theory. The meaning of theoretical content is determined by its place in a theory, and theories provide ways of seeing the world. In this section, I will explain two key pieces of terminology to the arguments in this chapter and the next. The first piece of terminology is 'theoretical concepts'. A theory is composed of claims placed in logical relation to one another to provide some explanation, description or understanding of the world. Theories make use of specific words and concepts, and these concepts' meanings are fixed within particular theories. Concepts whose meanings are fixed by the theories they are a part of are theoretical concepts. There are also concepts without clear or fixed meanings; these are ordinary concepts. They tend to be used in many areas of discourse and in ordinary life and their meaning has not been formalized. In this chapter, I argue that the discipline of philosophy studies ordinary concepts and helps to fix their meaning. Fixing the meaning of these concepts is a constructive step towards making progress thinking about them. This means that when students are faced with prominent and pressing questions that rest on ordinary concepts, their teachers should turn to the discipline of philosophy to help students make progress with ordinary-concept questions.

Post-war analytic philosophy was, at least initially, focused on the analysis of concepts. Ordinary concepts are contrasted with theoretical concepts and philosophers such as Ryle, Strawson and Wittgenstein provide accounts of the aims of philosophy that appeal to a distinction between ordinary and theoretical concepts. Ryle and Strawson describe analytic philosophy in terms of analysing ordinary concepts through a priori deductions; this is important for solving disputes, mapping logical relations between different propositions, relating theoretical content to ordinary concerns and relating theoretical content to other theoretical content. Wittgenstein sees analytic philosophy as therapeutic, dissolving apparent philosophical problems by 'throwing light on our concept of meaning something' (Wittgenstein, 1953, p. 125).

Ryle discusses ordinary concepts in detail in *Dilemmas* (1953). He distinguishes between technical or theoretical concepts which are employed by disciplinary sciences, and ordinary concepts which sit outside of disciplinary inquiry. Theoretical concepts are not, according to Ryle, within the scope of philosophy as philosophers have no expertise 'when discussing technicalities which they have not learned to handle on the job' (Ryle, 1953, p. 12). Theoretical concepts already have their meanings fixed by the technical theories that they play a role in. For example, the concept of 'dark matter' is studied and fixed by theories from theoretical physics; it is not the place of philosophers to claim expertise in this area. Ordinary concepts, on the other hand, are the proper subject of philosophical inquiry: 'I suspect that the most radical cross-purposes between specialist theories derive from the logical trickiness not of the highly technical concepts employed in them, but of the underlying non-technical concepts employed in them as in everyone else's thinking' (p. 12). Ordinary concepts are either loose and undefined because they do not play a fixed role in any theory, or they are unclear because they play many different roles in many different theories. Theoretical concepts are defined by their technical use within specific theoretical frameworks, and ordinary concepts are concepts that we use all of the time and that lack clearly defined technical meaning. Ryle thinks that ordinary concepts are the proper object of philosophical study.

To explain the importance of ordinary concepts, Ryle uses travelling and cartography as analogies. Ordinary concepts are like public roads:

> Different travellers use vehicles of highly intricate constructions and of very different makes for all the varying purposes of their dissimilar journeys, and yet are alike in using the same public roads and the same signposts as one another ... thinkers may use all sorts of specially designed concepts for their several purposes, but still have also to use the same way concepts. Usually, too, the traveller's doubts and mistakes about his bearings arise, not because anything in his private vehicle behaves awkwardly, but because the public road is a tricky road. (Ryle, 1953, p. 13)

Philosophers are engaged in a sort of cartography where 'once these key ideas are charted, the geography of the whole region is, at least in outline, fixed' (Ryle, 1971, p. 211). For example, in charting the meaning of the concept 'liberty', other concepts' logical relations to the concept and each other begin to emerge. Liberty stands in relations to 'law, obedience, responsibility, loyalty, government and the rest' (p. 201). A systematic inquiry into the concept of liberty involves making a map of how a range of central ordinary concepts lie in relation to one another. Ryle casts philosophical work on the problem of free will in this light. Philosophical inquiry into whether our actions are free or determined is the result of a lack of clarity about the ordinary concepts involved; these are 'event, before and after, truth, necessity, cause, prevention, fault and responsibility' (Ryle, 1953, p. 31). These are ordinary concepts that are used across many different disciplines and in non-disciplinary ordinary language. While the problem of free will provides an interesting way of investigating their meanings, the concepts involved are central to large swathes of human activity, both technical and non-technical. Clarifying their meanings clarifies any form of inquiry involving the concepts.

Strawson also draws a distinction between ordinary and technical concepts, something which he sees as drawing on both Ryle and Wittgenstein's work. Strawson describes the distinction using an analogy of learning the grammar of your mother tongue. Our understanding and use of ordinary concepts resembles our understanding and use of our native grammar; their meaning is implicit and requires study in order to make sense of, even if we are fluent in a concept's use:

> A vast and heterogeneous range of notions: ethical notions: good, bad, right, wrong, punishment; temporal and spatial concepts; the ideas of causality and explanation; ideas of emotions: sadness, anger, fear, joy; or mental operations of various kinds: thinking, believing, wondering, remembering, expecting, imagining; of perception and sense experience: seeing, hearing, touching, having sensations; whole ranges of classificatory concepts for types of people, animals, plants, natural objects, processes, or events, human artefacts, institutions, and roles; and the properties, qualities, doings, and undergoings of all these. Of course we learn the words which express these concepts in a variety of ways; but we learn them largely without benefit of anything which could properly be called general theoretical instruction. We are not introduced to them by being told their place in a general theory of concepts. Such instruction we do receive is severely practical and largely by example. We learn largely by copying and by occasional correction; as children learn to speak grammatically before they learn grammars. (Strawson, 1992, pp. 6–7)

Ordinary concepts are identifiable by their non-technical nature; they are not defined as part of a theory: 'A distinction must here be drawn, between what might be called pre-theoretical or non-technical concepts on the one hand and essentially theoretical concepts on the other; between the common vocabulary of men and the specialist vocabularies of physicists, physiologists, economists, mathematicians, and biochemists' (Strawson, 1992, p. 10). When we learn a theory from economics, its technical concepts are clearly defined through direct instruction; 'the scientific specialist, let us suppose, is perfectly capable of explaining what he is doing with the special terms of his specialism. He has an explicit mastery, within the terms of his theory, of the special concepts of his theory' (p. 12). Like Ryle, Strawson thinks that ordinary concepts play a role in both ordinary and theoretical discourse such that 'he is also bound to use certain concepts which have wider application than that of his specialism, concepts which are not really specialist concepts at all: for example, the concepts of explanation, demonstration, proof, conclusion, cause, event, fact, property, hypothesis, evidence, and theory itself – to mention only a few' (Strawson, 1992, p. 12). These ordinary concepts have implicit meanings which demand clarification, and are not studied explicitly through any particular disciplinary science.

Ordinary concepts shape our non-theoretical questions. They are commonplace outside of the disciplinary sciences, but they also play important roles within disciplinary theories because theories are in constant interaction with our ordinary concerns. We have a tacit understanding of ordinary concepts, but we do not have a systematic, technical grasp of them. This means that they necessarily sit outside of disciplinary sciences; their meaning is not defined by any particular disciplinary science, or any particular theory. Ordinary concepts are understood in terms of their ordinary usage. They mediate the boundaries between technical and ordinary thought, and underpin many areas of inquiry which fall outside of a disciplinary science. As Ryle points out, these are concepts which create the sort of conceptual confusion that analytic philosophers attempt to fix. They are often a focus of philosophical inquiry.

In summary, a theoretical concept has its meaning fixed by a specific theory. Ordinary concepts do not have clearly fixed meanings, either because they are used differently in many different theories, or because they do not play a role in any technical theory. This chapter rests on the claim that the discipline of philosophy systematically studies ordinary concepts, attempting to fix their meaning so that progress can be made towards answering ordinary concept questions.

The Argument

In this chapter, I argue that there is a body of theoretical content from the discipline of philosophy, which is best placed to address prominent and pressing questions based on ordinary concepts. Ordinary questions are those which might be described as non-technical, common-sense or pre-theoretical. I argue that analytic philosophy, in particular conceptual analysis, provides the best available resources for systematically addressing these questions. The argument can be summarized as follows:

(1) A theoretical education ought to provide students with the capacity to address prominent and pressing questions using the best available content;
(2) There is a distinction between ordinary and theoretical concepts;
(3) Ordinary concepts are essential to some prominent and pressing questions;
(4) The disciplinary science of philosophy, in particular conceptual analysis, systematically studies these ordinary concepts;
(5) The disciplinary science of philosophy is often best-placed to address prominent and pressing ordinary-concept questions;

> Therefore to conclude, philosophical content ought to be taught as part of a theoretical curriculum.

Premise (1) has been established in Chapter 4, and premise (2) has been addressed in the previous section of this chapter.

Premise 3: Ordinary Concepts are Essential to Some Prominent and Pressing Questions

Ordinary concepts should only be studied in schools if they underpin something of importance to students. In this section, I turn to Pring's account of the importance of ordinary concepts in education. I identify a set of prominent and pressing questions that rely on ordinary concepts for their meaning, and require the study of ordinary concepts to begin to address them. In order for philosophy to be educationally valuable, it needs to at least address prominent and pressing questions that people might be expected to deal with over the course of their lives.

Pring differentiates between theoretical ways of understanding the world and ordinary ways of understanding the world in the same manner as Ryle. He claims that 'the theoretician suggests that the world which is *ordinarily* described in terms of tables and chairs should be re-described in terms which are not *ordinarily* understood, namely, of molecules and particles, or atoms and electrons' (Pring, 1977, p. 59). Like Ryle, he is pointing out that technical theories create theoretical content with fixed concepts, such as 'atoms and electrons'. For example, when speaking about teacher education, Pring claims that trainees are 'asked to adopt a new conceptual framework' as part of their training. This contrasts with trainee teachers' common sense or ordinary understanding of the issues at hand where concepts such as 'learning' are only loosely defined in a common sense way. The significance of this distinction between common sense and theoretical understanding is that ordinary accounts 'are adequate for most practical purposes' and so should, in Pring's opinion, play a more central role in teacher education unless theoretical accounts are substantially better (p. 62).

Next, Pring sets out the significance of ordinary and theoretical ways of understanding the world to school-aged students. The issues that children face before they come to school are framed in ordinary or common sense ways; 'pupils bring to school … a wide range of common sense understandings. These understandings – common sense to them and those they mix with – form the student's view of the world and determine the many practical decisions he makes. These, then, are what above all need to be educated' (Pring, 1977, p. 73). Pring's view is that immediately teaching theoretical ways of understanding the world without considering students' existing common sense understandings of the world is problematic. Further, the focus of the curriculum on theoretical ways of understanding the world leaves important ordinary questions unaddressed. Pring does not go so far as to suggest that philosophy might address these ordinary questions, his point is limited to the claim that there are common sense or ordinary questions that are not systematically addressed by curricula that are primarily theoretical. I agree that within the class of ordinary questions arising from common sense ways of understanding the world, there are prominent and pressing questions which it would be worthwhile to address.

To illustrate what I mean by ordinary questions, the newspaper the *Guardian* runs a feature answering questions that people commonly ask Google. These include: 'what does grief feel like?' 'what is love?'; 'do people change?'; 'is the term 'mansplaining' sexist?'; 'can you be a socialist and rich?'; 'have I ruined my life?'; 'why do good people suffer?'; 'am I old?'; 'why don't unicorns exist?; 'am I a racist?'; ' is mental illness real?'; 'did I make the right decision?'; 'can technology replace teachers?' and 'am I just paranoid?' (*Guardian*, 2018). Although these questions have been selected by the *Guardian* for journalistic purposes, rather than as a representative sample, the list illustrates that there is a body of ordinary questions which people think about, but which schools do not address. Many of the questions share concerns about the meaning of ordinary concepts; for example, the concepts of 'sexism', 'racism', 'mental illness', 'teachers' or 'existence'. Others ask about morality, values and truth. These ordinary concepts play a role in many areas of thinking and are not systematically studied in schools. Not all of these questions are prominent and pressing; rather, the list illustrates the sorts of ordinary questions left off the curriculum because of their ordinary status. They are ordinary because they rest on ordinary concepts; by this I mean that without some understanding of the ordinary concepts they employ, the questions cannot be answered.

In considering ordinary questions, I suggest that they encompass at least: truth and knowledge; questions about beauty or aesthetics; questions about relationships; questions about morality; questions about the good life; questions about value; questions about the nature of reality and questions about life's meaning. Within these classifications there are trivial questions, excessively specialized questions, and prominent and pressing questions. For example, a prominent and pressing question about truth and knowledge is 'how ought I to judge different sources of information?'; this is particularly pressing given concerns about 'fake news' and its effect on democratic processes. An example of a prominent and pressing question in beauty and aesthetics is a question about body image and standards of human beauty. Standards of beauty and resulting concerns about body image can lead to mental and physical harm, particularly in young people. Examples of prominent and pressing questions about relationships include those about sexuality, monogamy, family and friendship. There are many prominent and pressing questions within the body of ordinary questions set out. Many of these do not have a defined place on the curriculum and are not addressed systematically during students' time at school.

Gareth Matthews illustrates the prominence of common sense questions in children's lives by using a series of anecdotes taken from young children: 'Tim (about six years), while busily engaged in licking a pot, asked, "Papa, how can we be sure that everything is not a dream?"' (Matthews, 1980, p. 1); 'Jordan (five years), going to bed at eight one evening, asked "If I go to bed at eight and get up at seven in the morning, how do I really know that the little hand of the clock has gone around only once?"' (p. 2); 'Ian (six years) found to his chagrin that the three children of his parents' friends monopolized the television ... "Mother," he asked in frustration, "why is it better for three people to be selfish than for one?"' (p. 28); and 'David worries about whether an apple is alive. He decides that it is when it's on the ground but not when it has been brought into the house' (p. 6). These questions ask about the nature of reality, and the possibility of knowledge (Tim and Jordan), the nature of morality (Ian) and the nature of life and death (David).

Matthews's examples are more abstract than those covered by the *Guardian*, but they are similar in that the questions rest on ordinary concepts. The questions are active concerns for children because they play a role in their lives. We talk about knowledge, belief, truth, death, goodness, value, life, time and space, dreaming, perception and so forth constantly and throughout our lives. Although Matthews's examples are not necessarily pressing, they do illustrate the importance of becoming competent users of ordinary concepts so that more pressing questions can be addressed in later life. Tim was asking questions about knowledge, Ian was asking questions about justice, and David was asking questions about life and death. These concepts ground prominent and pressing questions which they are likely to encounter in their future lives.

In Pring's opinion, 'to ignore such common sense views would be to leave the student, in those matters which chiefly preoccupy his mind, very much where he is' (Pring, 1977, p. 73). Since ordinary concepts are part of people's experiences of the world, and since they play a role in how a set of prominent and pressing questions are framed, it is worth addressing them as part of someone's education. To fail to address them would be to fail to educate students about issues which they are very likely to need to address either immediately, or in later life. Addressing ordinary prominent and pressing questions holds educational value.

Even if there is a body of questions which rest on ordinary concepts, it is only the case that they ought to be addressed by the curriculum if they are prominent and pressing enough. I think that it is clearly the case that some of these ordinary concept questions are prominent and pressing. Strawson's list of ordinary concepts is a starting point for identifying prominent and pressing questions that rest on them. Any question involving ethical notions is based on ordinary concepts; questions about whether an action is good or bad, whether someone ought to be punished and how they ought to be punished, how to live a good life, which political party to support, and so on, are prominent and pressing questions, which rest on ordinary concepts. There are also prominent and pressing questions about emotions; questions about how much weight to place on emotions, the meaning of different emotions, whether certain emotions are pathological or whether the pursuit of some emotions over others is worthwhile. Strawson also lists events, artefacts, institutions and roles as subjects which relate to ordinary concepts. There are corresponding prominent and pressing questions about political institutions, religious institutions, schools, prisons, money, vocation – all of which make use of ordinary concepts and underpin prominent and pressing questions about the nature of society.

In his paper 'On the Distinctive Educational Value of Philosophy', Michael Hand claims that 'justifying subscription to moral, political and religious standards' raises prominent and pressing questions, and 'the significance of these problems for everyone is sufficient to warrant the inclusion of philosophy in the school curriculum' (Hand, 2018, p. 4). Hand claims that questions about moral, political and religious standards are a 'significant subset of philosophical problems that feature prominently and pressingly in ordinary human lives' (p. 10). Furthermore, these are philosophical questions. In addition to Hand's line of reasoning, these questions fall within the domain of philosophy because they rest on ordinary concepts and fall into the class of prominent and pressing questions, which thereby justify the inclusion of philosophy on the curriculum. Hand thinks that it is the substantive work on these questions within the discipline of philosophy that makes philosophy worthwhile. My claim is that the sort of philosophical content needed to begin to answer them is analysis of ordinary concepts. This holds regardless of whether established philosophical theories in response to the questions exist. Philosophical inquiry rarely settles on established answers; in most cases, the discipline of philosophy presents a range of competing theories and tools to help arbitrate between those theories. However, at the same time, philosophers do seem to make progress towards clarifying ordinary concepts, or at least identifying different ways that ordinary concepts might be analyzed.

Questions resting on ordinary concepts are not ignored in schools, but they are marginalized, perhaps because they fall outside of particular disciplinary sciences that are commonly taught in schools. In England, they fall into marginal subjects such as PSHE, Citizenship or Religious Education which are often given very little curriculum time, make use of non-specialist teachers, are sometimes taught via assemblies and are rarely examined. It falls to these under-resourced subjects to cover a cacophony of ordinary concept questions. These are not trivial questions, but lie at the heart of what it is to live in the world we live in; they are prominent and pressing. In my previous role as a Religious Education teacher, a lot of class time was spent talking about justice, equality, fairness, human rights, poverty, faith, truth, God(s), reason, proof, evidence, relationships and other ordinary concepts. These are not clearly within the remit of other subjects taught in schools, however, to go through schooling without addressing questions based on these concepts seems to violate the principle of trying to include prominent and pressing questions that students are likely to come across on the curriculum. Similarly, when teaching PSHE, we covered mental health, bereavement, drug use and abuse, and the idea of a good life including vocation, lifestyle and values. To eschew addressing these questions disregards the aim of helping students to interact effectively with the world. A theoretical curriculum ought to address these questions, and ideally offer students something constructive to help them to answer them.

Alongside the questions often taught in marginalized parts of the school curriculum, there are also questions that are frequently left off the school curriculum. For example, very few schools address the concept of 'knowledge' despite 'knowledge' and its associated concepts underpinning questions about what to believe, when to doubt, how to identify the need to inquiry further, when to trust testimony, how to identify bias and other questions central to learning and human inquiry more generally. Students in England are rarely introduced to epistemological concepts and their associated questions, and they are not part of the National Curriculum.

There are, then, prominent and pressing questions that rest on ordinary concepts. Pring is right to say that 'to ignore such common sense views would be to leave the student, in those matters which chiefly preoccupy his mind, very much where he is' (Pring, 1977, p. 73). These questions ought to be addressed by the curriculum because addressing them would help students to interact effectively with the world.

Premise 4: The Discipline of Philosophy Systematically Studies these Ordinary Concepts

In this section, I will set out how conceptual analysis from the discipline of philosophy provides content which equips students to address prominent and pressing questions based on ordinary concepts. I will return to Strawson, who describes philosophy as the systematic study of ordinary concepts. I will then go through examples of conceptual analyses of prominent and pressing questions to demonstrate how conceptual analysis equips people to address questions premised on ordinary concepts.

In my analysis of theoretical education, I argued that the second guiding principle for curriculum selection should be that answers to prominent and pressing questions are drawn from some systematic area of study or disciplinary science. In this section, I will argue that philosophy provides the most systematic study of ordinary concepts and, therefore, the best available material for addressing ordinary concept questions.

By systematic study, I mean the sort of technical inquiry that works to fix the meaning of concepts. To exemplify technical inquiry, when asking 'what is a table made of?' there are many different technical ways of approaching the question. One is to look to technical content from carpentry to come to understand how tables are made, what they are made with, and which materials are most appropriate given different requirements for the table. Another is to look to technical theories from biology to learn about the properties of wood and the biological determinants of these properties such as the presence of a cell wall in plant cells. Physics and chemistry provide the answers discussed by Pring: that the table is constituted of 'of molecules and particles, or atoms and electrons' (Pring, 1977, p. 59). Each of these technical sources provides a distinctive set of theoretical concepts in response to a single question.

Furthermore, each of these different ways of answering the question is drawn from an area of systematic study. Carpenters have been making tables for generations, passing on wisdom, developing new technologies and methods and engaging in critical assessment of ideas. Biologists have developed methods for experimenting, observing and thinking about the biological world. They have collected and collated evidence, systematically debating and assessing biological theories and probing underlying principles of their subject matter. Physicists and chemists have their own methods, technologies, history, debates, standards of evaluation, underlying principles and substantive theories. Systematic study is fundamental to any disciplinary science. Answers to questions are provided by disciplines that systematically study the parts of the world being questioned. Disciplinary sciences provide the sort of transparency, focus, reproducibility and provenance for technical content which ties it to the best that humankind has to offer.

Answering questions about ordinary concepts, which, by their very nature, have not already been defined by a clear, technical theory risks providing students with poorly thought through, biased or ill-informed content. For example, relationships education ought not to be conducted exclusively through glossy magazines and agony aunt columns. It also encourages asking questions without having a fixed idea of the meaning of the questions, which is unlikely to be conducive to productive inquiry.

Within disciplines, definitions of theoretical concepts are learned through systematic study of the discipline. Conceptual clarification is an important preliminary to any organized inquiry and also an outcome of theorizing. Learning atomic theory is inseparable from learning the precise meaning of the concept 'atom' within that theory. Disciplinary sciences provide the clarity about concepts necessary to begin to systematically answer questions; and they do so explicitly. Strawson explains that 'it is certainly not true that we master the key concepts of specialist disciplines without explicit theoretical instruction. There are countless books and crowds of teachers whose function is precisely to introduce us to the key concepts of their disciplines by means of explicit instruction' (Strawson, 1992, p. 11). Clarity about theoretical concepts is part of properly understanding theories, and without clarity about these concepts, inquiry into questions based on them is hampered and prone to error or confusion.

When it comes to questions relying on ordinary concepts, a lack of clarity about their meaning can lead to difficulties. Midgley's analogy of philosophy as plumbing highlights this. When plumbing works well, we need not worry, but as soon as something goes wrong, if we do not understand how the plumbing works, we are incapable of making progress. She explains that 'systems of ideas which are working smoothly are more or less invisible' (Midgley, 1992, p. 143); however, 'when things go wrong … we must then somehow readjust our underlying concepts; we must shift the set of assumptions that we have inherited and have been brought up with. We must restate those existing assumptions – which are normally muddled and inarticulate – so as to get our fingers on the source of trouble' (p. 140). Without a clear understanding of the concepts that we ordinarily use, we cannot make progress on pressing questions that require an accurate understanding of ordinary concepts. What is required is some disciplinary science that provides content and methods for systematically studying ordinary concepts.

The discipline that provides this systematic study of ordinary concepts is philosophy, in particular, the parts of philosophy which engage in conceptual analysis. Strawson makes this point using an analogy with grammar: 'just as the grammarian, and especially the model modern grammarian, labours to produce a systematic account of the structure of rules which we effortlessly observe in speaking grammatically, so the philosopher labours to produce a systematic account of the general conceptual structure of which our daily practice shows us to have a tacit and unconscious mastery' (Strawson, 1992, p. 7). When philosophers engage in conceptual analysis, they are engaged in the systematic study of ordinary concepts with an aim of reaching conceptual clarity. As such, the methods and content associated with philosophy are well placed to contribute to helping students to effectively interact with the parts of the world which are understood and talked about using ordinary concepts. This is because the systematic study of ordinary concepts helps people to address and answer ordinary concept questions; and because there are ordinary questions which, if unanswered, hamper effective interaction with the world.

One reason why the systematic study of ordinary concepts is important when it comes to questions which are premised on ordinary concepts is that one way we interact effectively with the world is through theoretical content. The same is true of questions based on ordinary concepts, except unlike technical questions, the theoretical content that we have available to help us with such questions is often more imprecise and unsystematic. This means that we are left struggling to make sense of the available answers. We lack the means to criticise them, compare them with one another or make solid progress. For example, someone's parents might encourage them to pursue happiness in life. However, the concept of happiness is so murky that this provides little guidance. Furthermore, asking whether the pursuit of happiness is something worthwhile is an important question, but it remains difficult to solve due to a lack of systematic theoretical resources. Similar folk theoretical content underpins relationships advice: 'plenty more fish in the sea', 'marry for love', 'make sure you trust one another'. These platitudes are of little substantive value without clearer guidance about the meanings of the concepts employed and inquiry into whether the theoretical content underlying the meaning of the concepts is coherent.

I will go through two examples of how conceptual analysis contributes to the ability to answer prominent and pressing ordinary concept questions. The first is the contribution of analytic philosophy to epistemological questions. The second is Manne's recent analysis of misogyny. Between these two examples, I hope to illustrate how the philosophical canon contributes to the ability to address ordinary-concept questions, and its continued relevance particularly with the trend towards ameliorative conceptual analysis or conceptual engineering.

Analysis of the concept of knowledge is a philosophical staple. In his introduction to epistemology, Greco states,

> *Epistemology*, or the theory of knowledge, is driven by two main questions: 'what is knowledge?' and 'what can we know?' If we think that we can know something, as nearly everyone does, then a third main question arises: 'How do we know what we know?' Most of what has been written in epistemology over the ages addresses at least one of these questions. (Greco & Sosa, 1999, p. 1)

Epistemology starts with conceptual analysis of 'knowledge', on which a series of other ordinary questions and answers hinge.

Plato's analysis of knowledge provides a starting point for epistemology; the starting point provided is an analysis of knowledge as justified, true belief. Plato's *Theatatus* dialogically reaches the conclusion that the concept of knowledge could be defined in three ways: '(i) knowledge is the various arts and sciences; (ii) knowledge is perception; (iii) knowledge is true judgement and (iv) knowledge is true judgement with an "account" (*Logos*)' (Giannopoulou, 2019). Although Plato's dialogue in the *Theatatus* is inconclusive, it supports the basis of the tripartite account of knowledge where knowledge is defined as justified, true belief. This concept of knowledge dominated epistemology until Gettier's challenge in 1963; although arguably it is still the starting point for any analytic discussion in epistemology.

Gettier challenges the tripartite account of knowledge by offering counter examples, which demonstrate that a belief being justified and true is not sufficient for it to constitute knowledge (Gettier, 1963). Gettier asks us to imagine that Smith and Jones have applied for the same job, and Smith believes that 'Jones is the man who will get the job, and Jones has ten coins in his pocket' (p. 122). His belief is justified because the president of the company informed Smith that Jones will get the job, and Smith counted ten coins in Jones's pocket. Smith's belief can be simplified to the claim that 'the man who will get the job has ten coins in his pocket' (p. 122). However, as it turns out, Smith gets the job and Smith also has ten coins in his pocket. Smith's belief that 'the man who will get the job has ten coins in his pocket' is justified (he counted the number of coins in Jones's pocket and the president told him Jones would get the job); it is also true (Smith does have ten coins in his pocket and did get the job); however, Gettier contends that the justified, true belief that the man who will get the job has ten coins in his pocket does not constitute knowledge. There must be something wrong with the analysis of knowledge as justified, true belief.

Systematic work on the analysis of the ordinary concept of knowledge might not seem intuitively helpful when it comes to answering prominent and pressing questions; its dialogical nature casts doubt on whether it yields useful theoretical content. However, Gutting points out that conceptual analysis may not lead to settled and precise definitions, and that attempts to solve the Gettier problem have seemingly failed, however, 'they have helped produce new ways of thinking about knowledge that have revolutionized epistemology' (Gutting, 2009, p. 57). Goldman, for example, pointed out that the causes of the beliefs should be taken into an account, a move which founded reliabilism. Analytic philosophy, conducted through the use of examples and counter-examples, provides new ways of looking at the concept of knowledge and questions about how we know. This is similar to inquiry into other subject areas which provide new ways of looking at their particular subjects; a scientific theory is a way of looking at a particular aspect of the natural world; whether or not a single theory is settled upon does not detract from the value of the discipline in terms of insight shed on the world.

In terms of the contribution of analytic epistemology to prominent and pressing questions, how we understand the concept of knowledge plays a role in how we understand what to believe, how dogmatic or flexible to be in our beliefs and how to conduct inquiry.

One prominent and pressing question is about the proper attitude to take towards scientific findings. Chalmers introduces the field of philosophy of science with the following question:

> Science is highly esteemed. Apparently it is a widely held belief that there is something special about science and its methods. The naming of some claim or line of reasoning or piece of research 'scientific' is done in a way that is intended to imply some kind of merit or special kind of reliability. But what, if anything is so special about science? What is this 'scientific method' that allegedly leads to especially meritorious or reliable results? (Chalmers, 1978, p. xix)

Scientific knowledge is often presented to the public as knowledge defined in terms of justified, true belief. First, an understanding of the tripartite concept of knowledge can help people to distinguish good scientific claims from unscientific ones. Second, an awareness of issues with the tripartite definition of knowledge can help people to take a more nuanced approach to understanding the epistemological status of scientific claims. While Gettier cases appear to undermine scientific claims by pointing out that justification and truth are not adequate for knowledge; reliabilist accounts of knowledge allow for the possibility that we can trust careful inquiry to yield knowledge so long as the conditions are right. Furthermore, an understanding of the concept of knowledge can shape how we engage in inquiry. Philosophical study of scientific inquiry rests on how beliefs are justified, leading to the rejection of inductivism as a basis for knowledge and the idea that scientific beliefs can never be fully verified (Popper, 1959, 1963). A simpler example of the contribution of studying the concept of knowledge is that it helps us to take the correct attitude towards testimony, distinguish between opinion and knowledge and adopt appropriate levels of scepticism.

My claim is not that philosophy has definitively fixed the concept of knowledge, but that in systematically studying the meaning of the concept, the discipline of philosophy provides the best that humankind has to offer to clarify and fix its meaning. Through providing students with an overview of the philosophical analyses of knowledge undertaken within the discipline of philosophy, they are provided with the best available resources to help them to think clearly about knowledge for themselves.

The second example illustrates a more contemporary approach to conceptual analysis. Sally Haslanger gives an account of conceptual analysis which helps to explain how it can be constructive. She provides three separate analytical tasks:

> Conceptual inquiry which examines our use or ordinary concepts; descriptive projects which rely on 'empirical or quasi-empirical methods'; and analytical approaches to questions which ask What is the point of having these concepts? What cognitive or practical task do they (or should they) enable us to accomplish?

Are they effective tools to accomplish our (legitimate purposes); if not, what concepts would serve these purposes better? (Haslanger, 2012, p. 224)

Haslanger thinks that these tasks often go together, and that a question about, for example, gender, will need to take all three forms of inquiry into account. Between them they are able to clarify, deepen and ultimately alter our understanding of the world around us. Like scientific inquiry, this is a constructive methodology.

Kate Manne's *Down Girl* is a case in point. She undertakes an analysis of misogyny to engineer a fixed concept, which can improve society through giving an improved understanding of the effect of misogyny on women and society as a whole. Manne starts by saying that 'the term "misogyny" is … both a word we need as feminists, and one we are in danger of losing' (Manne, 2018, p. 12); her aim is to 'offer a useful toolkit for asking, answering, and debating such issues, as well as to provide room for detailed, substantive accounts of misogyny as they affect particular groups of girls and women' (p. 13). The toolkit that she develops is a conceptual framework for understanding what misogyny is and what is wrong with it.

Manne develops this conceptual framework by starting with an examination of what she calls the 'naïve conception' of misogyny where misogyny is the hatred of women (Manne, 2018, p. 19). She points out its inadequacies as a conception – it is too easy to dismiss as very few people hate women as a rule – and then develops a new conception which is better able to shed clarity on important questions. Her focus is firmly on analysis of the concept of misogyny. Here, 'as compared with the naïve conception, my account holds that misogyny primarily targets women because they are women in a man's world (ie. a historically patriarchal one, among other things), rather than because they are women in a man's mind, where that man is a misogynist' (Manne, 2018, p. 64).

Manne claims that the concept she develops as a result of this analysis has 'several important theoretical and practical advantages' (Manne, 2018, pp. 20–1). It 'enables us to understand misogyny as a relatively unmysterious, and epistemologically accessible, phenomenon'; 'It enables us to understand misogyny as a natural and central manifestation of patriarchal ideology'; 'It leaves room for the diverse range of ways misogyny works on girls and women given their intersectional identities'; 'It enables us to understand misogyny as a systematic social phenomenon, by focusing on the hostile reactions women face in navigating the social world'; It fits uses of misogyny in grassroots activist movements; 'It delivers plausible answers to many of the questions about misogyny that have been controversial recently'; and 'It enables us to draw a clean contrast between misogyny and sexism' (p. 21). All of these benefits constitute an opening up of understanding, insight and clarity about what we mean by misogyny. This allows for new dialogue about the concept, which in turn provides the potential for fruitful progress towards answering prominent and pressing questions.

Without a clear concept of misogyny, answering prominent and pressing questions about the experiences of women can become muddled, fractious and harmful. Manne points to the issue of misogyny in the 2016 US election; Trump's words and actions become transparently misogynistic on her analysis of the concept. This provides previously unavailable apparatus for talking about his words and actions in a constructive way. Without systematic analysis of ordinary concepts, we lack the clarity needed to properly address otherwise slippery prominent and pressing questions. If, as a teacher, I wanted to address prominent and pressing questions surrounding misogyny in a classroom, starting with Manne's analysis would present students with a systematic toolkit for making progress on the questions at hand. Manne's toolkit supports substantive theorizing in response to questions by fixing meanings, and providing clarity about what is at stake.

Studying the elements of philosophical work which engage in, and draw on the analysis of ordinary concepts can provide the sort of basis for the systematic study of ordinary-concept questions that other areas of the curriculum provide for their respective disciplinary questions. While studying philosophy might not always provide direct answers to questions, it can provide the resources needed to begin to construct answers.

Premise 5: The Disciplinary Science of Philosophy is Best-Placed to Address Prominent and Pressing Ordinary-Concept Questions

In order to argue that philosophy should be placed on the curriculum, it needs to be salient to prominent and pressing questions, but it also needs to be well, or best-placed to respond to them. Ideally, an argument for teaching philosophy in schools would establish that philosophy is the best placed discipline to draw answers from. In this section, I will argue that while philosophy is not the only discipline which addresses prominent and pressing ordinary-concept questions, there are reasons for thinking that it does so in the most systematic way available, and so is the best way of addressing them available. This means that it should be included on the curriculum.

I argue that while other disciplines raise and respond to prominent and pressing ordinary-concept questions, the disciplinary science of philosophy does so more systematically, and so ought to be a first port of call when looking for resources to provide guidance on a range of questions. There are plenty of contending disciplinary sciences that also address prominent and pressing ordinary-concept questions. The humanities and arts play a large role, and this should not be downplayed. I will rather show that the disciplinary science of philosophy adds clarity to the work of the arts and humanities and provides more systematic tools for exploring the same questions by clarifying the concepts in question. This is necessary for clear inquiry to proceed.

Nussbaum makes the case for teaching the humanities in response to prominent and pressing questions. She claims that 'even those issues that seem closest to home – issues, for example about the structure of the family, the regulation of sexuality, the future of children – need to be approached with a broad historical and cross-cultural understanding' (Nussbaum, 1997, p. 8). She suggests the study of non-Western cultures, women's studies, human sexuality studies, and literary contributions. While some of these disciplinary sciences involve the systematic study of prominent and pressing issues, such as women's studies, or human sexuality studies, others such as history and literature treat them in an unsystematic way. Studying history might provide some insight into gender, sexuality and relationships, but only as part of the systematic study of the past, not as the systematic study of those issues themselves. Similarly, studying literature sheds light on gender, sexuality and relationships, but not in a systematic way. Literature, as a disciplinary science, systematically studies literature itself, not gender, sexuality and relationships in their own right. Conceptual analysis, on the other hand, systematically studies the concepts grounding these questions and responses. Nussbaum alludes to this when she claims that Socratic dialogue should also be included on the curriculum.

As an example, take the relationship between studying literature and studying sexuality and gender, questions about which are likely to concern students at some point in their lives. Within the discipline of literature, the sort of content that might be used to inform answers to questions about sexuality and gender is very diverse. The University of Kent's reading list for its module on 'Contemporary Literature: gender and sexuality' offers a range of competing, contradictory and confusing views on gender and sexuality through Hollinghurst's *The Line of Beauty*, Bank's *The Wasp Factory*, Mammet's *Oleanna*, Winterson's *Written on the Body*, Nichol's *The Fat Black Woman's Poems*, Proulx's *Brokeback Mountain* and Munro's *Open Secrets* (Palmer, 2018). These works of literature cover a range of very different ideas about gender and sexuality. Even within a single work of literature, a range of different ideas might be juxtaposed and the work might perplex as much as it clarifies; this is certainly the case in *The Wasp Factory*. The aim of teaching literature is not to develop the ability to respond to difficult questions about gender and sexuality with clarity.

The disciplinary science of literature does not offer a systematic study of gender and sexuality; rather, it offers the systematic study of literature which deals with gender and sexuality. Students are left with the ability to systematically address questions about works of literature, but not the ability to systematically address questions about gender and sexuality. Nonetheless, studying literature about gender and sexuality certainly does provide students with a broader knowledge and understanding of the issues at hand; it ought to be included on the curriculum too. The additional role for philosophy is that some decision is needed about which views ought to inform answers, in other words, how to answer questions about gender and sexuality. This process requires a systematic approach to answering questions about key concepts to do with gender and sexuality. It involves an analysis of 'gender' and 'sexuality' as a first step. Systematic conceptual analysis of 'gender' and 'sexuality' is philosophical work. It is this preliminary conceptual clarity that philosophy is best placed to offer, and without conceptual clarity, further inquiry might lack care and direction.

Apart from literature, Nussbaum suggests drawing on non-Western cultures, women's studies, and the study of human sexuality to deal with the ordinary questions at hand. This is more promising since these fields and disciplines are engaged in the systematic study of the specific questions themselves. Here, however, it is still the case that conceptual analysis of underlying ordinary concepts is helpful for making progress. Some philosophical methodology (conceptual analysis) and content (the results of conceptual analysis) are needed to fully address questions about 'the structure of the family, the regulation of sexuality, the future of children' (Nussbaum, 1997, p. 8). This is made more important by Nussbaum's appeal to the importance of 'a broad historical and cross-cultural understanding' (p. 8). If students are presented with a broad set of different answers without being given guidance for figuring out how to assess and select from those answers, then they are more likely to be confused or lapse into relativism than to develop rational autonomy regarding those questions.

As an analogy, imagine studying all of the historical theories about the origin of species, including Darwinian evolution, without being provided with guidance on which theory is the most likely to be true, or how to decide between them. There would be a lack of standards for answers to live up to and a lack of methods of arbitrating between answers. The discipline of biology provides standards and means for arbitrating between competing theories. While philosophers often disagree about the answers to ordinary-concept questions, they have methods, tools and standards for determining which are viable and which are not. Conceptual analysis is a first step in this process. It is a systematic tool for reaching clarity about what the question at hand really means, and which available content addresses this precise meaning. Conceptual analysis is an area of systematic study in the same way that biology is, with its systematic account of theoretical terms such as 'evolution', 'origin', 'species', 'scientific' and 'evidence'. While philosophers present a large number of different theories about ordinary-concept questions such as 'what is a good life?', the discipline of philosophy includes methods and content which allow for arbitration between these competing theories. There are standards of debate built into the discipline, which add a level of systematization to any exploration of questions which rest on ordinary concepts.

The same applies to teaching students answers to ordinary pressing and prominent questions in Relationships and Sex Education (RSE) in schools in England. Curriculum guidance puts learning 'the facts and the law about sex, sexuality, sexual health and gender identity in an age-appropriate and inclusive way' (DfE, 2019, p. 26). A combination of studying the facts and the law about sex, sexuality, sexual health and gender identity is insufficient to answer the sorts of prominent and pressing questions that students are likely to have about these issues. For example, students are likely to run into questions about the morality of sexuality; particularly since religious organisations publicly make claims about this. This is going to bring up prominent and pressing questions, particularly for students whose sexuality is challenged by these organizations. Presenting facts about sexuality gives students little guidance about how to talk about or answer these questions. Without any suggested area of systematic study relating to questions about the morality of sexuality, teachers are left to piece together a range of different views, or to adopt a single poorly established view to teach children about these prominent and pressing issues. My recommendation is to turn to analytic philosophy for the sort of systematic resources needed to help students to address questions about morality stemming from issues about sexuality and relationships. This is because philosophy studies ordinary concepts, providing a systematic, disciplinary basis for them.

The risk of failing to turn to an area of systematic study is high, since poorly selected material has the potential to cause immense damage to how students feel about themselves and the world around them. For RSE teachers, selecting material without a systematic area of study to provide guidance is difficult; one systematic area of study which could provide guidance is analytic philosophy.

Conceptual analysis could provide RSE teachers with ways of understanding the concepts and questions associated with sex, gender identity and sexuality to present to their students. These would provide important starting points for discussions about the prominent and pressing questions which employ these concepts.

Conclusion

While it is certainly the case that existing subjects on the curriculum do address and provide content and discussion about prominent and pressing questions which rely on ordinary concepts, the resources provided by existing subjects do not provide a systematic basis for dealing with these questions. This is because history is the systematic study of the past, the natural sciences are engaged in the systematic study of the natural world, literature is primarily the systematic study of literature, sociology is the systematic study of society and so on. This means that while they address prominent and pressing ordinary-concept questions, they do not provide resources which constitute a systematic study of the underlying concepts to fix the meaning of these questions. Instead, they provide a systematic study of their own technical concepts, fixing these within their own sphere of study. The technical concepts that they discuss might not accord to the ordinary usage underlying the questions relevant to students. As Ryle points out, public, shared or ordinary concepts are left unclear and are prone to cause problems. On the other hand, studying philosophy at school, with the aim of learning how to engage in conceptual analysis and becoming acquainted with existing conceptual analyses of important ordinary concepts would provide the best systematic theoretical content and tools that humanity has to offer in order to make progress with questions and problems arising from ordinary concepts. That is not to say that philosophy offers complete responses to questions, rather that when it comes to the content available to humankind, conceptual analysis taken from the discipline of philosophy is, at least some of the time, the best there is.

6

Teaching Philosophy to Make Sense of the Curriculum

In Chapter 4, I presented a utility account of theoretical education:

1. Acquiring a broad array of theoretical content amounts to acquiring different ways of understanding the world;
2. Different ways of understanding the world contribute to a person's ability to act effectively within the world;
3. Providing students with the ability to act effectively within the world is a justifiable aim of education.

In this chapter, I argue that a further step is needed to ensure that a theoretical education meets its aim of helping students to interact effectively with the world. This required further step is an addition to point (2). In order to interact effectively with the world in the light of a theoretical education, students need to be able to make sense of the broad array of theoretical content they are taught and act on it appropriately. The full argument of is as follows:

(1) Acquiring a broad array of theoretical content amounts to acquiring different ways of understanding the world;
(2) Different ways of understanding the world contribute to a person's ability to act effectively within the world *if, and only if, they are applied, and applied appropriately*;
(3) Providing students with the ability to act effectively within the world is a justifiable aim of education.
(4) Teaching students how to apply theoretical content appropriately is central to meeting this aim;

> Therefore too conclude, students should be taught how to apply theoretical content appropriately.

This chapter argues that teaching philosophy in schools is the best way to teach students how to apply theoretical content appropriately. Since a theoretical education cannot help students to act effectively in the world to its full extent unless they have this ability, teaching philosophy is central to meeting the aim of theoretical education. I argue that any theoretical education ought to involve some theoretical content. Furthermore, since I argued in Chapter 4 that any education ought to involve at least some theoretical education, this chapter reaches the conclusion that philosophy ought to be taught at some point in every student's education.

The case for teaching philosophy in schools comes from the idea that a theoretical education provides students with a broad range of theoretical content taken from the best theories available in response to prominent and pressing questions. There are a plurality of theories that explain and describe the world around us in response to these prominent and pressing questions. This has the potential to create confusion when it comes to deciding which information to prioritize in response to questions, and how to draw on multiple sources of information to weave an effective response to a problem. I will outline existing discussions of this problem and subsequently characterize these in terms of problems caused by different conceptual schemes employed by different theories and disciplines. I will then explain how aspects of the discipline of philosophy address conceptual disparities and help students to think about how to solve the problems that they raise.

Fragmentation and Theoretical Education

There is an idea expressed by various philosophers of education that a broad theoretical curriculum is somehow fragmented and that this is problematic. Some refer to the inertness of curriculum content, others to the piecemeal nature of the curriculum, or the view that the curriculum fails to address students' concerns. This idea is expressed in lots of different ways, but I am going to use the term 'fragmentation'. I am going to characterize inertness, the piecemeal nature of the curriculum and the failure of the curriculum to address students' needs as stemming from the same problem of fragmentation. In this section, I will clarify this commonly identified problem of fragmentation. I will characterize it as a problem caused by the conceptual fragmentation of the different theories and theoretical frameworks which make up a theoretical curriculum.

One account of the fragmentation of a theoretical curriculum comes from Dewey, who explains that the traditional subject-based curriculum fails to address the interests and needs of children. He proposes, in contrast, a more child-centred curriculum. A subject-based curriculum falls short of educating children because 'the pupils are immersed in details; their minds are loaded with disconnected ideas' (Dewey, 1910, p. 96). He attributes this to the fact that a subject-based approach involves a canon which is not related to their own concerns. Here, 'the source of whatever is dead, mechanical and formal in schools is found precisely in the subordination of the life and experience of the child to the curriculum' (Dewey, 1967, p. 95). In providing students with the best theories that humankind has to offer without adequately considering what they are interested in or what they need to know, the curriculum bombards them with content without helping them to see what the content is for, or how it fits together. Dewey thinks that the curriculum is fragmented into subjects that seem unrelated to one another. It is also fragmented in relation to a child's experiences, which also seem unrelated to the curriculum. In being disconnected or fragmented in this way, the curriculum is inert to children. They do not know what it is for, and might be tempted to pay little attention to it.

Students, in Dewey's view, cannot be expected to weave a broad, fragmented theoretical curriculum into a meaningful body of knowledge. He says, 'it is certainly as futile to expect the child to evolve a universe of his own out of his own mere mind as it is for a philosopher to attempt the task' (Dewey, 1967, p. 102). Nor can they be expected to survey what they have been taught and select the relevant theoretical content in response to prominent and pressing questions. Dewey's solution is to allow children to shape what they learn themselves, so that theoretical content is always acquired in a meaningful way. This addresses the fragmentation between their own experiences and curriculum content. The child should shape their own curriculum, and in doing so they would fully understand how different theories relate to one another, thus easing the fragmentation between different areas of the curriculum as well. Addressing the fragmentation between subjects, and the fragmentation between a child's own experiences and what they learn in schools addresses the problem of inertness.

Phenix melds Dewey's emphasis on the importance of a meaningful curriculum with a commitment to a broad theoretical curriculum. In *Realms of Meaning*, he highlights and offers a solution to the same problem of fragmentation. To Phenix, 'the special office of education is to widen one's view of life, to deepen insight into relationships, and to counteract the provincialism of customary existence – in short, to engender an integrated outlook' (Phenix, 1964, pp. 3–4). However, traditional subject-based theoretical curricula fail to meet this educational aim:

> All too commonly the teacher teaches a particular subject or unit within a subject without reference to its relationships to other components of the curriculum. Similarly, the student may study one subject after another with no idea of what his growing fund of knowledge and skill might contribute to an integrated way of life. Students and teachers alike are prone to take the curriculum as they find it, as a traditional sequence of separate elements, without ever inquiring into the comprehensive pattern within which the constituent parts are located. (Phenix, 1964, p. 3)

Phenix thinks that students are exposed to a plurality of seemingly disparate ideas, but are given little guidance about what they mean or why they are important. Unlike Dewey, Phenix thinks that the solution is to make the theoretical curriculum more meaningful by paying attention to how each part fits together, and designing the curriculum accordingly. Interestingly, he thinks that teaching philosophy can contribute to solving the problem of fragmentation because philosophy is 'concerned with every kind of human experience and not with any one domain' (Phenix, 1964, p. 253). In creating a holistic, fully coherent curriculum in advance, Phenix thinks that students will no longer face the problem of fragmentation and will not need to do the work themselves.

Lipman, Sharp and Oscanyan's account of the value of philosophy for children draws on a similar account of fragmentation in education. They say that 'all too often students see no connection between what they are studying, what they do in their lives, and what society at large does' (Lipman et al., 1980, p. 22). In response, they think that philosophy, on a P4C model, encourages the intellectual resourcefulness and flexibility that can enable children and teachers alike to cope with the disconnectedness and fragmentation of existing curricula (p. 27).

Advocates of liberal education raise similar worries. Whitehead's description of the curriculum 'from which nothing follows' outlined in Chapter 2, is an example of the common intuition that a broad theoretical education can fail to transform a student (Whitehead, 1932, p. 9). Whitehead is pointing to the inertness of the curriculum, but in doing so, he describes a curriculum that does not fit together in a meaningful way. This description fits the idea that the curriculum is fragmented from both students' own experiences, and internally fragmented so that its constituent parts appear unrelated to one another. The problem of inertness stems from the problem of fragmentation.

Newman discusses the importance of a liberal education adding up to something and points to the possibility that it might fall short of this by asking us to imagine a seafarer who might range from one end of the earth to the other; but the multiplicity of external objects, which they have encountered, forms no symmetrical and consistent picture upon their imagination; they see the tapestry of human life, as it were, on the wrong side, and it tells no story. They sleep, and they rise up, and they find themselves, now in Europe, now in Asia; they see visions of great cities and wild regions; they are in the marts of commerce, or amid the islands of the South; they gaze on Pompey's pillar, or on the Andes; and nothing which meets them carries them forward or backward, to any idea beyond itself. Nothing has a drift or relation; nothing has history or promise. Everything stands by itself, and comes and goes in its turn, like the shifting scenes of a show, which leave the spectator where he was. (Newman, 1931, p. 59)

Similarly, a student in the midst of a theoretical curriculum might range from one classroom to another encountering the best that humankind has to offer, but without being transformed or impressed by what they encounter. Here, the inertness of their education is caused by its internal fragmentation, where one class seems to have little in common with another. It is also caused by the fragmentation between the experiences of the child and the school curriculum, where the curriculum appears to have little bearing on their own life. As a result, they might simply fail to engage in the aim of a theoretical education: to use theoretical content to help them to interact effectively with the world. It might come across as a purely academic activity; something to be liked or disliked, but nothing more than that.

Peters's analysis of education also touches on the fragmentation of the curriculum. In *Ethics and Education*, Peters describes a scientist who falls short of being considered an educated person because he 'could have a very limited conception of what he is doing. He could work away at science without seeing its connection with much else. For him it is an activity which is cognitively adrift' (Peters, 1966, p. 30). The scientist lacks what Peters calls 'cognitive perspective' because he only thinks of the world in terms of what he has learned about science' (p. 60). He fails to see that there are other angles by which the world around him can be understood and navigated. Peters's analysis of the concept of education focuses on what he calls its 'cognitive aspect'. This involves knowledge, understanding and cognitive perspective with 'the emphasis on "seeing" and "grasping" for oneself which is to be found both in Plato and in the "growth" theorists' (Peters, 1973c, p. 93). Peters acknowledges the importance of Dewey, as a growth theorist and his focus on the meaningfulness of theoretical activities or content to an individual. Peters points to the danger of the curriculum becoming 'a collection of disjointed facts' (Peters, 1973a, p. 18). Again, the curriculum risks being fragmented from students' own experiences and internally fragmented so that its parts are unrelated to one another.

This claim that the theoretical curriculum is prone to becoming fragmented and inert is common to Dewey, Phenix, Whitehead, Newman, Lipman and Peters. At one extreme, Phenix's account of the fragmentation of the curriculum leads him to claim that the curriculum ought to provide students with a readymade meaningful and coherent body of knowledge. This perhaps overestimates our ability to provide such a body of knowledge. It is quite possible that the body of theoretical content available to humankind forms no such meaningful unity. On the other hand, this does not mean that fragmentation ought to be accepted as a necessary companion to a broad theoretical education. Rather than demanding that students possess a unified body of knowledge, the problem of the fragmented curriculum can be addressed by helping students to think across different sorts of theoretical content. Students could be taught skills and content to help them solve the problem of fragmentation. This might involve connecting different theories to the world around them and putting them into action; or it might involve considering how different theories interact with one another; or how ordinary concerns relate to theoretical endeavours.

Clarifying the Problem

There is some general agreement that a broad theoretical education might become fragmented, both from students' experiences of the world and within the curriculum itself, so that different theories and disciplines become disconnected from one another; I have called this the problem of fragmentation. In this section, I will explain how and why this might be the case. If a broad theoretical education provides students with a plurality of theories, and theories employ their own conceptual schemes, then students are faced with a plurality of different conceptual schemes which they are expected to employ to understand the world around them. This means that students face conceptual problems when it comes to putting their broad theoretical education to good use. In this section, I aim to establish three claims:

(1) The meaning of a concept is defined by the role it plays in a theory;
(2) A theoretical curriculum is conceptually fragmented;
(3) Conceptual fragmentation causes problems for students.

I will characterize the problem of fragmentation in terms of the conceptual fragmentation of the curriculum. Adding clarity in this way will allow me to identify solutions to the problem of fragmentation.

Claim 1: The Meaning of a Concept is Defined by the Role it Plays in a Theory

In the previous chapter, I set out the idea that theoretical concepts are defined in terms of their technical role in a theory, whereas ordinary concepts lack a single, precise technical theoretical definition. I showed how analytic philosophy works to address the conceptual imprecision of ordinary concepts, providing them with fixed meanings in order to facilitate answering difficult questions, which rest on them. In this chapter, the idea that a concept is defined by the role that it plays in a theory is important because I will argue that the fragmentation of the curriculum is caused by the plurality of different conceptual schemes provided as part of a theoretical education. Theories employ different conceptual schemes and it is not always straightforward to work out how they relate to one another, or how they relate to ordinary concerns. This requires conceptual work.

Strawson talks about this conceptual confusion and claims that it is the result of concepts being taken out of the contexts or theories within which they have been defined. He says that 'we get into these muddles, encounter these problems, only when we allow the concepts or the words to become detached from their actual use, from the practical or theoretical concerns which give them their significance' (Strawson, 1992, p. 4). Concepts are precise and unproblematic while employed as parts of the theories or practices they were developed for. When a student is introduced to a theory, they are simultaneously introduced to its concepts: 'the scientific specialist … is perfectly capable of explaining what he is doing with the special terms of his specialism. He has an explicit mastery, within the terms of his theory' (p. 12). When a student is taught a broad theoretical curriculum, they master the concepts at work in each theory they are taught. However, since many of these concepts are defined by the role they play in theories, different theories become conceptually separate from one another and from real-world issues, and the curriculum fragments.

Furthermore, once concepts are removed from their respective theories, their meanings become confused, but 'distorting influences, though always latent, are neutralised so long as our words or concepts are actually being exploited in the various theoretical or practical spheres which are their true field of operation' (Strawson, 1992, p. 4). Strawson is interested in the origin of philosophical puzzles, but this level of conceptual confusion equally applies to students' understanding of aspects of the school curriculum. Whenever students are asked to think about a concept outside of its theoretical home, they are prone to running into conceptual confusion. Since a theoretical education is worthwhile if it helps students to interact with the world, the point where students are asked to apply ideas from a theory to the world around them is key to the value of theoretical education. This point is likely to cause difficulty wherever it is not simply a case of a very straightforward application of a single theory.

Ryle makes a similar point using an analogy involving Bridge and Poker. He says that 'the meanings of the terms used by Bridge-players and Poker-players are heavy with the systems and schemes of those games. It would be absurd to suppose someone learning what is meant by "straight flush" without learning even the rudiments of Poker, or learning all about Poker without learning what a "straight flush" is' (Ryle, 1953, p. 90). The concepts associated with Poker are learned as part of learning the 'theory' of Poker, or how to play it. These concepts are defined by the role that they play in the games. Ryle holds that the same is true of theoretical concepts:

> In the same general sort of way the special terms of a science are more or less heavy with the burden of the theory of that science. The technical terms of genetics are theory-laden, laden, that is, not just with theoretical luggage of some sort or other but with the luggage of genetic theory. Their meanings change with changes in the theory. Knowing their meanings requires some grasp of the theory. (Ryle, 1953, p. 90)

In this way, concepts are defined by their place in a theory. Similarly, what makes a theory distinct from other theories is its distinctive use of concepts.

This means that different theories can, and do, have different conceptual frameworks; they make use of and define concepts for their own purposes. The same word can refer to different concepts in different theories, theories might employ similar but subtly different concepts, or they might share little to nothing in common with one another. A broad theoretical education introduces students to the best theories available to answer prominent and pressing questions. Any student pursuing a theoretical education is going to spend their school time switching between different conceptual frameworks as they learn different theories. A theoretical education is conceptually fragmented in the same way that learning different card games is conceptually fragmented.

Claim 2: Conceptual Fragmentation Causes Problems for Students

There are two areas of fragmentation in a broad theoretical education which are likely to affect students. The first is the fragmentation between the ordinary or common sense ways of understanding of the world that students enter the classroom with and the theories that they are taught to see the world through in order to be well-informed about it. Here, ordinary concepts and theoretical concepts might be mismatched. This will cause problems when attempting to apply theories to one's own life, or when looking to answer any novel or pre-theoretical problem with existing theoretical content. This problem tracks that referred to as inertness in existing literature. The second is the fragmentation of different, potentially competing theories from one another. This might mean that students face conceptual difficulties when trying to employ different concepts in an interdisciplinary or synthetic way. This problem will also arise wherever there is a new pre-theoretical problem or a problem that sits outside of traditional subject disciplines.

The first issue that the conceptual fragmentation of the curriculum might cause for students is that the different conceptual schemes employed by technical theories do not always translate easily into the ordinary conceptual schemes underlying the sorts of prominent and pressing questions encountered by students. As an example, imagine a student at a party who is faced with the question of whether to join their peers and try taking drugs. At school, they may have been taught about the physiological and psychological effects of drug use. Maybe they are thinking about trying cannabis. They may have been taught that cannabis poses a risk of psychosis, or of inducing paranoia. They might have been taught that it carries risks for their respiratory or cardiac health or that it could cause changes in motivation and mood, which might impact their daily life. However, the student is also faced with a room full of peers, some of whom use cannabis regularly and seem to suffer no ill effects. What they can see in front of them suggests that cannabis use might be fun and risk-free. Their grasp of theoretical content seems at odds with their ordinary understanding of the world.

Perhaps more importantly, the student has various other considerations which are not about the physiology or psychology of cannabis use, but which fall much more into the realm of their ordinary conceptual schemes. The student might consider their social standing in a group of friends, their own curiosity about the new experience offered or insight into a cannabis subculture encountered in films and through social media. The student might also have moral concerns about trying cannabis, it might clash with their other values or with religious or political commitments. Considering whether to try cannabis is, after all, a normative task: should I try cannabis? In light of these concerns, the theoretical content about cannabis use provided to them in school falls short of helping them to navigate this particular situation effectively. It is fragmented from their other immediate concerns.

At least part of shortfall is a conceptual problem. One concept which is causing difficulty is the concept of risk. The information about the physiology and psychology of cannabis use explains what the risks of cannabis use are, but the student is left to their own devices to figure out what those risks mean in their circumstances and whether those risks outweigh perceived benefits of trying cannabis. Ordinary considerations about risk are about personal risk, and the physiology of cannabis use is about risk to the population. This is likely to be unclear to the student, and even if it was clear, the disparity between the two concepts of risk causes confusion. This means that what the student has been taught in school is conceptually fragmented from the circumstances in which they find themselves, and their theoretical education is falling short of helping them to effectively interact with the world.

Aside from the question about the concept of risk, the student finds themselves facing an interdisciplinary and relatively novel question: should they, at this time and in this place, try cannabis? The question requires a degree of self-knowledge, moral considerations, physiological considerations, sociological considerations and cultural considerations, which are beyond the scope of quick decision making at a party. In combination, they are difficult because each consideration comes with its own conceptual framework. Answering the question in an informed way requires working between and across different conceptual frameworks to reach a multifaceted conclusion which draws on all of them, weighing them up against each other, dismissing some and prioritising others, reflecting values and facts all at once. Even if the student had studied theoretical content about the morality, sociology, physiology and culture of drug use, they would still not be prepared to make a decision about whether to try cannabis. They need to be able to synthesise what they have learned into an answer; this is a task which sits outside of each individual theory. It is conceptually messy, and understandably very difficult.

This highlights the second problem of fragmentation for a theoretical education: that different theories are conceptually fragmented from one another, and wherever a plurality of different theoretical frameworks are brought to bear on a single issue, a student will need to work out how to prioritize, synthesize, categorize, assess and reach conclusions based on what they have been taught. The theoretical curriculum they have been taught falls short of providing straightforward answers about how to interact effectively with the world in all situations. This is not a shortcoming of the theoretical content itself; the content consists of the best available theories in response to the most prominent and pressing questions students are likely to face. It is an inevitable result of the nature of human inquiry, which draws on different conceptual frameworks to develop technical answers to specific questions. This means that sometimes a complex additional task involving thinking across a range of different theories, and their respective conceptual frameworks, is required.

Claim 3: The Need for Conceptual Work

Mary Midgley gives a detailed account of the problems caused by conceptual fragmentation using the analogy of plumbing:

> Plumbing and philosophy are both activities that arise because elaborate cultures like ours have, beneath their surface, a fairly complex system which is usually unnoticed, but which sometimes goes wrong ... each system supplies vital needs for those who live above it. Each is hard to repair when it does go wrong, because neither of them was consciously planned as a whole. There have been many ambitious attempts to reshape both of them, but existing complications are usually too widespread to allow a completely new start.
>
> Neither system ever had a single designer who knew exactly what needs it would have to meet. Instead, both have grown imperceptibly over the centuries, and are constantly being altered piecemeal to suit changing demands, as the ways of life above them have branched out. Both are therefore now very intricate. When trouble arises, specialised skill is needed if there is to be any hope of locating it and putting it right ...
>
> When the concepts we are living by function badly, they do not usually drip audibly through the ceiling or swamp the kitchen floor. They just quietly distort and obstruct our thinking. (Midgley, 1992, p. 139)

Given that a theoretical education introduces students to a wide range of theories, many with their own conceptual frameworks, the chances of concepts functioning badly or systems going wrong, are quite high.

Midgley holds that our conceptual schemes ground our ability to effectively interact with the world. When conceptual schemes go wrong we must then somehow readjust our underlying concepts; we must shift the set of assumptions that we have inherited and have been brought up with, We must restate those existing assumptions – which are normally muddled and inarticulate – so as to get our fingers on the source of the trouble. And this new statement must somehow be put in a useable form, a form which makes the necessary changes look possible. (Midgley, 1992, p. 140)

Midgley thinks that this task is the task of philosophers, who, like professional plumbers, are needed to fix the conceptual schemes causing problems. When it comes to theoretical education, I propose that there is at least some role for students, who have studied some of the tools and content developed by philosophers, to solve some conceptual problems themselves.

Ryle highlights the difficulty of working between and across the different conceptual schemes used by different theories:

An intelligent man may both know perfectly how to put a concept to its regular work within its appropriate field of employment, and thus have complete mastery of its domestic logical duties and immunities, and yet be quite at a loss to determine its external or public logic. He can, perhaps, think lucidly as a geometrician and still be perplexed about the relations between geometrical points and pencilled dots on paper or molecules and atoms; or he can, perhaps, think lucidly as an economist and still be perplexed about the identity or non-identity of his marginal farmer, with this or that unprosperous smallholder. Ability to use the private lingo of a theory does not necessarily carry with it the ability to render this lingo into public dictions which are neutral between theories or, perhaps more often, between it and common knowledge. (Ryle, 1953, pp. 128–9)

Whenever a theory is employed in response to an ordinary question, a new theory-neutral question, or a question that draws on multiple theories, then some conceptual work is needed to figure out how to do this. Since someone who has mastery of a theory has only mastered how to use it in certain specific ways, once they are asked to use it outside of these circumstances, they need to undertake additional work. In a theoretical education, students are taught theories within their respective disciplinary sciences. However, in order to be able to use what they have learned to effectively interact with the world, they are going to have to apply theories in ordinary, new or interdisciplinary circumstances. Whenever this is the case, they are going to have to perform an additional task, and this task is conceptual in nature.

Strawson highlights another situation in which conceptual work is required. This is where someone is faced with a meta-question about a theory:

A historian may produce brilliant historical explanations without being able to say, in general, what counts as a historical explanation. A natural scientist may be fertile of brilliantly confirmed hypotheses but at a loss to give a general account of the confirmation of a scientific hypothesis or even of the general nature of scientific hypotheses themselves. Again, a mathematician may discover and prove new mathematical truths without being able to say what are the distinctive characteristics of mathematical truth or of mathematical proof. So we have, besides history, the philosophy of history; besides natural science, the philosophy of science; besides mathematics, the philosophy of mathematics. (Strawson, 1992, p. 12)

Students are taught within disciplines, and can become adept historians, scientists and mathematicians without studying the value and meaning of work in those disciplines more holistically. Studying the meaning of the sort of work undertaken by different disciplines is important because if they are asked to answer an interdisciplinary question, such as the question about cannabis use, they are going to need to consider which theories to prioritize over others. Doing so requires some judgement about the nature and value of different theories from different disciplines. This is a meta-question about disciplines and theories. In part this turns on the relationship between theoretical conceptual schemes and the aspect of the world in question, alongside the relationships between the conceptual schemes of different theories to one another. It deals directly with the previously identified problem of fragmentation between students' experiences of the world, and what they are taught, and the fragmentation within the curriculum between different subjects.

This meta-question is one which is frequently asked by students in the form of 'what's the point of maths/religious education/history/etc.?' Given the amount of school time spent on theoretical education, this is a legitimate question and educators owe students an answer to why their time is being spent mastering the theories they are presented with. Asking what different theories and disciplines are for is also conceptual: How does the conceptual framework of a discipline relate to the conceptual frameworks I am interested in? These questions are particularly important when assessing and prioritizing different competing or complementary theories, which address the same question. It is important to stand outside of a discipline or theory and ask what exactly it is about, and how valuable it is in relation to the question being asked.

This meta-question about disciplines or theories is not something that sits within the remit of the discipline itself. As Lowe points out,

> No special science – not even physics – can have that concern because the subject matter of every special science is identified more narrowly than this: for instance, biology is the science of living things, psychology is the science of mental states, and physics – as I have already indicated – is the science of those states and processes (energetic states and dynamic processes for example) which are apparently common to all things existing in space and time. (Lowe, 2002, p. 3)

Lowe's point applies to teachers too; a physics teacher is not teaching physics when they explain the value of physics as a discipline. Similarly, Ryle says that 'the kind of thinking which advances biology is not the kind of thinking which settles the claims and counter-claims between biology and physics' (Ryle, 1953, p. 13). Since questions about the meaning and value of disciplines and theories fall outside of those disciplines and theories themselves, asking about their value or relationship to a question at hand requires an additional task. As Strawson points out, 'it is precisely in giving such explanations [about the nature and value of theories] and in bringing out the differences and resemblances between them that one can bring out also the relations which exists between the different departments of our intellectual and human life' (Strawson, 1992, p. 13). In identifying the nature and value of theories, their relationship to the non-theoretical or ordinary world is clarified, as are their relationships to each other.

These meta and conceptual questions that arise from the pluralistic nature of the best theories available and their respective disciplines track the fragmentation of the curriculum referred to by Dewey, Phenix, Lipman et al.; Newman; Whitehead; and Peters. The different departments of our intellectual life form the basic structure of a theoretical education. The aim of this sort of broad theoretical education is to provide students with ways of understanding the world around them, and interacting effectively with it. However, if a student is unable to work between and across these different departments of intellectual life, they are unable to select relevant theories, deal with conflicting theories, assess the relative value of theories or match theories with questions. As a result, they are unable to apply what they have been taught to help them to fully interact effectively with the world. This is not a problem in straightforward cases where theories are being used to directly answer the questions they were developed to respond to, for example, atomic theory straightforwardly answers questions about the reactivity of elements. However, whenever a question is new, is answered by a plurality of different theories, or is unclear, a theoretical education without additional conceptual work is insufficient.

Ryle describes this conceptual work as that of solving 'sovereignty disputes' and 'boundary disputes' (Ryle, 1953, p. 12). Jackson adds that conceptual analysis 'is in the very business of addressing when and whether a story told in one vocabulary is made true by one told in some allegedly more fundamental vocabulary' (Jackson, 1998, p. 28). Jackson has in mind the claim that theories about the world can all be reduced to physicalism, or the view that 'all natural phenomena are, in a sense to be made precise, physical' (Papineau, 1996, p. 1).

Jackson explains the task of marrying our understanding of the world with physicalism as a conceptual one:

> If some variety of serious metaphysics is committed to an account of how things are in one vocabulary being made true by how things are as told in some other vocabulary, it had better have to hand an account of how accounts in the two vocabularies are inter-connected ... surely it is beyond serious question that at least some of: rivers, inflation, explosions, buildings, and wars exist. Some existential claims expressed in a language other than the austerely physical are true.
>
> But why suppose that the interesting account that physicalists must give of how and why the physical account of the world makes true the psychological account (or the economic or the geographical or ...) of our world must involve conceptual analysis? The answer to this question turns on the importance of defining one's subject ... although metaphysics is about what the world is like, the questions we ask when we do metaphysics are framed in a language, and thus we need to attend to what the users of language mean by the words they employ to ask their questions. (Jackson, 1998, pp. 29–30)

According to Jackson, we talk about the world in lots of different ways, using different theoretical frameworks within different disciplines. However, we also find ourselves in circumstances where we have to translate between these different conceptual frameworks. Jackson argues that this translation is a conceptual task.

Two Worked through Examples of the Need for Conceptual Analysis

I have already worked through one example of the need for conceptual analysis by exploring the fragmentation of the curriculum in relation to drugs education and the difficulties a student might face marrying up what they had been taught with the issues they encounter in the world. In this section, I will discuss two further examples where a theoretical curriculum falls short of guiding effective interaction with the world despite, at least implicitly, providing students with the best theories in response to the questions at hand. The first example I will discuss is the climate crisis, which is a case where the interdisciplinary nature of the issue causes conceptual problems. The second is the Covid-19 crisis, which is a case where the newness of the issue causes conceptual problems. Overall, the drug use example highlights conceptual problems caused by the interplay between ordinary and theoretical conceptual schemes; the climate crisis example highlights conceptual problems caused by the different conceptual schemes employed by different disciplines; and the Covid-19 crisis highlights conceptual problems caused by entirely new problems where conceptual schemes are not yet clearly in place. It is worth noting that the sources of conceptual problems overlap, so Covid-19, drug use and the climate crisis are all interdisciplinary, all have an element of newness, and all require thinking about ordinary conceptual frameworks.

Normative Questions and Conceptual Questions

At this point, there is some overlap with the conclusions reached in Chapter 5 about the need for some education in philosophy to help students to address ordinary-concept questions. These three examples have normative elements. They ask about what someone *should* do. In fact, it is difficult to identify prominent and pressing questions that do not have a normative element. This is because an education that prepares people for their future lives prepares them to make decisions about what they should do based on what they have learned. In Chapter 5, I characterized normative questions as ordinary concept questions. The concepts of 'good', 'just', 'right' and 'wrong' are ordinary concepts that have been systematically studied by the discipline of philosophy. In this chapter, ethical theories and moral concepts should be thought of as part of theoretical content from philosophy that needs to be taken into account when trying to solve interdisciplinary and new questions. The need for some moral philosophy has already been established in Chapter 5.

Despite this, the case I want to make goes further. There is a need for further conceptual work, even when students have been taught relevant theories from moral philosophy. The conceptual frameworks employed by ethical theories cause their own conceptual problems in interaction with other areas of inquiry. The student thinking about whether to try cannabis will consider the morality of taking cannabis alongside a host of other considerations. Ideally, they would have been taught some philosophy to help them to think about moral concepts in a constructive way. This might have involved learning about different ethical theories. The argument in this chapter is that this is not sufficient, there is an additional conceptual task that needs to take place and that involves more than just the ethical theories and concepts involved.

The Climate Crisis

In his abstract to a paper about education and the climate crisis, Paul Standish summarises the problems and questions raised by the climate crisis to children and school as follows:

> The climate crisis is of a severity that fills many with a sense of hopelessness. The modest steps that ordinary citizens can take to reduce energy consumption and waste seem futile in relation to the massive changes that are needed from governments and industry, and inertia often results. (Standish, 2020, p. 927)

There are at least three prominent and pressing questions that people face when thinking about the climate crisis: (1) How might it affect me and others? (2) What should I do about it and (3) What can I, or others, do about it? Answers to the first question fall within the realms of various natural and social sciences. Answers to the second fall within the realm of moral philosophy. Answers to the third question are political, economic, scientific and personal. The climate crisis requires content from almost the full spectrum of a broad theoretical education. As a result, it is very difficult to work out the answers to these questions.

In response to these three questions, students might have been taught information from theories in physics and chemistry, which explain how climate change happens and makes predictions about how it might proceed. These theories, if well-selected and understood, will allow people to judge the testimony of others and assess media reports for themselves. They might also help students to think about some courses of action which they, individually, might take. They might have been taught something about geography and meteorology regarding changes in weather and natural disasters resulting from climate change. These might guide students to make long-term plans about, for example, whether to live on a flood plain. Students might also be taught the social geography of climate change, and how it is already affecting the lives of many people whose livelihoods have been threatened by changes in the climate. This might help them to think about how to protect themselves from similar threats, or it might help students to make decisions about supporting important causes around the world by raising awareness, or donating money or time to charity. This is already a standard education in the climate crisis. It provides information with direct applicability to a specified range of questions, but does not address some of the more prominent and pressing questions students will be considering.

The second question that students are likely to ask is what they ought to do about the climate crisis. The crisis poses an existential threat to themselves, to those they care about, to future generations and to others around the world, particularly people who are already socially or economically disadvantaged. At the same time, the sorts of actions available seem insufficient to deal with the climate crisis on their own, and many of them involve intrusive restrictions on their freedom to pursue their own interests. For example, avoiding air travel might involve lengthy separations from friends and family; or becoming vegan might come with health risks for some people. At an extreme, students might consider taking time out of school, or devoting their adult lives to campaigning in the way that Greta Thunberg has done, but this too would be hugely disruptive to the course of their lives. Given the apparent severity of the crisis, as indicated by the best theories in the natural and social sciences, how to respond as an individual without becoming a pariah is a very difficult question.

One solution to this difficult question is to add information about how to bring about changes in the world. Studying the history of social and political movements, or cases where activism has been effective, could help to clarify some of the options available. Information about existing political systems and structures could provide means to support wide scale change without making exceptional personal sacrifices in the name of that change. Students might consider a career in a field which directly or indirectly contributes to solving the climate crisis, such as working on windfarm technology, as an environmental lawyer or working for a charity dealing with the climate crisis. Information about the efficacy of these roles would be useful too; not only in determining whether to aim to work in these areas, but also in assessing what routes there are to solving to crisis.

Despite all of the available theoretical content relating to the climate crisis that could be taught in schools, students are still going to be left with the task of working out their response to it. Schools should teach children the best available theories pertaining to the prominent and pressing questions they will have in response to the climate crisis, because children need to be armed to live in a world facing such a crisis. However, there is no simple readymade response to living in a world in crisis. Responses range from buying a bike and composting kitchen waste, to doing a PhD in chemistry and working to remove carbon dioxide from the atmosphere, to spending time campaigning, to living as carbon-neutral a life as possible, to apathy and ignoring the crisis. How we each answer this question, even when faced with all of the same information, involves the complex task of figuring out how all of the best available theories stand when considered as a whole.

This requires moral reasoning, but moral reasoning alone is not sufficient. In fact, moral reasoning and ethical theories are just one set of conceptual frameworks for dealing with the climate crisis. They too need to be assessed in relation to all of the other pertinent theoretical resources available. This is exemplified in tensions between ethical claims about monogamy and scientific claims about the propensity of people to act promiscuously. Some people argue that scientific claims negate moral claims. Meta-ethical theories such as the naturalistic fallacy proposed by Moore deal exactly with this conceptual confusion: how do theories about the natural world interact with moral theories? Moore's claim is that when people appeal to properties of the natural world and purport that these equate to moral facts, they are wrong, 'when they named those other properties, they were actually defining good; that these properties, in fact, were simply not "other" but absolutely and entirely the same with goodness' (Moore, 1993, p. 65). This is not to say that Moore has the final word on this relationship between natural properties and moral properties, the point is merely that moral theories do not solve the problem of fragmentation. They are another set of theories that need to be used appropriately when answering difficult questions. The field of meta-ethics addresses how these theories stand in relation to each other, and to other areas of inquiry.

So, in the case of the climate crisis, conceptual analysis is needed to work out what the natural sciences, the social sciences, history, literature and moral theories tell us about how to interact with the world. The sort of conceptual work needed includes asking which theories, or which class of theories hold most authority in relation to each question. Philosophy of science can help to think about the relative value of what theories from the natural sciences tell us about how to react to the climate crisis. Conceptual work is needed to ask whether the natural sciences are the only sources of authority in relation to the climate crisis. Arguably, other sources of information are also important, including theories about the history of social change, or literature about similar situations, for example Le Guin's *The Lathe of Heaven* (2001). If students are going to work out what to do with what they have been taught, they are also going to have to relate what they have learned to their own lives, their own values and their own hopes and fears. Since theories are taught with their own conceptual frameworks, there will always be conceptual work to do in order to match the available theories with other theories, and with one's own experiences to allow for effective interaction with the world.

The climate crisis is conceptually difficult because most of the questions it raises are highly interdisciplinary, drawing on a wide range of different theories, and also on the ordinary conceptual frameworks we often use when considering how to live our day to day lives.

Covid-19

The second example I will give is the crisis resulting from the Covid-19 pandemic. This is not only conceptually difficult because of its interdisciplinary nature, but also because it is, at the time of writing, a new problem with few well-established conceptual frameworks in place to discuss it. Three prominent and pressing questions arising from Covid-19 are: (1) What should governments be doing about it? (2) What should I be doing about it? and (3) What can I expect from the future? The third question draws on the natural, social and political sciences, and the history of pandemics in the past. The first question requires political, historical and scientific theories, but also requires a worked through ethical framework for balancing economic and health considerations. The third question also rests on scientific theories about how to manage the virus, but these require balancing against an understanding of our rights and duties as members of society. Again, these questions have normative elements. These normative elements contribute to the case for teaching philosophy outlined in Chapter 5 because philosophy is needed to address ordinary-concept questions such as those involving moral language. But normative skills and content are not sufficient; a further conceptual task is needed.

The Covid-19 crisis is interesting because almost everyone has found themselves in the situation of having a broad education into the best theories available in response to the pandemic, but having no pre-existing framework for piecing together some idea of how to interact effectively with the world now that it has changed. Most people who have had some broad theoretical education have been taught basic information about viruses, the history of plagues and pandemics, how to stay healthy, the healthcare system, liberty and politics, and the global economy. Despite this, we have all found ourselves struggling to weave together a coherent response to the crisis since weighing up everything we know against our values, what we hope for, our own safety, the safety of those we care about and our effectiveness as an agent, presents a huge conceptual challenge. The problem is new, and this means that work needs to be done by everyone simultaneously. It has been interesting to see that experts have struggled, or where they have presented clear opinions and answers, other experts have disagreed with them. A broad theoretical education is insufficient for answering new questions. Conceptual work is required to work out how theory ought to guide action.

Questions raised by Covid-19 are wide-ranging. Vaccine developers, medics, regulatory bodies, politicians, business owners, teachers, shop-workers, delivery drivers, dog-walkers, parents, children and the elderly are all examples of people who have had to make sense of what incoming news means to them, to judge whether that news is accurate, to build a working model for themselves of what is going on in the world, to make predictions about the future, to react appropriately to other people's views, to consider moral questions arising from the crisis and to use what they already know, their education and theoretical understanding of the world to interact effectively with it. The questions are not only about what should be done, but also how to do it and what options are available. Theoretical content can guide answers to these questions, and I imagine that people have appealed to their theoretical education for at least some understanding of solutions. However, people will have had to think hard about how the theoretical content they have acquired works in the current situation. This requires the conceptual task that I am describing, and that I think the discipline of philosophy can help with.

Combined, the three examples, drug use, the climate crisis and the Covid-19 pandemic, illustrate three situations where a broad theoretical education falls short of guiding effective interaction with the world. First, when a prominent and pressing question is posed in an ordinary-concept framework, theoretical conceptual frameworks need to be translated in response. This relates more clearly to the drug use example. Second, when a prominent and pressing question is highly interdisciplinary and different theoretical frameworks need to be considered simultaneously. This relates most clearly to the climate change example. Third, when a new prominent and pressing question arises and existing theoretical frameworks do not readily fit the issue at hand. This primarily relates to the Covid-19 example. These situations are not mutually exclusive, all of the examples discussed draw on ordinary conceptual frameworks and require interdisciplinary thinking. The climate crisis and the Covid-19 pandemic are also both relatively new. This highlights the fact that people are constantly facing new prominent and pressing questions that they will not have addressed in school or thought about before. Despite having a broad theoretical education, and potentially one which has already provided them with the best theories in response to the questions they face, answers about how to respond and act are not readily available. A further conceptual task is required.

Philosophy and the Conceptual Task

A broad theoretical education is fragmented into different theories, many of which are conceptually distinct from one another. These different conceptual frameworks cause problems when students are faced with questions arising from their own ordinary conceptual frameworks, when they are faced with interdisciplinary questions that draw answers from the different conceptual frameworks employed by different relevant theories or when they are faced with new questions where the appropriate conceptual frameworks for thinking about how to answer the questions have not yet been developed. Analytic philosophers including Midgley, Ryle, Strawson, Lowe and Jackson have proposed that this conceptual task falls within the disciplinary science of philosophy.

To return to Chapter 4, a broad theoretical education ought to provide students with the best available theories to address prominent and pressing questions. I have discussed how addressing prominent and pressing questions requires some conceptual work. This means that the conceptual work required to answer some questions is prominent and pressing in its own right. Conceptual work is a necessary step in addressing directly prominent and pressing questions, and so it is prominent and pressing too. Conceptual questions ought to be addressed by the curriculum if they are prominent and pressing. They ought to be addressed in such a way that the best available theoretical content is taught in response to them. The means for establishing whether something is the best available content is to take it from a disciplinary science which systematically studies the question(s) at hand. If philosophy is the disciplinary science that systematically studies conceptual questions, then relevant philosophical theories and methods ought to be taught as part of the school curriculum. In this section, I will show that at least some philosophers see themselves as systematically studying the conceptual problems arising from a broad theoretical education.

Ryle discusses the value of philosophy in relation to solving conceptual problems arising from interdisciplinary areas of study. He calls these 'inter-theory' questions:

> When intellectual positions are at cross-purposes ... the solution of their quarrel cannot come from any further internal corroboration of either position. The kind of thinking which advances biology is not the kind of thinking which settles the claims and counter-claims between biology and physics. These inter-theory questions are not questions internal to those theories. They are not biological or physical questions. They are philosophical questions. (Ryle, 1953, p. 13)

He diagnoses this interdisciplinary conceptual task as arising from the fact that different theories use different conceptual frameworks, but still share ordinary concepts whose precise meaning is not clearly fixed in the way that a theoretical concept would be. This means that:

> The most radical cross-purposes between specialist theories derive from the logical trickiness not of the highly technical concepts employed in them, but of the underlying non-technical concepts employed as well in them as in everyone else's thinking. Different travellers use different vehicles of highly intricate constructions and of very different makes for all the varying purposes of their very dissimilar journeys, and yet are alike in using the same public roads and the same signposts as one another … Usually, too, the traveller's doubts and mistakes about his bearings arise, not because anything in his private vehicle behaves awkwardly, but because the public road is a tricky road. (Ryle, 1953, pp. 12–13)

Ryle thinks that the conceptual problems can and ought to be solved by reaching clarity about the meaning of shared ordinary concepts. Since conceptual analysis, as practiced in analytic philosophy, often involves the systematic study of ordinary concepts, it is central to solving boundary disputes arising from interdisciplinary questions:

> What is often, although not very helpfully, described as 'the analysis of concepts', is rather an operation – if you like a 'synoptic' operation – of working out the parities and disparities of reasoning between arguments hinging on the concepts of one conceptual apparatus and arguments hinging on those of another. (Ryle, 1953, p. 129)

Ryle holds that classical philosophical problems and dilemmas in the philosophical canon serve as case studies of situations where different conceptual frameworks clash in obvious ways. Ryle goes through five dilemmas which he thinks play this role: the problem of freewill, Achilles and the tortoise, questions raised by the concept of pleasure, the relationship between 'the world of science and the everyday world' and questions about perception. When studying these, philosophers are directly engaged in the task of trying to solve boundary disputes between the different conceptual frameworks employed by different theories. The answers developed by philosophers, and the methodologies involved form the best available content for addressing the conceptual problems raised. In doing this, they are applying the content of a theoretical education to an interdisciplinary question. Ryle thinks that the dilemmas studied by philosophers are not interesting just for their own sake, but also because of what they reveal about similar conceptual difficulties that arise elsewhere.

In relation to the conceptual issues raised by the climate crisis, it is likely that Ryle would advocate examining the relationship between ordinary concepts and the different theories at play. If someone was to ask, 'how should I live my life, based on what I know about the climate crisis', Ryle would point out that the concept of 'should' is a tricky public road, which is used by a range of theories in different ways. The environmental activist, politician, economist, physicist or school child might all mean very different things by 'should', and it is only through working out some clear shared meaning, that any sort of answer to the question can be reached. As Ryle points out, there is plenty of existing philosophical work on the concept 'should' within the sub-disciplines of moral philosophy and ethics. Here, philosophers systematically examine the concept, providing a wealth of theoretical content.

Midgley sees a similar role for philosophy when it comes to conceptual questions like those arising from a theoretical education. She asks:

> What is the aim, the proper object of philosophising? What are we trying to do?
>
> We are not, of course, starting from nowhere, nor are we just riffling through ideas at random. We are always looking for something – a link, a connection, a context that will make sense of our present muddled notions. Thoughts that are not blundering around loose and detached need somehow to be drawn into a pattern.
>
> But this doesn't always work.
>
> Often we seem to be trying to resolve a complex jigsaw, one which has mistakenly brought together parts of several different pictures; trying to give a single shape to a manifold vision. Indeed, we are bound to keep doing this, because our minds are never quite empty at the start. They always contain incomplete world-pictures, frameworks to which loose scraps of experience and of various studies, such as geology, history, mathematics, astronomy and so forth, can be attached. And these various frameworks do not fit together spontaneously. (Midgley, 2018, pp. 3–4)

A theoretical education is fragmented in the way described by Midgley. When we face ordinary questions, interdisciplinary or new questions, we need to piece together our jigsaw of information and theories in a new way to reach an answer. Since different frameworks do not fit together spontaneously, this requires work. Although Midgley might be interpreted as claiming that the aim is to create a coherent body of knowledge within which all conceptual problems are solved, and theoretical frameworks are made consistent with one another, this need not be the case. Rather than attempting to complete the whole jigsaw, all that a theoretical education requires from conceptual analysis is the ability to look at a few jigsaw pieces at a time and work out how to fit them together in response to specific questions. Making a decision about attending a protest during the Covid-19 pandemic does not require a full understanding of the pandemic, but does require consideration of a range of factors in relation to the specific question. Midgley sees philosophy as directly engaged with this task.

Similarly, Strawson thinks that the solution to conceptual problems is to study the philosophy of different disciplinary sciences. He says that 'we have, besides history; the philosophy of history, besides natural science, the philosophy of natural science; besides mathematics, the philosophy of mathematics' (Strawson, 1992, p. 13). These philosophies provide answers to meta-questions about disciplines that arise when trying to work out how the different theories provided by theoretical education relate to one another, or relate to the prominent and pressing questions at hand. The philosophical canon in each of these areas of philosophy provides some answers about how to solve conceptual problems arising from a theoretical education. The philosophical canon provides examples of useful distinctions and classificatory schemes, which can go some way towards guiding students to appropriately deploy their theoretical education to answer conceptually puzzling questions.

Lowe describes the philosophical sub-discipline of metaphysics as the study of the sorts of conceptual problems raised by a theoretical education:

> One of the roles of metaphysics, as an intellectual discipline, is to provide a forum in which boundary disputes between other disciplines can be conducted – for instance, the dispute as to whether the subject-matter of a special science, such a psychology or economics, can be properly said to be subsumed under another, allegedly more 'fundamental' science, such as physics. According to one traditional and still widespread conception of metaphysics – which is basically the concept of metaphysics which informs the present book – metaphysics can occupy the interdisciplinary role described because its central concern is with the fundamental structure of reality as a whole. (Lowe, 2002, pp. 2–3)

According to Lowe, metaphysics involves the systematic study of the conceptual puzzles raised by the boundary disputes between different disciplines and theories which are:

> All concerned, at least in part, with the pursuit of truth, but pursue it according to their own methods of inquiry within their own domain. None the less, the indivisibility of truth means that all these forms of inquiry must, if they are to succeed in their aim, acknowledge the need to be consistent with each other. Nor can any one of them presume to adjudicate such questions of mutual consistency because none of them has any jurisdiction beyond its limited domain. Such adjudication can only be provided by practitioners of an intellectual discipline which aspires to complete universality in its subject matter and aims – and that discipline is metaphysics – traditionally conceived. (Lowe, 2002, p. 3)

Regardless of whether we accept the account of the unity of truth provided by Lowe, metaphysics remains the study of the relationships between different disciplines, theories and conceptual frameworks. If this is the case, then metaphysics is the systematic study of the conceptual problems arising from a theoretical education and since these pose prominent and pressing questions, whatever Lowe means by metaphysics ought to be included on the curriculum.

Finally, Jackson agrees that conceptual analysis is central to solving conceptual problems arising from a theoretical conflict:

> The role for conceptual analysis that I am defending in these lectures is the modest role: the role is that of addressing the question of what to say about matters described in one set of terms *given* a story about matters in another set of terms. Conceptual analysis is not being given a role in determining the fundamental nature of our world; it is, rather, being given a central role in determining what to say in less fundamental terms given an account of the world stated in more fundamental terms. (Jackson, 1998, p. 44)

A theoretical education provides students with many different descriptions of the world using different sets of terms. Jackson thinks that conceptual analysis is not necessarily about creating a holistic, true story about the fundamental nature of the world, but can more modestly be said to address conceptual difficulties which arise from the plurality of theories we have about the world around us. These conceptual difficulties map onto the conceptual difficulties raised by a theoretical education.

These accounts of the nature of some fields of analytic philosophy lend credence to the view that the discipline of philosophy is, at least in part, concerned with the systematic study of the sorts of conceptual difficulties raised by a theoretical education. This is sufficient to ground the claim that philosophical content is the best available content to answer this set of prominent and pressing questions that students will face. It is sufficient because the best answers to questions come from areas where those questions have been systematically studied; philosophy is the only discipline that involves the systematic study of conceptual problems arising from the plurality of conceptual schemes taught in schools. Teaching philosophy in schools with this aim in mind is needed to help students to interact effectively with the world whenever they are faced with conceptual problems.

My claim is that the discipline of philosophy is unique in its study of conceptual problems arising from the nature of human inquiry. A student being taught a broad theoretical education is bound to run into these conceptual problems. When faced with these, they will need to solve the conceptual problems if they are to make full use of their theoretical education to interact effectively with certain aspects of the world. Philosophers have a well-developed arsenal of tools and theories about how to deal with conceptual difficulties. This stems from a systematic study of various different conceptual difficulties, both abstract and applied, over the history of the discipline. Teaching children a course in philosophy is the best available way of arming them to be able to deal with conceptual difficulties on their own.

A Philosophy Course for Addressing Conceptual Problems

In principle, it seems that there is theoretical content from the discipline of philosophy that is best suited to solving the conceptual problems raised by a theoretical education. In this section, I will return to the examples of drug use, the climate crisis, and the Covid-19 pandemic to explore some philosophical content that could help students to effectively interact with these aspects of the world in light of their theoretical education. For each issue, I will outline some areas of philosophy that are relevant, and one dilemma or thought experiment that explores a conceptual issue at play. Again, it is worth bearing in mind that there is considerable overlap with the argument for teaching philosophy to address ordinary concept questions. This is because ordinary concepts play a role in all of these questions, alongside problems that result from conceptual fragmentation.

I do not want to claim that philosophy has direct answers available to students' conceptual difficulties. The conceptual difficulties are very complex, will change from one student to another, and when they are new, they are unpredictable. The best that schools can do is teach students how to deal with these sorts of questions, and acquaint them with relevant theoretical content where some is available. As in other areas of inquiry, the theoretical content available from philosophy takes the form of a plurality of different theories. There are no straightforward solutions to the conceptual difficulties presented by a theoretical education; there is, however, guidance taken from a field of systematic study of those questions.

Drug Use

The first example is the student at a party who is considering smoking cannabis for the first time. In this case, the student might struggle to understand how to square what they have learned at school with the immediate decision at hand. It is also an interdisciplinary question, drawing on a range of different theories from disciplines such as physiology, chemistry, economics, geography, politics, law, ethics and arts and literature. I propose that a student who has studied a basic introduction to ethics, philosophy of law and philosophy of science would be better equipped to answer this question than someone who had not. This is partially because of the ordinary concept elements of the question, but it is also because of the conceptual problems posed by the fragmentation between disciplinary content and the student's immediate concerns and experiences.

Since drug use involves ordinary concept questions, an introduction to ethics would begin to address these. Alongside basic discussions about the meaning of moral concepts, this would draw on constructive theories including the three dominant categories of ethical theories: deontological theories, consequentialist theories and virtue ethics theories. In doing so, the student would start to consider the consequences of their actions on others, and their duties towards themselves and to others. A virtue ethics approach would help them to think about what it is to live a good life, and whether drug use can play a role in that good life. In covering these theories, they would be prompted to think about their values and what matters to them using a technical language which facilitates clearer reasoning.

In response to conceptual problems arising between different ethical theories, they should study relativism in order to ask whether ethical theories should be taken seriously and which theories are more appropriate to the question being asked.

Next, there are conceptual problems arising from the interplay between different disciplines. An introduction to philosophy of law would help students to explore the purpose of laws about drugs, whether following the law is a moral obligation, whether the law always tracks morality, and questions about how they want society to look and what they can do to influence laws that they disagree with.

Studying an introduction to philosophy of science would help students to consider the relationship between scientific and medical studies about cannabis in relation to themselves. Studying the concept of 'evidence' in science, and 'truth' when it comes to scientific theories might help them to consider their attitude towards the science of cannabis use.

Furthermore, it would be useful to introduce students to contemporary literature on the philosophy of drug use, such as Lovering's work on the topic published in *Philosophy Now* (Lovering, 2016), a journal aimed at the general public. Lovering examines common arguments against drug use, and questions whether they lead to the conclusion that drug use is immoral. He asks whether the fact that drug use can harm health makes it wrong, whether the idea that drug use is unnatural would make drug use wrong, whether the idea that drug use suppresses personal autonomy makes it wrong, or whether using drugs shows a disregard for the self. Exploring these questions exemplifies the conceptual work required to make sense of how to apply a broad theoretical education to the question of cannabis use.

Another source of theoretical material about drug use comes from relevant dilemmas. Ryle thinks that a well-chosen dilemma highlights and explores relevant conceptual problems. One such dilemma is exemplified by Roger Crisp's thought experiment of the Haydn and the Oyster. Crisp asks us to:

> Imagine you are a soul, waiting to be allocated a life. You are offered either the life of the composer, Joseph Haydn, or that of an oyster. Haydn's life is quite long, involving great success and enjoyment. The life of the oyster consists only in the most simple and primitive pleasurable experience possible. Of course, you ask for the life of Haydn; but you are then told that the life of the oyster can be as long as you like – millions of years, if you so desire. (Crisp 1997, pp. 10–11)

This thought experiment helps students to focus on the concept of the good life, considering the value of pleasurable experiences in contrast to success and fulfilment. A focused discussion on this issue clarifies the ordinary concept of a good life, and whether drug use can be part of a good life. Furthermore, studying the literature about this question helps students to see different possible answers, their strengths and shortcomings, and different ways of reasoning about conceptual problems.

All of this theoretical content is useful when it comes to working out how to translate a broad theoretical education into effective interaction with the world in a conceptually complex situation. Since readymade answers do not exist when it comes to the precise situation the student is facing, the best available content in response to their situation is a set of theories and guided thought about how to balance all of the competing considerations at hand. This is offered by areas systematically studied by philosophers, and could be taught as part of a philosophy course in schools.

The Climate Crisis

Theoretical content associated with the discipline of philosophy can also help students to answer questions about the climate crisis.

Again, an introduction to ethics would help to work out what to value and how to live a good life. This is relevant to questions about how they ought to live, what they ought to avoid doing and what they can permissibly do even if they know it might have a negative effect on the environment. It will help them to explore their duties to themselves and others, and how to balance this with considerations about the consequences of their actions.

An introduction to the philosophy of science will help students to assess the status of different scientific theories about climate change. Studying political philosophy will allow students to consider the role of the state, and its limitations. They will be able to consider the value of personal liberty and autonomy against the welfare of society as a whole. This sort of exploration, even if not directly about the climate crisis, will equip students with theoretical content which will help them to tease out different issues and develop answers to them.

One dilemma which highlights a relevant conceptual problem is Parfit's discussion of future lives and the non-identity question. Since the climate crisis requires us to consider the consequences of our actions for future generations, we also need some understanding of how to balance our duties to future generations with our duties towards existing people. Furthermore, there is growing disquiet about the idea of having children in an increasingly uncertain world. The anti-natalism movement questions the morality of bringing new lives into a world where their quality of life might be significantly reduced, and where the act of reproducing places even more pressure on the environment. Parfit presents three thought experiments which explore this conceptual space:

> Ruth, who is pregnant, knows that, unless she takes some painless treatment, the child she is carrying would have some disease that would kill this child at the age of forty. If Ruth takes this treatment, this child would live to eighty.

Sarah must decide whether to have a child. Sarah knows that any child whom she conceives would have this same disease, and would live to only forty. She also knows that, because this disease would have no earlier effects, any such child's life would be likely to be well worth living. Sarah and her husband strongly want to have a child, and there is no existing child whom they could adopt.

Clare knows that, if she conceives some child now, this child would have this same disease, and would live to only forty. If Clare waits for two months, she would later conceive a child who would not have this disease, and would live to eighty. (Parfit, 2017, p. 121)

These cases highlight conceptual problems. First, it seems that Ruth has a duty to take a painless treatment to improve her child's future life. Second, Sarah seems justified in bringing a child into the world, even if that child would have a shortened life, so long as that child's life was worth living. The difficulty is Clare's case; Clare decides not to bring one potential child into the world, but decides to bring a second potential child into the world instead. This is clearly bad for the first potential child, who she could conceive now but chooses not to. Between them, these cases explore questions about how we make choices about having children. We are led to discuss whether we have any duties to future lives, whether we ought to have children, whether choosing not to conceive causes any sort of harm or benefits. Despite presenting no clear answers, this is the beginning of the systematic study of questions about having children arising from the climate crisis.

The Covid-19 Pandemic

Recent events bring into focus questions about the adequacy of education in response to the current pandemic. I have proposed that some education in philosophy would help us to better interact with the changes we are currently seeing in the world. The question I need to answer is: What philosophical content do I think we should all have been taught in schools to help us to deal with the current pandemic? Most of the questions that policymakers, politicians and the public have dealt with have involved the tension between the economy, political freedom, individual liberty, the nature of scientific inquiry and questions about the good life. Like the previous questions, an education in ethics, political philosophy, philosophy of science and epistemology would have helped many people to at least begin to piece together other relevant parts of their theoretical education to help them to effectively interact with the world.

For example, many of us have had our first real experience of watching scientific inquiry in action. Uncertainty about the possibility of a vaccine, debates about standards for vaccine approval, conspiracies about vaccine development and reluctance to trust scientists has all been brought to the fore of public debate. Philosophy of science has a lot of say about how theories develop, how inquiry can move both backwards and forwards in the search for answers, how to interpret evidence and when to hold that a scientific theory is true or at least a good tool for making technological progress. This could help people to manage their expectations, without trusting too much to quick scientific progress, nor losing hope in science altogether. It also seems fairly clear that an introduction to deontological, consequentialist and virtue ethics would help people to think about the sacrifices they have been asked to make in relation to broader outcomes.

Another conceptual problem in relation to Covid-19 has involved different discourses about the pandemic, including conspiracy theorists' responses to the crisis. Epistemological work is needed to work out how to treat these different approaches to the pandemic. Questions about authority and testimony are important for selecting who to listen to and what to make of what they say. Furthermore, questions about how to weigh up political versus scientific beliefs come into play, with anti-maskers sometimes arguing that scientific knowledge about Covid-19 is inadequate to justify restricting liberty. Then there are questions about what we mean by 'truth' and 'fake news', which are relevant to how we listen to and respond to what the media, politicians, scientists and social-influencers are telling us.

One example of a relevant dilemma that would help people to think about the pandemic is Rawls' veil of ignorance. Here, Rawls asks us to consider how we would set out social and political institutions if we were in a situation where we did not know what sort of circumstances we would be born into. This sort of reasoning is designed to develop a just society. It focuses attention on conceptual difficulties arising from the newness of current events and their interdisciplinary nature: What should our priorities be? Will they be fair? How are new policies effecting all members of society, including those who are already underrepresented? Should countries protect their own citizens first, or cooperate to find a global solution? How should we change society in light or what has happened? Rawls's veil of ignorance thought experiment focuses discussion on a narrow area of conceptual difficulty and allows people to clarify the terms of the debate. This can help facilitate decision-making.

Between the three examples, what emerges is that many different areas of philosophy can be useful when it comes to the conceptual problems raised by the combination of theoretical education and the need to interact with the world. If the findings of Chapter 5 are added, then further philosophical content concerned with the analysis of a broad range of ordinary concepts also has a place on the curriculum. Additionally, the methods, tools, or skills associated with philosophical thinking and integral to learning about philosophical theories are a central part of learning how to move from the theories acquired during a broad theoretical education to effective interaction with the world in conceptually complicated cases.

Conclusion

A theoretical education, understood as an education that aims to provide students with theoretical content to help them to interact effectively with the world, falls short of meeting its aims unless students are helped to solve conceptual problems which arise from the conceptually fragmented nature of human inquiry. Disciplines employ different conceptual schemes, different theories define concepts differently too and so become conceptually fragmented from one another. This conceptual fragmentation raises questions for students about how to use what they have been taught to answer the prominent and pressing questions they are faced with. Since solving conceptual problems is a necessary condition for answering some prominent and pressing questions, these conceptual problems track the prominent and pressing nature of the initial questions they arise from. There are aspects of the discipline of philosophy that can help students to navigate these conceptual problems. Since philosophy is often conceived as the systematic study of both ordinary concepts, and conceptual problems, it is either well-placed, or the best placed discipline to play this role. I conclude with the proposal that, primarily for practical reasons, students should be taught a broad introductory philosophy course.

This chapter also completes my analysis of theoretical education:

(1) Acquiring a broad array of theoretical content amounts to acquiring different ways of understanding the world;
(2) Different ways of understanding the world contribute to a person's ability to act effectively within the world if, and only if they are applied, and applied appropriately;

(3) Providing students with the ability to act effectively within the world is a justifiable aim of education.

This analysis of theoretical education justifies teaching a broad introductory philosophy course at some point during a students' theoretical education in order to meet the aim of helping students to interact effectively with the world.

Conclusion

Given the variety and range of theoretical content from the discipline of philosophy that has been identified as important to a theoretical education, I propose that schools should teach any student undertaking a theoretical education an introductory course focusing on conceptual analysis taken from the discipline of philosophy at some point during their theoretical education.

Teaching a discrete, focused, philosophy course is advantageous over alternatives, such as embedding philosophy in other lessons, for a number of reasons. First, it allows for the recruitment of subject-specialists to teach a complex discipline. Second, it is not possible to select conceptual problems and teach students clear answers to them. Clear answers do not exist; instead, the best available theoretical content is pluralistic and requires independent thinking, which needs to be taught. Third, the sort of independent thinking needed is best developed through practice, for example, by tackling the sorts of dilemmas promoted by Ryle. Finally, disciplinary sciences are convenient vectors for teaching theoretical content. They contextualize it, and set out clearly the standards it is subjected to by specialists. This is important for teaching philosophy too.

This discrete approach to philosophy teaching is exemplified by the French *Baccalaureat*, and secondary education systems influenced by it, including the International Baccalaureate's *Theory of Knowledge* course. In these cases, the course is taught during students' last two years of school, which is sufficient to help students to make good use of their theoretical education as they leave school.

Another precedent for teaching philosophy in schools in a more limited but similar way is the A-level in Religious Studies taught in schools in the UK. This is limited because it only covers one area of conceptual difficulties, namely those arising from religious beliefs. However, in doing do, the course draws on broad philosophical content, including a range of theories, dilemmas and skills. Since there are many more conceptual difficulties arising from a theoretical education and from students' ordinary lives than just religious ones, this sort of treatment of conceptual difficulties ought to be much broader in schools.

The sort of course taught in schools should be a discrete, focused course looking at (1) the meanings of ordinary concepts; (2) theories developed in response to ordinary concept questions; (3) conceptual difficulties arising from the need to consider conceptually diverse theoretical frameworks alongside one another and in relation to ordinary concerns and (4) existing philosophical theories that attempt to clarify applied conceptual difficulties. The best available theoretical content, as it stands, consists of a plurality of different philosophical theories, analyses, dilemmas, applied answers, dialogues and thought-experiments. The discipline of philosophy can also provide the methods and tools for engaging in philosophical inquiry in order to sort through philosophical content. Any course taught in schools ought to mirror this disciplinary complexity, whilst ensuring that it aims to meet the educational good of effective interaction with the world. Practically speaking, a discrete philosophy course is best placed to meet this aim.

The recommendation that schools introduce a discrete introductory philosophy course would require some investment. This might not be as drastic as it first seems. It is likely that many schools already have teachers with some philosophical training. For example, in English schools many Religious Education teachers have philosophy degrees. Alternatively, schools could bring in external specialists to run courses for them if need be. Organizations such as *SAPERE* might be well placed to provide some of the expertise if required. However, overall it would be better to have philosophy specialists embedded within schools, to reflect the centrality of philosophy teaching in theoretical education. It should not be taught as some tagged-on extracurricular activity, but as essential to meeting the aims of education.

Furthermore, the conclusion that schools are broadly justified in following a discipline-based broad theoretical education means that I am not advocating for wholesale changes to the curriculum, only the addition of an introductory philosophy course at some point over the course of students' theoretical education. Given the importance of teaching philosophy to make sense of a theoretical education, and to provide students with guidance about ordinary concept problems, some investment in specialist philosophy teaching is urged.

In summary, this book provides a rationale for why philosophy should be on the curriculum. It is a response to an absence of systematic thinking about teaching philosophy in schools. The hope is that the conclusions reached, or at least the discussions presented along the way, will help to advocate for teaching philosophy in schools. Philosophy is not just a valuable addition to the curriculum, but a central part of any education. If this conclusion is accepted then it straightforwardly follows that philosophy ought to be included on school curricula, even if finding curriculum space for it might be difficult.

In summary, in Chapter 1 I provide an overview of the history of philosophy teaching in schools and its current status. This is followed in Chapter 2 by a discussion of different arguments for teaching philosophy in schools. While there is a large body of literature on Philosophy for Children (P4C), I argue that the reasons given for bringing P4C into schools do not transfer very well to the case for a broader, more disciplinary approach to teaching philosophy. Other arguments for teaching philosophy in schools require development in order to substantiate their conclusions. Furthermore, a developed account of the aims of education and the role of the curriculum is needed to ground a good argument for teaching philosophy in schools. This argument needs to appeal to the aims of education, and explain why philosophy is well placed to meet those aims.

Curriculum guidance is important because many children spend large amounts of their time in compulsory education. If the curriculum they follow is poorly thought through or educational activities are not justified, then this time spent in schools is at worst, a waste of their time, or at best, a sub-optimal use of their time. An argument for including philosophy in schools needs to be able to appeal to why philosophy is a good use of students' time. This requires an appeal to some education goods that teaching philosophy can provide students with, and some reasons why teaching philosophy is the optimal way of providing those educational goods.

In Chapter 3, I explore the nature and aims of theoretical education. A theoretical education is one which focuses on informing students about the world. This sort of education has dominated the history of schooling, and continues to dominate policy today. This means that, for the most part, schools spend at least some of their time providing students with a theoretical education. I ask why this might be the case, and explore possible justifications of teaching a broad theoretical curriculum. Much of the existing discussion of theoretical education focuses on the idea of a liberal education which is often described as a broad and balanced theoretical education. I conclude that further work is needed on the nature and aims of theoretical education.

This is the task tackled in Chapter 4, where I argue that a broad theoretical education aims to help students to interact effectively with the world by providing them with the best available theoretical content in response to the prominent and pressing questions that they are likely to face. This analysis of the aims of theoretical education yields basic curriculum guidance. A theoretical curriculum should deal first and foremost with the sorts of questions students are likely to face in their lives, and it should be pluralistic, drawing on the broad spectrum of the best available theories in response to these questions. Nonetheless, I argue that following a discipline-based approach to the curriculum is justified given the importance of disciplinary standards, the value of contextualising theories and role these disciplinary standards and contexts play in helping students to come to fully understand theories. I characterize a discipline as the systematic study of a set of related questions about the world.

In the latter half of Chapter 4, I argue that a theoretical education provides valuable educational goods. Furthermore, the sorts of goods provided are those which ground other possible goods. Framed in terms of Rawlsian goods, effective interaction with the world is a primary good, which facilitates acquisition of other goods. Since a theoretical education provides educational goods, which play a role in broader conceptions of the good life, such as flourishing, all students ought to be provided with at least some theoretical education. Informing students about the world around them is an important aim of education, and curriculum time ought to be spent on it.

This groundwork about the nature and aims of theoretical education provides the basis for two arguments for teaching philosophy in schools. It does so by specifying the aims of education, so that these can be appealed to by any argument for teaching philosophy. It also does this by providing a basis for establishing whether philosophy is best placed to meet these aims. Philosophy would be best placed if it offered the best available theories in response to questions; and the best available theories are those that are sourced from a discipline which systematically studies the questions at hand. An argument for teaching philosophy in schools needs to identify prominent and pressing questions that need answering, and then philosophical content which is best placed to answer those questions. Since all students ought to be taught some theoretical education, if such an argument can be provided, then all students ought to be taught some philosophy at some point during their education.

The first argument that I provide for teaching philosophy in schools is that there is a range of prominent and pressing ordinary-concept questions. Philosophy systematically studies ordinary concepts, and so is well placed to help students to answer these questions. I demonstrate how studying ordinary concepts using the philosophical canon can provide constructive ways of answering prominent and pressing ordinary questions.

The second argument for teaching philosophy in schools identifies a set of conceptual problems arising from any theoretical education. These are problems caused by the different conceptual schemes employed by different theories. I explain that these problems are particularly likely to arise when students are asked to translate between ordinary-concept questions and theoretical answers; when students are faced with interdisciplinary questions; and when students are faced with new questions which lack established conceptual frameworks. In many cases, these problems overlap with one another. I argue that philosophy is often understood as the systematic study of conceptual problems which track those raised by a broad theoretical education. I also identify a range of philosophical content taken from the disciplinary canon which helps students to tackle these conceptual problems.

Together, these two arguments make the case for teaching a broad introduction to philosophy at some point during a child's education. A broad introduction to philosophy would help students to interact effectively with the world in two ways: first, by helping them to think clearly and systematically about ordinary-concept questions and second, by helping them to navigate conceptual problems caused by the nature of a theoretical education. Both of these roles for philosophy answer to the aims of theoretical education, and since these aims are well-founded, they extend to an argument for teaching all children some philosophy.

Since philosophy as a discipline is the main place where ordinary concepts, and conceptual problems are systematically studied, philosophy provides at least some of the best available theoretical content in response to a set of prominent and pressing questions which schools ought to help students to answer. While further work is needed to develop a detailed philosophy course to meet these curriculum needs, this provides a robust case for teaching philosophy in schools.

I conclude that students ought to be taught philosophy in schools. Philosophy courses should not shy away from the philosophical canon, nor should they focus exclusively on thinking skills. The discipline of philosophy has substantive theoretical content which ought to sit at the heart of any theoretical curriculum. Philosophy is a discipline in its own right, with its own standards and instruments of inquiry, and it ought to be taught as such, including the skills and tools that philosophy as a discipline rests on. I have argued that a theoretical education is incomplete without some education in philosophy. Philosophy ought to be taught, because, without it, any theoretical curriculum is suboptimal. Since many students take part in compulsory schooling, using their time in a suboptimal way, when an easy solution is available, is unjustified. In conclusion, philosophy ought to be taught in schools.

References

Adler, M., and Mayer, M. (1958). *The Revolution in Education*, Chicago: University of Chicago Press.

Adler, M. J. (1940). *How to Read a Book*, London: Jarrolds.

Aldrich, R. (1988). 'The National Curriculum: An Historical Perspective', in D. Lawton and C. Chitty (eds), *The National Curriculum*, London: Institute of Education, pp. 21–33.

Alexander, H. (2007). 'What Is Common about Common Schooling? Rational Autonomy and Moral Agency in Liberal Democratic Education', *Journal of Philosophy of Education*, 41(4), pp. 609–24.

Arnold, M. (1962). *Democratic Education*, Toronto: University of Michigan Press.

Attwater, D. (1927). 'Athenian Education', *Irish Monthly*, 55(645), pp. 132–7.

Bailey, C. (1984). *Beyond the Present and the Particular*, London: Routledge & Kegan Paul.

Bialystok, L. (2017). 'Philosophy across the Curriculum and the Question of Teacher Capacity; or What Is Philosophy and Who Can Teach It?' *Journal of Philosophy of Education*, 51(4), pp. 817–36.

Bonnet, M., and Cuypers, S. (1998). 'Autonomy and Authenticity in Education', in M. Blake, P. Smeyers, R. Smith and P. Standish (eds), *The Blackwell Guide to Philosophy of Education*, Oxford: Blackwell Publishing, pp. 326–40.

Bradley, B. (2002). 'Is Intrinsic Value Conditional?' *Philosophical Studies*, 107, pp. 23–44.

Brandt, R. (1988). 'On Philosophy in the Curriculum: A Conversation with Matthew Lipman'. *Educational Leadership*, 46(1), pp. 34–7.

Brighouse, H. (2006). *On Education*, London: Routledge.

Brighouse, H. (2019). *'How Can We Understand "Liberal Arts Education?"'* available at: https://mellon.org/news-blog/articles/how-can-we-understand-liberal-arts-education/ (accessed 5 March 2020).

Brighouse, H., Ladd, H., Loeb, S. and Swift, A. (2018). *Educational Goods*, Chicago: University of Chicago Press.

Brighouse, H., and Schouten, G. (2014). 'To Charter or Not to Charter: What Questions Should We Ask and What Will the Answers Tell Us?' *Harvard Educational Review*, 84(3), pp. 341–64.

Briseid, O., and Caillods, F. (2004). *Trends in Secondary Education in Industrialized Countries: Are They Relevant for African countries?* Paris: International Institute for Educational Planning.

Buchanan, A. (1980). 'Rawls on Justice as Fairness', in G. Blocker and E. Smith (eds), *John Rawls' Theory of Social Justice: An Introduction*, Athens: Ohio University Press, pp. 5–11.

Burnet, J. (1936). *Aristotle on Education*, Cambridge: Cambridge University Press.

Cam, P. (1995). *Thinking Together*. Sydney, NSW: Primary English Teaching Association and Hale & Iremonger.

Canguilhem, G. (1953). 'The Teaching of Philosophy in France', in G. Canguilhem (ed.), *The Teaching of Philosophy: An International Inquiry of UNESCO*, Paris: UNESCO, pp. 17–27.

Carlsmith, C. (2002). 'Struggling toward Success: Jesuit Education in Italy, 1540–1600', *History of Education Quarterly*, 42(2), pp. 215–46.

Carr, D. (2009). 'Curriculum and the Value of Knowledge', in H. Siegel (ed.), *The Oxford Handbook of Philosophy of Education*, Oxford: Oxford University Press, pp. 281–99.

Carr, W (ed.). (2005). 'Philosophy and Education', in *The Routledge Falmer Reader in Philosophy of Education*, Oxford: Routledge, pp. 34–49.

Chalmers, A. F. (1978). *What Is This Thing Called Science*, Milton Keynes: London University Press.

Clayton, M., and Stevens, D. (2018). 'What Is the Point of Religious Education?' *Theory and Research in Education*, 16(1), pp. 65–81.

Collingwood, R. G. (1940). *An Essay on Metaphysics*, Oxford: Clarendon Press.

Collingwood, R. G. (1999). *The Principles of History*, Oxford: Oxford University Press.

Conway, D. (2010). *Liberal Education and the National Curriculum*, London: Civitas.

Corbeill, A. (2001). 'Education In the Roman Republic: Creating Traditions', in Y. Lee Too (ed.), *Education in Greek and Roman Antiquity*, Boston: Brill, pp. 261–87.

Core Knowledge. (2016). *The Core Knowledge Foundation 2016 Annual Impact Report*, available at: https://www.coreknowledge.org/wp-content/uploads/2017/10/CKF-Annual-Report-2016.pdf (accessed 13 October 2020).

Crisp, R. (1997). 'Introduction', in J. S. Mill (ed.), *Utilitarianism*, London: Oxford University Press.

Dewey, J. (1910). *How We Think*, Boston: DC Heath.

Dewey, J. (1916). *Democracy and Education: An Introduction to the Philosophy of Education*, New York: Macmillan.

Dewey, J. (1967a). 'The Child and the Curriculum', in M. Dworkin (ed.), *Dewey on Education: Selections*, New York: Teachers College Press, pp. 91–111.

Dewey, J. (1967b). 'My Pedagogic Creed', in M. Dworkin (ed.), *Dewey on Education: Selections*, New York: Teachers College Press, pp. 19–32.

DfE. (2019). *Relationships Education, Relationships and Sex Education (RSE) and Health Education: Draft Statutory Guidance for Governing Bodies, Proprietors, Head Teachers, Principals, Senior Leadership Teams, Teachers*, available at: https://assets.publishing.service.gov.uk/government/uploads/system/uploads/attachment_data/file/781150/

Draft_guidance_Relationships_Education__Relationships_and_Sex_Education__RSE__and_Health_Education2.pdf (accessed 9 July 2019).

Droit, R. (1995). *Philosophy and Democracy in the World: A UNESCO Survey*, Paris: UNESCO.

Edexcel. (2015). *GCSE (9–1) History Specification*, available at: https://qualifications.pearson.com/content/dam/pdf/GCSE/History/2016/specification-and-sample-assessments/GCSE_History_(9-1)_Specification_Issue_2.pdf (accessed 10 September 2019).

Elgin, C. (2007). 'Understanding and the Facts', *Philosophical Studies*, 132, pp. 33–42.

Elgin, C. (2012). 'Understanding's Tethers', in C. Jaeger and W. Loeftke (eds), *Epistemology: Contexts, Values and Disagreements*, Kirchberg: De Gruyter, pp. 131–46.

Elliott, V. (2021). *Knowledge in English Canon, Curriculum and Cultural Literacy*, Abingdon: Routledge.

Elungu, P. (1980). *Philosophy in Zaire: Consultation on Teaching and Research in Philosophy in Africa*, Paris: UNESCO.

Fensi, X. (1986). 'China', in UNESCO (ed.), *Teaching and Research in Philosophy: Asia and the Pacific*, Paris: UNESCO, pp. 80–8.

Ferrar, F. W. (1868). *Essays on a Liberal Education*, London: Macmillan.

Fisher, R. (2008). *Teaching Thinking: Philosophical Inquiry in the Classroom*, London: Bloomsbury.

Gatley, J. (2020a). 'The Educational Value of Analytic Philosophy', *Journal of the American Philosophical Association*, 7(1), pp. 59–77, doi: 10.1017/apa.2020.9.

Gatley, J. (2020b). 'Philosophy for Children and the Extrinsic Value of Philosophy', *Metaphilosophy*, 51(4), pp. 548–63, doi: 10.1111/meta.12445.

Gatley, J. (2020c). 'A Utility Account of Liberal Education', *Philosophy of Education*, 74(2), pp. 28–38, available at: https://www.philofed.org/copy-of-issue-2.

Gatley, J. (2021). 'Intrinsic Value and Educational Value', *Journal of Philosophy of Education*, 55(4-5), pp. 675–87, doi: 10.1111/1467-9752.12555.

Gatley, J., Woodhouse, E. and Forstenzer, J. (2020). 'Youth Philosophy Conferences and the Development of Adolescent Social Skills', *Precollege Philosophy and Public Practice Journal*, 1(2), pp. 107–25.

Gaudin, P. (2016). 'Neutrality and Impartiality in Public Education: The French Investment in Philosophy, Teaching About Religions, and Moral and Civic Education', *British Journal of Religious Education*, 39(1), pp. 93–106.

Gettier, E. L. (1963). 'Is Justified True Belief Knowledge?' *Analysis*, 23, pp. 121–3.

Giannopoulou, Z. (2019). 'Plato: Theaetatus', in *Internet Encyclopedia of Philosophy*, available at: https://iep.utm.edu/theatetu/ (assessed 9 October 2019).

Glock, H. (2008). *What is Analytic Philosophy*, Cambridge: Cambridge University Press.

Gorard, S, Siddiqui, N. and See, B. H. (2015). *Philosophy for Children: SAPERE*, Evaluation Report and Executive Summary, EEF.

Gov.uk. (2014). *Statutory Guidance National Curriculum in England: English Programmes of Study*, available at: https://www.gov.uk/government/publications/national-curriculum-in-england-english-programmes-of-study (accessed 23 February 2017).

Gov.uk. (2016). *The National Curriculum*, available at: https://www.gov.uk/national-curriculum/key-stage-1-and-2 (accessed 12 January 2017).

Gove, M. (2009). *What Is Education For*, Speech to the Royal Society for the Arts, available at: https://www.thersa.org/globalassets/pdfs/blogs/gove-speech-to-rsa.pdf (accessed 3 August 2019).

Greco, J., and Sosa, E. (1999) *The Blackwell Guide to Epistemology*, Oxford: Blackwell.

Gregory, M., Haynes, J. and Murris, K. (2016). *The Routledge International Handbook of Philosophy for Children*, London: Routledge.

Gutmann, A. (1987). *Democratic Education*, Princeton: Princeton University Press.

Gutting, G. (2009). *What Philosophy Can Do*, New York: W.W. Norton.

Hand, M. (2006a). 'Against Autonomy as an Educational Aim', *Oxford Review of Education*, 32(4), pp. 535–50.

Hand, M. (2006b). *Is Religious Education Possible?* London: Bloomsbury.

Hand, M. (2010). 'On the Worthwhileness of Theoretical Activities', *Journal of Philosophy of Education*, 43(1), pp. 109–21.

Hand, M. (2018a). 'On The Distinctive Educational Value of Philosophy', *Journal of Philosophy in Schools*, 5(1), pp. 4–19.

Hand, M. (2018b). *A Theory of Moral Education*, London: Routledge, Taylor & Francis Group.

Hand, M., and Winstanley, C. (2008). *Philosophy in Schools*, London: Continuum.

Haslanger, S. (2012). *Resisting Reality: Social Construction and Social Critique*, Oxford: Oxford University Press.

Haynes, J. (2008). *Children as Philosophers: Learning through Enquiry and Dialogue in the Primary Classroom*, London: Routledge.

Haynes, J., and Murris, K. (2011). 'The Provocation of an Epistemological Shift in Teacher Education through Philosophy with Children', *Journal of Philosophy of Education*, 45(2), pp. 285–303.

Hirsch, E. D. (1984). *Cultural Literacy*, Conference Paper at National Institute of Education, Washington: Adult Literacy Conference.

Hirsch, E. D. (2017). *Why Knowledge Matters*, Cambridge, MA: Harvard University Press.

Hirsch, E. D. (2020). *Core Knowledge*, available at: https://www.coreknowledge.org (accessed 14 October 2020).

Hirst, P., and Peters R. (1970). *The Logic of Education*, London: Routledge and Kegan Paul.

Hirst, P. (1973). 'Liberal Education and the Nature of Knowledge', in R. S. Peters (ed.), *The Philosophy of Education*, London: Oxford University Press, pp. 87–110.

Hirst, P (ed.) (1974). 'Liberal Education and the Nature of Knowledge', in *Knowledge and the Curriculum*, pp. 30–53.

Hirst, P. (1993). 'Education, Knowledge and Practices', in B. Robin and W. Patricia (eds), *Beyond Liberal Education*, London: Routledge, pp. 184–99.

Hobbs, A. (2018). 'Philosophy and the Good Life', *Journal of Philosophy in Schools*, 5(1), pp. 20–37.

Hospers, J. (1990). *An Introduction to Philosophical Analysis*, Oxford: Blackwell.

Hountondji, P. J. (1984). 'Aspects and Problems of Philosophy in Africa', in UNESCO (ed.), *Teaching and Research in Philosophy: Africa*, Paris: UNESCO.

Huxley, T. (1868). 'Liberal Education and Where to Find It', in H. Thomas (ed.), *Collected Essays Volume 3: Science and Education*, Cambridge: Cambridge University Press, pp. 81–2.

IBO. (2017a). *International Baccalaureate, Theory of Knowledge Syllabus Outline*, available at: http://www.ibo.org/programmes/diploma-programme/curriculum/theory-of-knowledge/ (accessed 20 August 2017).

IBO. (2017b). *Philosophy Guide*, available at: https://www.fjuhsd.org/cms/lib/CA02000098/Centricity/Domain/233/Philosophy%20guide%20exams%20from%202016.pdf (accessed 13 October 2020).

IBO. (2019). *What Is ToK*, available at: https://www.ibo.org/programmes/diploma-programme/curriculum/theory-of-knowledge/what-is-tok/ (accessed 10 January 2019).

ICPIC. (2019). *International Council of Philosophical Inquiry with Children*, available at: https://www.icpic.org (accessed 9 November 2019).

Jackson, F. (1998). *From Metaphysics to Ethics: A Defence of Conceptual Analysis*, Oxford: Clarendon Press.

Kallendorf, C. (2003). 'Humanism', in R. Curren (ed.), *A Companion to the Philosophy of Education*, Oxford: Blackwell Publishing, pp. 62–72.

Kitchener, R. (1990). 'Do Children Think Philosophically?' *Metaphilosophy*, 21(4), pp. 416–31.

Korsgaard, C. (1996). 'Two Distinctions in Goodness', in C. Korsgaard (ed.), *Creating the Kingdom of Ends*, Cambridge: Cambridge University Press, pp. 249–74.

Kotzee, B. (2018). 'Applied Epistemology of Education', in D. Coad and J. Chase (eds), *The Routledge Handbook of Applied Epistemology*, London: Routledge, pp. 211–30.

Kuhn, T. (1962). *The Structure of Scientific Revolutions*, Chicago: University of Chicago Press.

Lawton, D., and Gordon, P. (2002). *A History of Western Educational Ideas*, London: Woburn Press.

Le Guin, U. (2001). *The Lathe of Heaven*, London: Gollancz.

Le Parisien. (2019). *Bac 2019: Les Sujects Complets de Philosophie*, available at: http://etudiant.aujourdhui.fr/etudiant/info/bac-2019-les-sujects-complets-de-philosophie.html (accessed 19 December 2020).

Levison, M. (2002). *The Demands of Liberal Education*, Oxford: Oxford University Press.

Lipman, M. (2003). *Thinking in Education*, Cambridge: Cambridge University Press.

Lipman, M., Sharp, A. M. and Oscanyan, F. S. (1980). *Philosophy in the Classroom*, Philadelphia: Philadelphia Press.

Llera, H. P. (1953). 'The Teaching of Philosophy in Cuba', in UNESCO (ed.), *The Teaching of Philosophy: an International Inquiry of UNESCO*, Paris: UNESCO, pp. 27–38.

Long, M. (2000). *The Psychology of Education*, Abingdon: Routledge.

Lord, P., Dirie, A., Kettlewell, K., and Styles, B. (2021). *Evaluation of Philosophy for Children: an Effectiveness Trial*, London: Educational Endowment Foundation.

Lovering, R. (2016). 'On Moral Arguments against Recreational Drug Use', *Philosophy Now*, p. 113.

Lowe, E. J. (2002). *A Survey of Metaphysics*, Oxford: Oxford University Press.

Lyle, S. (2014). 'Embracing the UNCRC in Wales (UK): Policy, Pedagogy and Prejudices', *Educational Studies*, 40(2), pp. 215–32.

MacKinnon, D. (1953). 'The Teaching of Philosophy in the United Kingdom', in G. Canguilhem, *The Teaching of Philosophy: An International Inquiry of UNESCO*, Paris: UNESCO, pp. 119–48.

Makaiau, A. (2017). 'A Citizen's Education: The Philosophy for Children Hawai'i Approach to Deliberative Pedagogy', in M. Gregory, J. Haynes and K. Murris, *The Routledge International Handbook of Philosophy for Children*, London: Routledge, pp. 19–27.

Manne, K. (2018). *Down Girl: The Logic of Misogyny*, Oxford: Oxford University Press.

Matthews, G. (1980). *Philosophy and the Young Child*, Cambridge, MA: Harvard University Press.

McGinn, C. (2015). 'The Science of Philosophy', *Metaphilosophy*, 46(1), pp. 84–103.

McPeck, J. (1990). *Teaching Critical Thinking: Dialogue and Dialectic*, London: Routledge.

Michaela Community School. (2020). *About Us*, available at: mcsbrent.co.uk (accessed 14 October 2020).

Midgley, M. (1992). 'Philosophical Plumbing', *Royal Institute of Philosophy Supplements*, 33, 139–51.

Midgley, M. (2018). *What Is Philosophy For?* London: Bloomsbury.

Mill, J. S. (ed.). (1924). 'Speech: The Utility of Knowledge', in *Autobiography*, London: Oxford University Press, pp. 267–75.

Moore, G. E. (1993). *Principia Ethica*, Cambridge: Cambridge University Press.

Morgan, T. (1918). 'Literate Education in the Hellenistic and Roman Worlds', *Classical Quarterly*, 49(1), pp. 46–61.

NATRE. (2018). *Religious Studies A-level Entries Decline by 22% as the Subject Is Squeezed Out of the Curriculum*, available at: https://www.religiouseducationcouncil.org.uk/news/religious-studies-a-level-entries-decline-by-22-8-as-the-subject-is-squeezed-out-of-the-curriculum/ (accessed 20 October 2019).

Newman, J. (1902). *The Idea of a University*, Cambridge: Cambridge University Press.

Newman, J. (1931). *Landmarks in the History of Education*, Cambridge: Cambridge University Press.

Nightingale, A. W. (2001). 'Liberal Education in Plato's Republic and Aristotle's Politics', in Y. Lee Too (ed.), *Education in Greek and Roman Antiquity*, Boston: Brill, pp. 133–74.

Nikam, N. A. (1953). 'The Teaching of Philosophy In India', in UNESCO (ed.), *The Teaching of Philosophy: An International Inquiry of UNESCO*, Paris: UNESCO, pp. 89–104.

Nozick, R. (1981). *Philosophical Explanations*, Cambridge, MA: Harvard University Press.

Nussbaum, M. (1997). *Cultivating Humanity: A Classical Defense of Reform In Liberal Education*, London: Harvard University Press.

O'Hear, A. (1981). *Education, Society and Human Nature. An Introduction to the Philosophy of Education*, London: Routledge & Kegan Paul.

Oakeshott, M. (1989). *The Voice of Liberal Learning*, London: Yale University Press.

OCR. (2012). *GCSE Religious Studies B (Philosophy and/or Applied Ethics) Specification*, available at: https://www.ocr.org.uk/Images/82571-specification.pdf (accessed 19 September 2022).

OCR. (2015). *GCSE 9–1 Specification: English Literature*, J352, available at: https://www.ocr.org.uk/Images/168995-specification-accredited-gcse-english-literature-j352.pdf (accessed 10 September 2019).

OCR. (2016a). *Gateway Science Chemistry a Specification*, J248, available at: https://www.ocr.org.uk/Images/234598-specification-accredited-gcse-gateway-science-suite-chemistry-a-j248.pdf (accessed 10 September 2019).

OCR. (2016b). *GCSE 9–1 Specification: Religious Studies*, J625, available at: https://www.ocr.org.uk/Images/240547-specification-accredited-gcse-religious-studies-j625.pdf (accessed 10 September 2019).

OCR. (2018). *GCSE Markscheme*, available at: https://www.ocr.org.uk/Images/537340-mark-scheme-islam-beliefs-and-teachings-practices.pdf (accessed 13 October 2020).

OCR. (2019). *Specification at a Glance*, available at: https://www.ocr.org.uk/qualifications/as-and-a-level/religious-studies-h173-h573-from-2016/specification-at-a-glance/ (accessed 14 February 2019).

Olsson, E. (2011). 'The Value of Knowledge', *Philosophical Compass*, 6(12), pp. 874–83.

Palmer, B. (2018). *Contemporary Literature: Gender and Sexuality ELI2012*, University of Surrey Reading List, available at: https://rl.talis.com/3/surrey/lists/3916F402-332A-A6DE-20C3-23A9ED73D916.html?lang=en-GB (accessed 26 November 2018).

Papineau, D. (1996). *The Philosophy of Science*, New York: Oxford University Press.

Parfit, D. (2017). 'Future People, the Non-Identity Problem, and Person-Affecting Principles', *Philosophy and Public Affairs*, 45(2), pp. 118–57.

Parker, H. (1890). 'The Seven Liberal Arts', *English Historical Review*, 5(19), pp. 417–61.
Pascal, N. (1984). 'The Legacy of Roman Education', *Classical Journal*, 79(4), pp. 351–5.
Pepin, C. (2010). *Les dix Philosophes Incontournables du Bac Philo*, Paris: Librio.
Peters, R. S. (1966). *Ethics and Education*, London: George Allen & Unwin.
Peters, R. S. (1973a). 'Aims of Education – a Conceptual Inquiry', in R. S. Peters (ed.), *The Philosophy of Education*, London: Oxford University Press, pp. 11–58.
Peters, R. S. (1973b). 'Education as Initiation', in R. S. Peters (ed.), *Authority, Responsibility and Education*, Plymouth: George Allen & Unwin, pp. 81–107.
Peters, R. S. (1973c). 'Education and Seeing What Is There', in R. S. Peters (ed.), *Authority, Responsibility and Education*, Plymouth: George Allen & Unwin, pp. 108–22.
Peters, R. S. (1973d). 'The Justification of Education', in R. S. Peters (ed.), *The Philosophy of Education*, London: Oxford University Press, pp. 239–69.
Phenix, P. (1964). *Realms of Meaning*, London: McGraw-Hill Book.
Plato, and Waterfield, R. (1998). Republic, Oxford: Oxford University Press.
Popper, K. (1959). *The Logic of Scientific Discovery*, London: Hutchinson of London.
Popper, K. (1963). *Conjectures and Refutations: The Growth Of Scientific Knowledge*, London: Routledge.
Priestley, M., and Biesta, G. (2013). *Reinventing the Curriculum*, London: Bloomsbury.
Pring, R. (1973). 'Curriculum Integration', in R. S. Peters (ed.), *The Philosophy of Education*, London: Oxford University Press, pp. 123–50.
Pring, R. (1977). 'Common Sense and Education', *Journal of Philosophy of Education*, 11(1), pp. 57–77.
Pring, R. (2005). *Philosophy of Education: Aims, Theory, Common Sense and Research*, London: Continuum.
Rawls, J. (1971). *A Theory of Justice*, Cambridge: Cambridge University Press.
Reay, D. (2004). 'Education and Cultural Capital: The Implications of Changing Trends in Education Policies' Cultural Trends, 13(2), pp. 73–86.
Reeve, C. D. C. (2008). 'The Socratic Movement', in R. Curren (ed.), *A Companion to the Philosophy of Education*, Oxford: Blackwell Publishing, pp. 7–24.
Reeve, C. D. C. (2010). 'Blindness and Reorientation', in M. McPherran (ed.), *Plato's Republic, a Critical Guide*, Cambridge: Cambridge University Press, pp. 203–27.
Reiss, M., and White, J. (2013). *An Aims Based Curriculum: The Significance of Human Flourishing for Schools*, London: IOE Press.
Rush, P. (2016). 'Myriad Philosophical Methodologies', *Metaphilosophy*, 47(4–5), pp. 680–95.
Ryle, G. (1953). *Dilemmas: The Tarner Lectures*, Cambridge: Cambridge University Press.
Ryle, G. (1971). 'Philosophical Arguments', in G. Ryle (ed.), *Collected Papers: Volume II, Collected Essays 1929–1968*, London: Hutchinson, pp. 203–22.
SAPERE. (2018). *What Is P4C*, available at: https://www.sapere.org.uk/Default.aspx?tabid=162 (accessed 9 June 2018).

Siddiqui, N., Gorard, S., and Huat See, B. (2017), 'Can Programmes Like Philosophy for Children Help Schools to Look Beyond Academic Attainment?' *Educational Review*, 71(2), pp. 1–20.

Siddiqui, N., Gorard, S., and Huat See, B. (2017). *Non-Cognitive Outcomes of Philosophy for Children*, Durham: Durham Research Online.

Standish, P. (2020). 'Exhausted: Education and the Response to the Planetary Crisis', *Journal of Philosophy of Education*, 54(4), pp. 927–43.

Strawson, P. F. (1992). *Analysis and Metaphysics: An Introduction to Philosophy*, Oxford: Oxford University Press.

Suissa, J. (2008). 'Philosophy in the Secondary School – a Deweyan Perspective', in M. Hand and C. Winstanley (eds), *Philosophy in Schools*, London: Continuum, pp. 132–44.

The Guardian. (2018). *The Autocomplete Questions*, available at: https://www.theguardian.com/commentisfree/series/the-autocomplete-questions (accessed 5 November 2018).

The Philosophy Foundation. (2018). *P4C*, available at: https://www.philosophy-foundation.org/p4c (accessed 18 June 2018).

Thinking Space. (2020). *Projects,* available at: https://www.thinkingspace.org.uk/portfolio (accessed 13 October 2020).

Topping, K. J., and Trickey, S. (2006). 'Collaborative Philosophical Enquiry for School Children: Socio-emotional Effects at 10–12', *School Psychology International*, 27(5), pp. 599–614.

Topping, K. J., and Trickey, S. (2007). 'Collaborative Philosophical Inquiry for Schoolchildren: Cognitive Gains at 2-Year Follow Up', *British Journal of Educational Psychology*, 77(4), pp. 787–96.

Trickey, S., and Topping, K. J. (2006). 'Philosophy for Children: A Systematic Review', *Research Papers in Education*, 19(3), pp. 365–80.

UNESCO. (1980) *Consultation on Teaching and Research in Philosophy in Africa*, Paris: UNESCO.

UNESCO. (1984). *Teaching and Research in Philosophy: Africa*, Paris: UNESCO.

UNESCO. (1986). *Teaching and Research in Philosophy: Asia and the Pacific*, Paris: UNESCO.

UNESCO. (2005). *Creation of a World Philosophy Day,* available at: https://unesdoc.unesco.org/ark:/48223/pf0000138818_eng (accessed 25 February 2020).

UNESCO. (2007). *Philosophy a School of Freedom*, Paris: UNESCO.

UNESCO. (2009a). *Teaching Philosophy in African Anglophone Countries*, Paris: UNESCO.

UNESCO. (2009b). *Teaching Philosophy in Latin America and the Caribbean*, Paris: UNESCO.

UNESCO. (2011). *Teaching Philosophy in Europe and North America*, Paris: UNESCO.

Van der Straten Waillet, N., Roskam, I., and Possoz, C. (2015). 'On the Epistemological Features Promoted by "Philosophy for Children" and Their Psychological

Advantages When Incorporated into RE', *British Journal of Religious Education*, 37(3), pp. 273–92.

White, J. (1973). *Towards a Compulsory Curriculum*, London: Routledge & Kegan Paul.

White, J. (2004). *Rethinking the School Curriculum: Values, Aims and Purposes*, London: RoutledgeFalmer.

White, J. (2005). *Curriculum and the Child: The Selected Works of John White*, London: Psychology Press.

White, J. (2012). 'Philosophy in Primary Schools?' *Journal of Philosophy of Education*, 46(3), pp. 449–60.

Whitehead, A. N. (1932). *The Aims of Education*, London: Ernest Benn

Whittle, S. (2015). 'Philosophy In Schools: A Catholic School Perspective', *Journal of Philosophy of Education*, 49(4), pp. 590–606.

Williamson, T. (2007). *The Philosophy of Philosophy*, Oxford: Blackwell.

Wilson, J. (1992). Philosophy for Children, a Note of Warning, *Thinking*, 10(1), pp. 17–18.

Winch, C., and Gingell, J. (1999). *Key Concepts in the Philosophy of Education*, London: Routledge.

Wittgenstein, L. (1953). *Philosophical Investigations*, trans. G. Anscombe, Oxford: Basil Blackwell.

Wolfe, E. (1994). 'Cicero and the Liberal Arts Tradition in America', *Ciceronia Online*, 8, pp. 93–102.

Worley, P. (2018). 'Plato, Metacognition and Philosophy in Schools', *Journal of Philosophy in Schools*, 5(1), pp. 76–91.

Young, M. (2009). 'What Are Schools For', in H. Daniels, H. Lauder and J. Porter (eds), *Knowledge, Values and Educational Policy: A Critical Perspective*, Abingdon: Routledge, pp. 10–18.

Index

academic disciplines 107
  disciplinary sciences 86, 110, 113–15, 131–2, 137–9, 144–6, 170
  discipline of philosophy 19, 20, 23, 44–5
academic skills 31, 34–5, 36
advanced-level (A-levels) 13, 19, 39–40, 44, 183
  Religious Studies 19
  philosophy 19, 23
aims of education 17, 27, 29–33, 35–8, 42, 49–51, 55–123, 184, 186
ameliorative analysis 140–3
Aristotle 11, 39, 58–9, 63, 78
autonomy 57, 60, 64–5, 78, 80–5, 89–90, 92–7, 105–6, 146, 177–8
  autonomy as an educational good 117–22

Bailey, Richard 83–4, 92, 94–6, 105, 108
  general utility 92, 94, 96–7, 106, 108, 112, 119
best available content 43, 51, 56, 92, 103, 110–14, 121, 123, 127, 132, 137, 142, 144, 159, 166–7, 170, 172, 178, 183–4, 186–7
Brighouse, Harry (*see* Educational Goods) 63, 74, 121
broad and balanced education 56, 73, 83–4, 89–90, 95, 101, 105, 185

Catholic education 9–11, 14–15, 39–41, 60
character education 46, 57–60, 63
  virtues and education 30–3, 35–7, 43, 58, 79
children's interests 28, 30, 63, 67, 69, 151, 166
climate crisis 164–9, 172, 175, 178–9
cognitive ability 31, 34–6
Collingwood, Robin George 86–7, 109

Community of Inquiry 14, 20–2, 32, 37–8, 43
conceptual analysis 44, 49, 131–2, 137, 139, 140–2, 145–8, 163, 167, 171, 173–4, 183
conceptual problems 154, 160, 164, 170–81, 183, 187
conceptual schemes 4, 48, 92–3, 127, 150, 154–5, 157–8, 160–1, 164, 175, 181, 187
Covid-19 112, 164, 168–9, 173, 175, 179–80
critical thinking 1, 3, 18, 31, 34–5, 86–7, 89
culture, cultural capital 8, 27, 47, 57, 61, 64, 66, 71–80, 114
curriculum coherence 1, 3, 27–8, 38, 45–7, 83, 90, 101–2, 104, 140, 152, 154, 173
curriculum integration 48, 86, 102, 104, 152

democratic education
  citizenship 16, 17, 27, 56, 63, 78, 79, 122, 136
  citizens 33, 37, 56, 58, 67, 72, 76, 78–80, 180
  civic education 16, 25, 30–1, 33, 36–7, 39, 42–3, 60, 63, 74, 79
  liberal democracy
Dewey, John 21, 29–30, 33, 37, 38, 73, 79, 86, 151–2, 154, 162
dialogue 14, 18, 21–3, 33–4, 36–8, 79, 122, 140, 144–5, 184
discrete philosophy course 183–4
drugs education 157–8, 161, 163, 165, 176–7

economic considerations 2, 12, 17–18, 20, 26, 61, 69, 78, 117–18, 120–2, 130, 160, 163, 165, 174, 168, 173, 176, 179

educational goods 3, 25–7, 29–30, 33–8, 41, 44, 48–51, 55–7, 64, 84, 91, 104–5, 116–22
educational value 3–4, 27, 30, 36, 45, 48, 50, 66–7, 70–1, 95, 135
effective interaction with the world 4, 71, 107, 115–8, 120–1, 139, 164, 168–9, 178, 181–2
Elgin, Catherine 102–3
empirical research 30–4, 47, 110, 142
English National Curriculum 27–8, 56, 61–3, 90, 111, 114, 137
ethics 10, 14, 16, 18–19, 39, 43, 49–50, 58, 130, 136, 153, 164–5, 167–8, 172, 176–80

facts 40, 46, 78, 98–102, 110, 147, 154, 158, 167
flourishing 4, 58, 63, 65, 76, 79, 82, 84, 117–18, 120–1, 186
fragmentation of the curriculum 4, 47, 150–81
freedom 85, 89–91, 104, 166, 179
French *Baccalaureat* 11, 12, 14–15, 183

General Certificate of Secondary Education (GCSEs) 15, 19, 40, 115

Hand, Michael 15, 21–2, 40–1, 43, 82, 86, 92, 107, 135–6
Hirst, Paul 27, 29, 45, 50–1, 58, 65, 80–1, 83–110
  Forms of knowledge 29, 45, 80–1, 83–110
Huxley, Thomas Henry 61–2, 96–7, 105

industrial revolution 61, 62, 95
inert ideas 95, 98–102, 150–4, 165
instrumental value 12, 67–74, 83–4, 94–5, 105–6, 120, 122
interdisciplinarity 157–8, 161, 164, 168–73, 176, 180, 187
International Baccalaureate 19, 44–6
International Council of Philosophical Inquiry with Children (ICPIC) 14–15
intrinsic value 45, 64, 73–9, 83–4

knowledge 7, 11, 40–2, 47, 58, 65–7, 72–5, 79–81, 83–110, 140–2

justified, true belief 98, 100, 102, 140–2
propositional knowledge 88, 98–102, 104, 128

leisure 58–61, 72–3, 82
liberal arts 56, 60, 62–3
liberal democracy 63–4, 78–9
liberal education 3, 45, 55, 57–106, 121, 152, 153, 185
liberty 2, 28, 91, 129, 168, 178–80
Lipman, Matthew 14, 20–1, 31–2, 35, 37–8, 47, 152, 154, 162

Manne, Kate 140, 143–4
Matthews, Gareth 23, 29, 134
memorization 93–4, 98–9, 101, 103
metaphysics 43, 89, 163, 173–4
Midgley, Mary 47–8, 139, 159–60, 170–3
Mill, John Stuart 76, 96
misogyny 140, 143–4
moral education 8, 25, 27, 30, 39, 41–3, 61, 86
morality 1, 3, 7, 21, 41, 133–6, 147, 158, 164–5, 167–8, 172, 177–8

Newman, John Henry 40–2, 45, 66, 70, 153–4, 162
normative questions and claims 1, 9, 28, 69, 158, 164, 168
Nussbaum, Martha 60, 64, 78–9, 145–6

Oakeshott, Michael 72, 75
ordinary concepts 43, 127–48, 155, 157, 164, 171–2, 175, 181, 184, 186–7

pedagogy 14, 20, 23, 32–3, 37–8, 43
personal, social, health education 136
  relationships education 26, 32, 66, 88, 107–8, 113–15, 117–8, 122, 134, 136, 138, 140, 145, 147, 152
Peters, Richard Stanley 28–9, 45, 65–70, 80–1, 84, 86, 91–3, 95, 98–106, 110, 153–4, 162
  cognitive perspective 81, 84, 153–4
  transcendental argument 65, 67, 70
  worthwhile activities 28, 35, 95
Phenix, Phillip 110, 153–4, 162
philosophical traditions 15, 16, 39, 49, 50

analytic philosophy 4, 12–14, 128, 131, 140–2, 147, 155, 170–1, 174
Anglo-American philosophical tradition 9, 12, 14–15, 144
continental philosophy 15, 49
Philosophy for Children (P4C) 7, 9, 12, 14–25, 31–43, 152, 185
piecemeal curriculum content 1, 112, 150, 159
Plato 10–11, 39, 58–9, 63, 65, 78, 80, 140, 154
political ideologies 15–16
powerful knowledge 75
pre-theoretical concepts 130–1, 157
primary educational goods 116, 119–20, 122–3
Pring, Richard 86, 95–6, 132–3, 135, 137–8
prominent and pressing questions 92, 107–15, 121–3, 127–8, 131–51, 157–9, 164–70, 173–5, 181, 186–7

rationality 67, 80–1, 84–5, 88–90, 97, 103–4
rational autonomy 57, 60, 64–5, 80–90, 92, 97, 105–6, 146
Rawls, John 118–20, 180, 186
religion 1, 18–19, 39–42, 72, 86, 88
Religious Studies 19, 39–40, 115, 183
Religious Education 2, 14, 40–3, 136, 161, 184
Ryle, Gilbert 49, 128–32, 148, 156, 160, 162–3, 170–3, 177, 183

schooling 28, 36, 55, 56–7, 64, 82–3, 112, 114, 116, 119–20, 123, 136, 185, 188
social skills 1–3, 18, 31–2, 35–6
Society for Advancing Philosophical Enquiry and Reflection in Education (SAPERE) 14, 22, 184

Strawson, Peter Frederick 128, 130–1, 135, 137–9, 155–6, 161–2, 170, 173
students' time 26, 82, 90, 134, 185
subject based curriculum 62, 151–2

technical concepts 129–30, 148, 171
theoretical concepts 127–8, 130, 132, 138, 155–7
theory 40, 50, 100–13, 127–32, 136–8, 146–7, 150–1, 154–87
Theory of Knowledge (ToK) 19, 46
training 29, 46, 56, 58–9, 74, 81, 94, 117, 122, 132
transformative education 99, 102
transmission of ideas 65, 71, 72, 99, 103, 111
truth 29, 45, 59, 65–7, 70–1, 78, 82, 85, 96, 100, 102, 107, 112, 115, 133–4, 136, 142, 161, 174, 177, 180

understanding 3–4, 8, 39, 41, 44–5, 48, 60, 72–4, 80–5, 87, 92–112, 120–2, 128, 130–48, 149–51, 154, 156–7, 159, 162–3, 168–9, 173, 178, 181, 186
United Nations Educational, Scientific and Cultural Organization (UNESCO) 7–18, 39, 44, 46, 56
utility 3, 83–4, 91–123, 149

virtues 14, 30–5, 37, 43–4, 58, 63, 70, 79, 91, 176, 180
vocational education 30, 59, 78, 81, 94, 117, 135–6

White, John 18, 27–8, 30, 35, 45, 61–2, 67, 70, 81–2, 84, 120–1, 152, 154

Young, Michael 75

www.ingramcontent.com/pod-product-compliance
Lightning Source LLC
Chambersburg PA
CBHW061830300426
44115CB00013B/2316